PLATO'S
THEORY OF IDEAS

PLATO'S THEORY OF IDEAS

BY

SIR DAVID ROSS

SECOND EDITION

OXFORD
AT THE CLARENDON PRESS
1953

Oxford University Press, Amen House, London E.C. 4

GLASGOW NEW YORK TORONTO MELBOURNE WELLINGTON
BOMBAY CALCUTTA MADRAS KARACHI CAPE TOWN IBADAN

Geoffrey Cumberlege, Publisher to the University

FIRST EDITION 1951

Reprinted lithographically in Great Britain
at the University Press, Oxford, 1953
from corrected sheets of the first edition

PREFACE

IN 1948 the Queen's University, Belfast, did me the honour of appointing me to deliver the Memorial Lecture established in memory of the notable historian of ancient thought, Sir Samuel Dill. I welcomed the opportunity of saying something about Plato's theory of Ideas, at which I had been working for some time, and the substance of the lecture is embodied in the final chapter and in other parts of the present book.

I have not thought it necessary, as a rule, to print in the original Greek passages from Plato and other Greek writers, but have been content to translate or to use a good existing translation. I must in particular thank Messrs. Routledge and Kegan Paul for permission to quote from Cornford's excellent translations of the *Parmenides*, the *Theaetetus*, the *Sophistes*, and the *Timaeus*. To facilitate the turning up of Platonic passages in the original I have given precise references to the lineation in Burnet's text.

W. D. R.

CONTENTS

ABBREVIATIONS
USED IN REFERRING TO MODERN BOOKS

Cherniss, H., *A.C.P.A.* = *Aristotle's Criticism of Plato and the Academy*, i (1944).

Cherniss, H., *R.E.A.* = *The Riddle of the Early Academy* (1945).

Cornford, F. M., *P.T.K.* = *Plato's Theory of Knowledge* (1935).

Cornford, F. M., *P.P.* = *Plato and Parmenides* (1939).

Diels, H., *F.V.* = *Fragmente der Vorsokratiker* [5] (1934, 1935, 1937).

Field, G. C., *P.C.* = *Plato and his Contemporaries* (1930).

Hackforth, R., *A.P.E.* = *The Authorship of the Platonic Epistles* (1913).

Ritter, C., *P.L.S.L.* = *Platon, sein Leben, seine Schriften, seine Lehre* (1910, 1923).

Robin, L., *T.p.I.N.* = *La Théorie platonicienne des Idées et des Nombres* (1908).

Taylor, A. E., *P.M.W.* = *Plato, the Man and his Work* (1926).

Taylor, A. E., *P.S.* = *Philosophical Studies* (1934).

Van der Wielen, W., *I.P.* = *De Ideegetallen van Plato* (1941).

Wilpert, P., *Z.a.F.I.* = *Zwei aristotelische Frühschriften über die Ideenlehre* (1949).

References to Plato are to Burnet's text.

References to Aristotle, where no work is named, are to the *Metaphysics*.

I

THE ORDER OF THE DIALOGUES

ANYONE who tries to trace the history of the theory of Ideas is bound to consider the dialogues in some particular order; and the right order is very hard to ascertain, and must remain at many points still a matter of conjecture. Plato's works contain very few allusions to recent historical events, except the trial and imprisonment of Socrates; and where there are such references it is sometimes difficult to say to which of two events they refer. Again, the dialogues rarely refer, even in the most general way, to one another, or to recent works of other writers. Were we confined to evidence of these two kinds we should know very little about the order of writing of the dialogues. The attempt has often been made to date them by another method; by assuming that the development of the doctrine must have followed a certain order, and that the dialogues may be dated according to the comparative maturity of the doctrines they contain. But this method has led to very different conclusions in different hands, and, while not in principle unsound, is apt to be too subjective in its application.

The method that has proved most fruitful, and has led to the most harmonious results when used by different scholars, has been the stylometric method. Starting with the tradition reported by Diogenes Laertius,[1] that Plato left the *Laws* unpublished, and with the universally accepted view that it is the latest of Plato's works (unless the *Epinomis* be accepted as his and dated later), taking the style and vocabulary of the *Laws* as a standard, and testing the affinity of other dialogues to the *Laws* in respect of a large number of independent points (the use of particular particles or combinations of particles, the choice of this or that one of two synonyms, the avoidance of hiatus, &c.), different scholars have arrived at results which partly agree and partly disagree, about the order of the dialogues. The following table summarizes the views of five leading students of the subject. Each of the other

[1] iii. 37 (25).

lists omits, for reasons which do not concern us, some of the dialogues included in Raeder's list. In the case of Ritter I give the order which he assigns in his latest work, *Kerngedanken der platonischen Philosophie*, translated under the title *The Essence of Plato's Philosophy*.

Arnim	Lutoslawski	Raeder	Ritter	Wilamowitz
	Apol.	Apol.	Hipp. Mi.	Ion
Ion		Ion		Hipp. Mi.
Prot.		Hipp. Mi.	Lach.	Prot.
Lach.	Euthyph.	Lach.	Prot.	Apol.
Rep. 1	Crito	Charm.	Charm.	Crito
Lysis	Charm.	Crito	Euthyph.	Lach.
Charm.		Hipp. Ma.	Apol.	
Euthyph.	Lach.	Prot.	Crito	Lysis
Euthyd.	Prot.	Gorg.	Gorg.	Charm.
Gorg.		Menex.	Hipp. Ma.	Euthyph.
Meno	Meno	Euthyph.	Euthyd.	Gorg.
Hipp. Mi.	Euthyd.	Meno	Crat.	Menex.
Crat.	Gorg.	Euthyd.	Meno	Meno
Symp.	Rep. 1	Crat.	Menex.	Crat.
Hipp. Ma.	Crat.	Lysis	Lysis	Euthyd.
Phaedo	Symp.	Symp.	Symp.	Phaedo
Crito	Phaedo	Phaedo	Phaedo	Symp.
Rep. 2–10	Rep. 2–10	Rep.	Rep.	Rep.
Theaet.	Phaedr.	Phaedr.	Phaedr.	Phaedr.
Parm.	Theaet.	Theaet.	Theaet.	Parm.
Phaedr.	Parm.	Parm.	Parm.	Theaet.
Soph.	Soph.	Soph.	Soph.	Soph.
Pol.	Pol.	Pol.	Pol.	Pol.
Phil.	Phil.	Phil.	Tim.	Tim.
	Tim.	Tim.	Critias	Critias
	Critias	Critias	Phil.	Phil.
Laws	Laws	Laws	Laws	Laws
		Epin.		

Two things leap to the eye if one surveys these lists—that as regards the early dialogues there is much disagreement between the five scholars, and that as regards the later dialogues, from the *Republic* onwards, there is almost complete agreement. If one were to quote the orders adopted by other recent scholars, the same two features would at once become noticeable. This is due to the fact that while the views of scholars about the order of the early dialogues are for the most part based on subjective theories about the probable development of Plato's thought, their views about the order of the late dialogues are in the main based on the sure ground of the stylometric tests initiated by Lewis Campbell. It may be added that the late dating of the dialogues from the *Parmenides* and *Theaetetus* onwards, first established by stylometric tests, in fact offers a far likelier order of development of Plato's thought than the view which treated them as belonging to Plato's youth.

Several comments must be made on these lists:[1]

1. They agree in omitting a large number of dialogues which were included in Thrasyllus' list of tetralogies or in the appendix to it, but which are now almost universally regarded as spurious. The *Letters* were, till recently, also so regarded, but recent opinion has tended to treat several of them as genuine. It is impossible to be sure of the genuineness of any of them, but it seems probable that the only one which is philosophically important, the seventh, is genuine, and that it may be dated about 353 or 352 B.C.

2. The genuineness of the *Hippias Major* has been denied by many scholars. In the Platonic canon there is only one other pair of dialogues bearing the same name, *Alcibiades I* and *Alcibiades II*, and these are now almost universally rejected. This creates a slight, but only a slight, presumption against the belief that Plato wrote two dialogues called *Hippias*. There is also the fact that Aristotle in *Met.* 1025a6 uses the phrase 'the argument in the *Hippias*' of an argument which is to be found in the *minor Hippias*;[2] it has been argued that he could hardly have referred to the slighter dialogue as 'the *Hippias*' if Plato had also written the other. But if Plato wrote two *Hippias*'s, Aristotle would know which one he meant by 'the *Hippias*' and could probably count on his hearers' knowing too. The arguments against the authenticity of the dialogue drawn from points of style and grammar[3] are not very strong.

On the other hand, the first example of definition quoted by Aristotle in *Top.* 146a21–3 seems to be as clear an allusion to

---

[1] I omit discussion of the dialogues which do not throw light on the theory of Ideas.　　　　　　　　　　　　　　　　　　　　[2] 365 d 6–369 b 7.

[3] For these see Miss Tarrant's edition, lxxv–lxxx. These and other objections to the dialogue have been ably met by Prof. G. M. A. Grube in *Class. Quart.* xx (1926), 134–48 and in *Class. Philol.* xxiv (1929), 369–75.

Hippias Major 297 e 3–303 a 11, where the definition of the beautiful as 'that which gives pleasure through hearing or sight' is discussed, as the second example is to *Soph.* 247 d 3–e 4. Similarly the suggested definition of the beautiful as 'the fitting' in *Top.* 102ª6 and 135ª13 is probably a reminiscence of *Hippias Major* 293 d 6–294 e 10. Further, the dialogue shows signs of a development in the theory of Ideas which it is hard to assign to anyone but Plato. Here, for instance, and nowhere else, Socrates points out the difference between most Ideas, which are true of each and all of a number of individual things, and Ideas of number, which are true of a group but not of its individual members.[1] Taking along with this comparative maturity of doctrine the fact that von Arnim on purely stylistic grounds places the dialogue later even than the *Symposium*, I go so far as to place it, tentatively, after the *Euthyphro*.

3. Since the *Apology*[2] presupposes the trial of Socrates in 399 B.C., the order adopted by Lutoslawski and by Raeder clearly assumes that Plato wrote no dialogues before that date. Grote argued strongly for this view, chiefly on the ground that military service in the Peloponnesian War, and the troubled state of Athens thereafter, must have made literary activity on Plato's part before 399 impossible; but it seems by no means impossible that by that time (when he was already twenty-eight or twenty-nine) Plato should have written a few dialogues. The argument of Burnet and Taylor, that it is psychologically impossible that he should have written dialogues about Socrates while his master was still alive, is far from convincing. If we suppose that a few dialogues were written before the *Apology*, we are not necessarily dating them before 399 (for we do not know that the *Apology* was written immediately after the trial of Socrates); we are only leaving the possibility open.

4. There is a serious doubt about the date of the *Cratylus*. Most scholars date it not long after 390, and put it in the same sort of position in the series that the lists we have quoted assign to it. But Prof. Jaeger has pointed out[3] the partial correspondence of the names

---

[1] 300 d 5–302 b 3.   [2] Like the *Euthyphro* and the *Crito*.
[3] In *Sitzb. Preuss. Akad.* xxv (1928), 402 n. 2.

for qualities of mind in *Crat.* 411 d 4–412 b 8—φρόνησις, γνώμη, νόησις, σωφροσύνη, ἐπιστήμη, σύνεσις, σοφία—with those which occur in a very late dialogue, *Phil.* 19 d 4–5—νοῦς, ἐπιστήμη, σύνεσις, τέχνη. M. Warburg[1] has argued for the view that the affinities of the dialogue are really with the *Theaetetus*, and that it was written between 380 and 370, and E. Haag[2] and E. Weerts[3] have expressed similar views. On the other hand, stylistic details suggest an earlier date. The question remains an open one.

5. Taylor places all the dialogues down to and including the *Republic* before the foundation of the Academy in 388–7. His ground for this is that in the Seventh Letter,[4] where Plato is describing the state of mind in which he paid his first visit to Sicily, he says that he had been driven to say, in a eulogy of genuine philosophy, that humanity will never escape its sufferings until either true philosophers occupy political office or political rulers, by some happy providence, turn to philosophy. This looks like an allusion to *Rep.* 473 c 11–e 2, where the same thing is said, in almost the same words, as part of a eulogy of true philosophy. Since Plato, who was born about 428, says[5] that he was about forty years old at the time of his voyage, that *seems* to point to the *Republic*'s having been written before 388.

Plato, however, does not say directly that when he first went to Sicily he had already used these words, still less that he had written them in a dialogue. What he says is that he already had these thoughts in mind when he went to Sicily,[6] and that is compatible with his expression of them in the *Republic* having been later. We must consider the general probabilities. Taylor's view credits Plato with having written by the age of forty, i.e. within a space of at most about twenty years, the whole range of dialogues down to and including the *Republic*, which cover nearly 1,200 pages,[7] and in the remaining forty years of his life dialogues covering less than 1,050; which, while not impossible, is not likely. It involves also ignoring the reference in the *Symposium*[8] (which is admittedly earlier than the *Republic*) to an event of the year

---

[1] *Zwei Fragen zur 'Kratylos'*, 31–61.　　　　[2] *Platons Kratylos*, 86–90.
[3] In *Philol.* Supplementband xxiii (1932), 1–84.
[4] 326 a 5–b 4.　　　　[5] 324 a 6.　　　　[6] 326 b 5.
[7] In Burnet's text.　　　　[8] 193 a 1–3.

385 or 384, and the other indications that point to the dating of the *Symposium* after those years. There is also force in Ritter's suggestion[1] that the description of the tyrant in the ninth book of the *Republic* owes much to Plato's experience at the court of Dionysius, and presupposes at least Plato's first visit to it in 389–8.

6. The *Parmenides*, *Theaetetus*, *Sophistes*, and *Politicus* form what is from some points of view a single group; in the attempt to determine their relations several lines of evidence have to be borne in mind.

(*a*) In the *Theaetetus*, as in all the earlier dialogues, Socrates is the chief speaker. In the 'first part' of the *Parmenides* he plays an important part, but Parmenides is the chief speaker; and in the 'second part' Socrates is a silent listener. In the *Sophistes* and the *Politicus* he appears only at the beginning, and these dialogues are virtually monologues by an 'Eleatic Stranger', with Theaetetus in the *Sophistes* and 'the younger Socrates' in the *Politicus* doing little more than say 'yes' or 'no' to the Stranger's questions. In the *Timaeus* and the *Critias* Socrates appears at the beginning, but the *Timaeus* is virtually a monologue by Timaeus, and the *Critias* a monologue by Critias. In the *Laws* Socrates does not appear at all, and the dialogue is conducted in the main by an 'Athenian Stranger'. Of all the late dialogues, the *Philebus* is the only one in which Socrates is the chief speaker; and that is no doubt because, alone among the late dialogues, the *Philebus* is mainly occupied with Socrates' primary subject, the subject of ethics. On the whole, then, the late works are characterized by the absence of lively dialogue, and by the fact that Socrates has ceased to be the chief speaker.

(*b*) At the beginning of the *Theaetetus* (143 b 5– c 5) the narrator says that he proposes to omit the tedious phrases 'and I said' and 'he agreed', and simply to present the actual words of the speaker. Teichmüller deduced from this that any dialogue in which such phrases occur must be earlier, and any dialogue in which they do not occur later, than the *Theaetetus*. He greatly overstated his case; many of the dialogues which on all other grounds must be dated early follow in fact the prescription of the *Theaetetus*, for

[1] *P.L.S.L.* i. 203.

which Greek drama had set a precedent. But it would be surprising if in the very next dialogue he wrote Plato had gone back to the method of presentation which he renounces in the *Theaetetus*; now he actually uses it in the first, though not in the second, part of the *Parmenides*.[1]

(*c*) The *Parmenides* professes to relate a conversation between Parmenides, Zeno the Eleatic, and Socrates. The conversation purports to have taken place at a time when Parmenides was about sixty-five (127 b 3), Zeno close on forty (ibid. 4), and Socrates very young (127 c 4). Since Socrates is credited with having already arrived at the theory of Ideas, and with having reflected a good deal about it, we cannot suppose the age assigned to him to be less than twenty at the very least; and since Socrates was born in 469, Plato evidently represents Parmenides as having been born not before *c.* 515, and Zeno not before *c.* 490. The traditional dates of birth assigned to Parmenides and Zeno respectively are 544–540 and 504–500.

It is impossible to believe that, if Parmenides and Socrates ever met, they could have had such a conversation as they have in the dialogue; we have no reason to suppose Parmenides capable of the kind of dialectical discussion which forms the later part of the dialogue, and it is contrary to all probability to suppose that Socrates at the age of twenty already held the theory of Ideas as it is depicted in the 'first part'. But if the course of the dialogue is imaginary, we have no reason to regard the setting as historical. Burnet and Taylor, it is true, attack the traditional dates of Parmenides and Zeno as resting on arbitrary assumptions; but that is because they are committed to belief in the accuracy of Plato's 'biography' of Socrates, and if we are right in rejecting that view we are justified in treating the meeting as fictitious. Now both in the *Theaetetus* (183 e 7) and in the *Sophistes* (217 c 4–7) Socrates describes himself as having as a young man met Parmenides. If we are right in treating the conversation in the *Parmenides* as fictitious, these allusions refer not to an actual meeting, but to the fictitious meeting depicted in that dialogue.

---

[1] The best discussion of the variations of the dialogue form used by Plato is that by Raeder (*Platons Phil. Entw.* 44–61).

(*d*) The only clear allusions to the Eleatics, so far as I know, in dialogues earlier than these four are two unimportant ones in *Symp.* 178 b 9 and *Phaedr.* 261 d 6. But there are three allusions in the *Theaetetus.* In 152 e 2 Parmenides is significantly mentioned as the only one of 'the wise' who does not subscribe to the view that 'nothing ever is, but all things are always becoming'. In 180 d 7–181 b 5 Plato expresses his conviction that he must come to grips not only with the Heracliteans, but also with the 'partisans of the immovable whole', among whom he names Melissus and Parmenides. In 183 e 5–184 a 1 Parmenides is described as 'a reverend and awful figure' and as having 'a sort of depth that was altogether noble'. In the *Parmenides*, as we have seen, he plays the leading part. In the *Sophistes* and the *Politicus* (which present themselves as continuations of the dialogue begun in the *Theaetetus*)[1] a member of the Eleatic school plays the chief part.

Thus these four dialogues are linked together by various cross-references, and by a new interest in the Eleatic philosophy. It would seem natural, at first sight, to treat them as a single group, and to suppose that Plato's interest in Eleaticism had been stimulated by meetings with members of the school in Magna Graecia while he was on his way to Sicily about 367 B.C. But linguistically the four dialogues fall into two strongly contrasted groups; the *Parmenides* and the *Theaetetus* stand close to the later books of the *Republic* and to the *Phaedrus*, the *Sophistes* and the *Politicus* close to the *Timaeus* and the *Philebus*. This can best be explained by supposing the last two of the four dialogues to be separated from the first two by the lapse of time and the distraction of interests involved in Plato's long second visit to the court of Dionysius in Syracuse, in 367–6.

At the same time, to allow for the transition from the confident assertion of the theory of Ideas in the *Republic* to the self-questioning mood of the *Parmenides*, it is natural to suppose some years to have elapsed between the finishing of the one and the writing of the other. Finally, the facts mentioned in (*b*) above can be best explained by supposing either that the first part of the *Parmenides* was written before the *Theaetetus*, and the second part after it, or

---

[1] *Theae* . 210 d 3, *Soph.* 216 a 1, *Pol.* 257 a 1.

that the *Theaetetus* simply enunciates a principle which Plato had already in fact adopted in the second part of the *Parmenides*.

7. On the question of the relative dates of the *Timaeus* and the *Philebus* the opinion of scholars is pretty evenly divided. Linguistic tests have done nothing to resolve the question, and on the whole the other arguments put forward for either view carry no great weight. But there is one argument which points definitely, though not decisively, in one direction. The derivation of the ideal numbers from the One and the 'great and small' of which we hear so much from Aristotle, and which clearly belongs to Plato's latest phase, links up much more closely with the 'limit' and the 'unlimited' (or the 'greater and less') of the *Philebus* than it does with anything in the *Timaeus*. This seems to me to turn the scale in favour of regarding the *Philebus* as the later of the two dialogues.[1]

The definite data for the time of writing of individual dialogues are very scanty. The *Menexenus*, a funeral oration on the dead in battle, cannot have been written before 390, and is more likely to have been written after the Peace of Antalcidas in 386; the *Symposium* refers to an event of the year 385 or 384,[2] the *Theaetetus*[3] to one of the year 369, the *Laws*[4] to one of about the year 356. The industry and ingenuity of scholars have discovered many hints which suggest limits of date for this dialogue or that, but none of these conjectures approaches certainty.

There are two general points that must be borne in mind by anyone who tries to determine the order of the dialogues. One is that the composition of each of the two long works, the *Republic* and the *Laws*, must have occupied a period of some years, and that some of the shorter dialogues may have been written during the composition of the longer. The other is that Plato is known to have been assiduous in revising his works,[5] so that touches which suggest a late date may well be much later than the main sub-

---

[1] The *Philebus* is placed after the *Timaeus* also by Baeumker, *Probl. d. Materie in d. gr. Philos.* 114, 197, by Bury in his ed. of the *Philebus*, lxxx, by L. A. Post in *Trans. of the American Philological Assn.*, lx (1929), 12, by C. Ritter in his latest book, *The Essence of Plato's Philosophy*, 27, by Robin, *La Place de la Physique dans la Philos. de Platon*, 10 n. 2, by Taylor, *A Comm. on Plato's Timaeus*, 9 n., and by Wilamowitz, *Platon*, i. 628.

[2] 193 a 3.   [3] 142 a 6.   [4] 638 b 1.

[5] Dion. Halic. *Comp.*, pp. 208–9.

stance of the dialogue in which they occur. In view of these difficulties, any order of the dialogues that may be proposed is bound to be very tentative. With these provisos, the following may be offered as a probable order of those of the earlier dialogues which throw light on the theory of Ideas, and of all the later works.

Birth of Plato, 429–427
  Charmides
  Laches
  Euthyphro
  Hippias Major
  Meno
First visit to Sicily, 389–388
  ? *Cratylus*
  Symposium, 385 or later
  Phaedo
  Republic
  Phaedrus
  Parmenides
  Theaetetus, 369 or later

Second visit to Sicily, 367–366
  Sophistes
  Politicus
Third visit to Sicily, 361–360
  Timaeus
  Critias
  Philebus
  Seventh Letter, 353–352
  Laws
Death of Plato, 348–347

II

THE BEGINNINGS OF THE THEORY

AMONG the early dialogues there are four whose main object is to discuss the definitions of certain things. The *Charmides* asks 'what is temperance?', the *Laches* 'what is courage?', the *Euthyphro* 'what is piety?', the *Hippias Major* 'what is beauty?' In the very asking of such a question, the germ of the theory of Ideas is already latent; for to ask it is to imply that there is a single thing for which such a word as 'temperance' stands, and that this is different from any of the many persons or actions that can rightly be called temperate.

Of these dialogues, the one in which Plato shows the least consciousness of the more general significance of what he is saying about one virtue in particular is the *Charmides*, and that is a reason, though not a compelling one, for regarding it as the earliest of the four.

The seeds of the theory of Ideas appear more definitely in the *Laches*. In that dialogue[1] Socrates, after enumerating various circumstances in which courage may be shown, asks 'what is it that, being in all these things, is the same?', thus assuming that there is something that *is* the same; and he makes the same assumption about quickness in 192 a 1–b 3. Here we have in germ the view that to every common name there answers a single entity which is referred to in every occurrence of the name.[2] But in the *Laches*, and long after the writing of the *Laches*, Plato's interest is not in the metaphysical status of this entity. His interest is that which characterized Socrates himself—interest in the answer to the particular question in hand, What is courage? But this interest in courage, both in Socrates and in Plato, is twofold. Primarily, perhaps, it is a practical interest; both Socrates and Plato want to know what courage is, because they are interested in their fellow citizens' becoming brave. But it is equally character-

[1] 191 e 10.   [2] *Rep.* 596 a 6.

istic of both that, unlike merely practical moralists, they are convinced that it is by *knowledge* of what virtue is, and by that alone, that men can become truly virtuous.[1] And to this practical interest there is added an intellectual curiosity aroused by two facts—that a variety of very different things are all alike instances of courage,[2] and that many things that have much in common with these are yet *not* instances of courage.[3] It was this combination of interests that led to the metaphysical doctrine of the Ideas. This may be added, that, while in the *Laches* as in other early dialogues it is in ethical terms that Plato is directly interested, he already recognizes, in mentioning the common nature of *quickness*, that the relation of universal to particular is not confined to ethical terms.

Plato does not discuss the implications of such a question as 'what is courage?', but it is not difficult to see what its implications are.[4] In the first place, it implies that there is not merely the word 'courage', nor merely this and the thought of courage, but a real thing of which 'courage' is the name. Secondly, it implies that this is one thing and not several. Plato was alive to the possibility of ambiguity in the meaning of a name. But apparently he regarded this as only occurring somewhat rarely, and was not fully alive to the varying shades of meaning which even the most seemingly innocent word may have. Thirdly, it is implied that courage is a complex thing capable of being analysed into elements; for if it were not so, the question 'what is courage?' would be a stupid one, the only true answer being that courage is courage. The answers which from time to time he gives to questions of this form show that in principle he was assuming, as Aristotle proceeded to do explicitly, that definition is analysis *per genus et differentiam*. But it is not till we come to the *Sophistes* that we find him explicitly saying this.

It seems probable that the *Euthyphro* is the first dialogue in which either of the words ἰδέα and εἶδος appears, in its special Platonic sense; and both appear there. The passages are as fol-

---

[1] *Lach.* 190 b 3–c 2.   [2] 190 e 7–191 e 8.   [3] 192 b 9–193 d 10.
[4] The meaning and implications of the 'what is X?' question in Plato are well discussed by Mr. R. Robinson in *Plato's Earlier Dialectic*, 51–62.

lows: 5 d 1–5 'Is not piety in every action always the same? and impiety, again, is it not the opposite of all piety? Is not everything that is to be impious the same as itself, having, as impiety, a single Form (ἰδέα)?' 6 d 9–e 6 'Do you remember that I did not ask you to give me one or two examples of piety, but to explain that very Form (εἶδος) which makes all pious things to be pious? Do you not remember that you said there was one Form (ἰδέα) which made impious acts impious, and pious acts pious? ... Tell me, then, what is the nature of this Form (ἰδέα), so that by looking to it and using it as a pattern I may say that any act done by you or another that has such a character is pious, and any act that has it not is impious.'

Both εἶδος and ἰδέα are derived from ἰδεῖν, 'to see', and the original meaning of both words is no doubt 'visible form'. Taylor made in *Varia Socratica*[1] a comprehensive study of the usage of the words in Greek literature before Plato, and came to the conclusion that the usage which we find in Plato and occasionally elsewhere has its origin in a Pythagorean use of these terms in the sense of geometrical pattern or figure. Taylor's list of quotations was carefully surveyed by C. M. Gillespie,[2] who came to a different conclusion, viz. that

in the time of Socrates the words ... show two trends of meaning in the general vocabulary of science. The first is mainly physical, but without mathematical associations: including many gradations of meaning from the popular to the technical: the *form* of a bodily object—occasionally used for the bodily object itself, like our own words 'form' and 'shape', but always distinct from σῶμα: sometimes the outer visible form or *shape*: often the inner form, the structure, nature, φύσις, a specifically physical conception: often extended to the nature of objects other than bodily: in one treatise of rhetorical character passing, by an easy transition, nearly, if not quite, into the metaphysical notion of essence. The second is semi-logical, classificatory: used especially in such contexts as 'there are four forms, kinds' of anything, whether a substance like the 'moist' or a disease or what not. ... In this line of development the later meaning of *species* is but a single step farther. Prof. Taylor seems to have made out a case for the employment of εἶδος in the Pythagorean mathematics in the sense

[1] 178–267.   [2] *Class Quart.* vi (1912), 179–203.

of geometrical 'pattern' or 'figure'. But there is no evidence whatsoever to show that this highly specialized meaning was a determining factor in the other developments; it seems to have been a collateral growth.

The two uses specified by Gillespie are natural enough developments from the original meaning. Sight is the most informative of our senses, and it is not surprising that words which originally meant visible form should come to mean visible nature, and then to mean nature in general; nor that from meaning nature they should come to mean 'class marked off by a nature from others'.

Mr. H. C. Baldry has suggested[1] that Plato's usage of the terms εἶδος and ἰδέα, and indeed 'the fundamental principle of Plato's metaphysics', were reached by a fusion of Socrates' teaching about moral values with the Pythagorean teaching about number-patterns. But our ignorance about the history of Pythagoreanism, and about the dating of developments in it, is profound. We do not know that at the time of Plato's youth the Pythagoreans called the number-patterns εἴδη or ἰδέαι. We do not know that Plato visited Italy before 389 or 388 B.C., and we can be pretty sure that the earliest dialogues in which the ideal theory is found were written long before this. Though Aristotle says that Plato assigned to Ideas the same sort of function that the Pythagoreans attached to numbers,[2] and that in later life he identified the Ideas with numbers,[3] he does not suggest that the number-patterns had anything to do with the inception of the ideal theory. Above all, there is nothing in the early dialogues to suggest this. The position seems rather to be that Socrates' inquiries as to 'what virtue is', 'what courage is', and the like, led Plato to recognize the existence of universals as a distinct class of entity, and that he took over as names for them the words εἶδος and ἰδέα, which in ordinary Greek had already begun to be used in the sense of 'quality' or 'characteristic'. What was original was not the use of the words, but the status he assigned to the things for which the words stood.

For Plato's use of the words we have an exhaustive study in Ritter's *Neue Untersuchungen*.[4] He distinguishes[5] six senses:

1. The outward appearance.

[1] *Class. Quart.* xxxi (1937), 141–5.   [2] *Met.* 987[b]9–13.
[3] 1078[b]9–12.   [4] 228–326.   [5] Ibid. 322.

2. The constitution or condition.

3. 'The characteristic that determines the concept.'

4. The concept itself.

5. The genus or species.

6. The objective reality underlying our concept.

To enable us to judge of the value of the distinctions he draws between senses (2), (3), (4), and (6), we may look at some typical examples. Ritter considers that in many passages it is doubtful which of these meanings is in question: I therefore take passages to which he assigns without hesitation one meaning or another:

Sense (2): *Meno* 72 d 7 'Do you think there is one health of a man, another of a woman? Or is it the same Form (εἶδος) everywhere, if it is health, whether it is in man or in anything else?'

Sense (3): *Meno* 72 c 6 'So, too, then, with the virtues; even if they are many and of all kinds, all surely have one identical Form (εἶδος) by reason of which they are virtues, with an eye to which the respondent should indicate to the questioner what virtue actually is.'

Sense (4): *Phaedo* 104 e 1 'So the Form (ἰδέα) of evenness will never enter into a set of three things.'

Sense (6): *Phaedo* 102 a 11 'Since it was agreed that each of the Forms (εἴδη) is something real and that it is by virtue of sharing in these that other things are called after them.'

Look not only at these passages but at their context, and you will be convinced that Plato means one and the same thing in every case; that nowhere is he speaking of concepts or of 'the content of concepts', but in every case of something which he considers perfectly objective, existing in its own right and not by virtue of our thinking of it. Ritter's attempt to distinguish between these four senses is a product of nineteenth century conceptualism which is far removed from the simple realism of Plato's thought.

What we find is that Plato not seldom uses both words in their original meaning 'visible form', that he uses both words in various non-technical senses in which they had been used by earlier writers, and that he uses both words in the two technical senses of 'Idea' and 'class'. While in the dialogues from the

Phaedo onwards, with the exception of the *Parmenides*, the meaning
'class' is the commonest meaning of εἶδος, it is only rarely that
ἰδέα is used in this sense. ἰδέα is the more vivid of the two words,
and tends to be preferred in the more highly coloured and
imaginative passages. It may be added that Plato often uses οὐσία
and φύσις as ways of referring to an Idea, and that he so uses
γένος in the *Sophistes*, and ἑνάς and μονάς in the *Philebus*.

In the *Hippias Major* an interesting hint may be found as to
what led Plato to his interest in definitions. 'Some one lately',
Socrates says in 286 c 5, 'when I was blaming certain things as
ugly and praising others as beautiful, threw me into confusion by
asking me, and very insolently too, "tell me, how have you come
to know what kind of things are beautiful or ugly. Come, could
you tell me what the beautiful is?"'
What led Plato to his interest in definition, if we take this hint,
was the conviction that no one can apply a word correctly unless
he can frame to himself some general account of its meaning. Not
only, as he often says, is pointing to instances no true answer to
the problem of definition; we cannot be sure that we are pointing
to genuine instances unless we first know what the definition is;
knowledge of connotation must precede knowledge of denotation.
'Teach me', Socrates says to Hippias, 'what the beautiful itself
(αὐτὸ τὸ καλόν) is.'[1] The question conceals a certain ambiguity,
of which Plato was perhaps not aware. It might mean 'what is
that very characteristic which the word "beautiful" stands for?',
or it might mean 'what is the characteristic or set of characteristics, other than beauty, which a thing must have in order to be
beautiful?' But the phrase 'the beautiful *itself*' points to the first
interpretation; and a hint in favour of this may be seen in a
passage of the *Charmides*,[2] in which Socrates is asking the parallel
question about self-control. He there says 'we have failed to discover what that is to which the imposer of names gave the name
of self-control'. It is not, then, the connexion between beauty and
its conditions that Socrates wants to know, but the nature of the
very characteristic for which the word 'beauty' stands.

[1] 286 d 8.   [2] 175 b 3.

The passage of the *Hippias Major* furnishes one of the earliest instances of the phrase αὐτὸ τό, which became one of the standard expressions for an Idea; the phrase is repeated elsewhere in the dialogue.[1] εἶδος makes its appearance in 289 d 4 and in 298 b 4.

At this stage the relation of the Idea to the particular is thought of simply as that of universal to particular; there is as yet no mention of the failure of the particular to be a true instance of the Idea. The Idea of beauty is 'that identical thing which makes pleasures of sight and pleasures of hearing beautiful, that which is present to both together and to each separately'.[2] The point is made that individual things are not always or in all relations instances of the same universals—that in some relations gold will appear no more beautiful than fig-wood;[3] but the point is not made that no particular is ever a true instance of an Idea, that the Idea is a standard or limit rather than a universal, and the relation of the individual to it that of imitation, not of participation.

There is one passage of the *Hippias Major*[4] which seems to be evidence of a further development of the theory of Ideas than anything to be found in the *Laches* or the *Euthyphro*. In his search for an answer to the question 'what is the beautiful?', Socrates suggests that it is the pleasant, apprehended by hearing and sight, and adds that the word 'beautiful' is applicable alike to both forms of the pleasant and to each of them. Hippias asserts that any term applicable to both together of two things is also applicable to each. Socrates hints that there are many exceptions, and finally points out that the term 'one' is applicable only to one thing at a time and not to both of two, while 'two' is applicable to both together and not to each, and again that each is odd and not even, while both together are even and not odd. The passage is interesting on two accounts; first because it foreshadows the problem raised in the *Parmenides* as to whether it is the whole or only a part of each Idea that is possessed by the individuals falling under it, and secondly, because it indicates an early interest in the Ideas of number, which engrossed Plato in his very latest period.

[1] 288 a 9, 289 c 3, 292 c 9; *Prot.* 360 e 8 may be earlier.
[2] 300 a 9–b 1. [3] 291 c 7. [4] 300 d 5–302 b 3.

In the *Meno* there is a good deal of reference to the Ideas, under the name of οὐσία or εἶδος. It is still the immanence of the Ideas in particulars that is insisted on: 'All the virtues *have* an identical Form.'[1] There is one phrase which may be the origin of Aristotle's term καθόλου and of our term 'universal'—'saying about virtue, as about a whole (κατὰ ὅλου), what it is'.[2] What is absent from the *Meno* is perhaps more striking than what is present in it; no attempt is made to connect the Ideas with the doctrine of anamnesis. Not only is there no reference, explicit or implicit, to the Ideas in the passage dealing with anamnesis,[3] but the method by which the slave-boy is got to discover what square has twice the area of that of a given square is a purely empirical one; it is on the evidence of his eyesight and not of any clearly apprehended relation between universals that he admits that the square on the diagonal of a given square is twice the size of the given square. He admits that certain triangles have areas equal, each of them, to half of the given square, and that the figure which they make up is itself a square, not because he sees that these things must be so, but because to the eye they look as if they were. For the establishing of a relation between the Ideas and anamnesis we have to look to the *Phaedo*, and in the *Meno* the theory of Ideas is carried no farther than in earlier dialogues.

The *Cratylus* plays an important part in the development of Plato's metaphysics; for it is here that he opposes himself most explicitly to complete subjectivism. He insists that 'things have a secure being of their own, not relative to us, nor dragged up and down by the force of our fancy, but in themselves related to their own being as they are by nature'.[4] But though we find the Idea elsewhere described as the being (οὐσία) of its particulars, and we find the word 'οὐσία' here, it would probably be a mistake to suppose that there is a direct reference here to the theory of Ideas. For by the οὐσία of a thing Plato seems to mean here its whole actual nature, as opposed to the nature which human opinion may ascribe to it; but no Idea is ever thought to be the *whole* nature of any of its instances; a particular just act, for

[1] 72 c 7; cf. 74 a 9.   [2] 77 a 6.   [3] 81 a 5–86 b 5.   [4] 386 d 8–e 4.

example, has something in it that distinguishes it from other just acts, and this must be something other than the Idea of justice. Elsewhere, indeed, there are references to the Ideas;[1] but they contain nothing new, except that it is definitely in opposition to the Heraclitean doctrine of universal flux that the doctrine of Ideas is put forward. As Aristotle says,[2] Plato accepts the Heraclitean doctrine so far as sensible things are concerned, but points out that there are non-sensible things *not* subject to flux.

At one point, perhaps, there is a trace of something new; there is one passage which suggests more clearly than anything we have hitherto found the transcendence of the Ideas. 'To what does the carpenter look', says Socrates,[3] 'in making the shuttle? Does he not look to something that was naturally fitted to act as a shuttle? ... And suppose the shuttle to be broken in the making, will he in making another look to the broken one? Or will he look to the Form according to which he made the other?' And this he proceeds to describe as 'precisely that which a shuttle is' or 'the Form of the shuttle'. It looks as if there were a suggestion here of a Form of shuttle which can be contemplated, and therefore must exist, before it is embodied in any particular shuttle. We can hardly suppose that that to which the maker looks in making the shuttle is necessarily a universal abstracted from existing shuttles for that would make the *invention* of the shuttle impossible. Yet while Plato *seems* to be thinking of a Form of shuttle as existing in its own right before it is embodied in particular materials, he does not ascribe to it a merely transcendent existence; for he goes on to speak of the carpenter as succeeding, when he is skilful, in embodying the Form in particular materials.[4] He has not yet reached the point of thinking that an Idea is never perfectly exemplified, but only imitated. And perhaps on reflection we ought to admit that though his language may be interpreted as implying the existence of the Form before it is embodied, that is not a necessary interpretation. When he says that the carpenter looks to the Form, he may not think of the Form as pre-existing

[1] 389 d 6–7, e 3, 439 c 8.   [2] *Met.* 987ª32–b1.   [3] 389 a 6–c 1.
[4] 389 c 3–6; cf. 390 b 1–2.

any more than, when we say we aim at some end, we think of that end as existing already.

The most interesting passage of the *Cratylus*, for our purposes, is that which comes at the end.[1] According to Aristotle,[2] Plato's earliest philosophical association was with Cratylus the Heraclitean, and he retained the belief that all sensible things are in constant flux; but when he had come under Socrates' influence he held that because of their changeability not they but something else must be the object of knowledge. This is just what we find in the *Cratylus*.

The knowledge of things is not to be derived from names. No; they must be studied and investigated in themselves. . . . Tell me, whether there is or is not any absolute beauty or good, or any other absolute existence. . . . Then let us seek the true beauty, not asking whether a face is fair, or anything of that sort . . . let us ask whether the true beauty is not always beautiful. . . . Then how can that be a real thing which is never in the same state (for obviously things which are ever in the same state cannot change while they remain the same; and if they are always the same and in the same state, and never depart from their original form, how can they change or be moved?) . . . Nor yet can they be known by anyone; for at the moment that the observer approaches, then they become other and of another nature, so that you can no longer know their nature or state; surely no knowledge knows what it knows, if that has no state. . . . Nor can we reasonably say, Cratylus, that there is knowledge at all, if everything is in a state of transition and there is nothing abiding. For if knowledge does not fall away from being knowledge, it continues always to abide and to be knowledge; but if the very nature of knowledge changes, it will change to another nature than knowledge and no longer be knowledge; and if the transition is always going on, at the time when the change occurs there will be no knowledge, and, according to this view, there will be no one to know and nothing to be known; but if there are always that which knows and that which is known, and the beautiful and the good and every other thing also exist, then I do not think that they can resemble a process of flux, as we were just now supposing.

This is the first distinct appearance in Plato of the argument from the existence of knowledge to the existence of unchangeable, non-

---

[1] 439 b 4–440 c 1.   [2] *Met.* 987a32–b7.

sensible objects. It is what Aristotle calls[1] the argument 'from the sciences', just as that which we have found in earlier dialogues is the argument of the 'one over many'.

A more definite assertion of transcendence than any we have found hitherto occurs in a famous passage of the *Symposium*:[2]

He who has been instructed thus far in the things of love . . . will suddenly perceive a beauty of wondrous nature . . . a beauty which in the first place is everlasting, not growing and decaying, or waxing and waning; secondly, not fair in one point of view and foul in another, or at one time or in one relation or at one place fair, at another time or in another relation or at another place foul, or in the likeness of a face or hands or any other part of the bodily frame, or in any form of speech or knowledge, or existing anywhere in any other being, as for example in animal, or in earth, or in heaven, or in any other thing; but beauty absolute, separate, simple, and everlasting (αὐτὸ καθ' αὑτὸ μεθ' αὑτοῦ μονοειδὲς ἀεὶ ὄν), while all other beautiful things share in it in some such fashion as this: while the others come into being and pass away it neither becomes greater or less nor suffers any change.

That certainly is a strong assertion of the transcendence of the Idea of beauty, but we have to remember that these are not the words of Plato nor of Socrates. They are put into the mouth of Diotima the wise woman of Mantinea, and their tone is that of a prophet rather than of a philosopher. It is legitimate to suppose that, translated into the language of philosophy, the passage only affirms, not the separate existence of the Idea of beauty, but its difference from all its embodiments, and its eternity and purity in contrast to their transitoriness and imperfection.

Apart from this one passage, this whole group of early dialogues treats the Ideas as being immanent in particular things. It is 'present' in them; it is placed 'in them' by the craftsman; it comes to be 'in them'; it is 'common' to them; the particulars, in turn, 'possess' it or 'share in' it.[3]

[1] Ibid. 990ᵇ11–14.   [2] 210 e 2–211 b 5.   [3] For the evidence, cf. pp. 228–30.

III

THE *PHAEDO*

IN the *Phaedo* the Ideas play a much larger part than in any previous dialogue. They are indeed almost omnipresent in the dialogue; but the introduction of them is always subordinate to the proof of immortality, and much of what is now said of them throws no fresh light on Plato's views about their own nature. The first passage in which they are mentioned[1] tells us only that they do not come to be known by the use of any of the senses, but by pure thought (αὐτῇ καθ' αὑτὴν εἰλικρινεῖ τῇ διανοίᾳ). Later, however, Plato describes more definitely than he has hitherto done the process of coming to know the Ideas. We saw that in the *Meno* the theory of anamnesis is not connected with the knowledge of the Ideas; in the *Phaedo* it is. Plato first points out[2] that recollection 'may be derived from things either like or unlike', i.e. that there may be association either by resemblance (as when by seeing a picture of Simmias we are led to remember Simmias),[3] or by contiguity (as when by seeing a lyre we are led to remember its owner);[4] and that in the former case we note in addition whether the thing perceived falls short, in any respect, of that of which it reminds us.[5] Now we maintain (he continues) that there exists equality itself, and we know what it is. And this knowledge we have been led to by seeing equal pieces of wood, stones, and the like.[6] These are very different from equality itself, as is proved by the fact that sticks or stones, while remaining the same, sometimes appear equal to one person and not to another, but 'equals themselves' never appear unequal, nor equality to be inequality.[7] Perfect particular instances of an Idea are here distinguished both from imperfect, sensible particulars and from the Idea itself; this is important as the earliest hint of a belief in mathematical entities as something intermediate between Ideas and sensible particulars.[8] But, while

---

[1] 65 d 4–66 a 8.   [2] 74 a 2.   [3] 73 c 9.   [4] 73 d 5–10.
[5] 74 a 5–7.   [6] 74 b 4–7.   [7] 74 b 7–c 6.
[8] The belief ascribed to Plato by Aristotle in *Met.* 987^{b}14–18.

Plato distinguishes between perfect particulars and the Idea, he does not stress the distinction, and it plays no part in his argument.

The recognition of Ideas is thus brought under the heading of association by resemblance, and under that sub-form of it in which the resemblance is very imperfect. It would be easy for a modern thinker to say that what suggests to us the idea of equality is the experience of *inequality*; for we are familiar with the fact that exact instruments of measurement reveal inequalities where the eye does not detect them, and that in all probability we have never seen two physical bodies that were exactly equal. But though it is true to say that probably no two physical bodies are exactly equal in their dimensions, it is not true to say that only the experience of unequals suggests the idea of equality; for we certainly have many experiences between whose objects we can *detect* no difference of size, and this is more correctly called an experience of apparent equals than an experience of unequals. The truth seems to be that an experience of apparent equals and an experience of apparent unequals are equally capable of bringing into our minds the thought of equality.

Plato, at all events, does not take the line of saying that it is the experience of unequals that suggests the thought of equality. He refers to the experience, throughout the passage, as the experience of equals; yet he stresses their imperfection. The point in which he finds them imperfect is that they 'seem equal to one person and unequal to another' (74 b 7–9) ; he is thinking, perhaps, of the effects of perspective. There is a certain inconsistency in his thought here. For in view of his emphatic statement, in the *Protagoras* and the *Cratylus*, that bodily things have a nature of their own and may be different from what they seem to us, it follows that things which seem to some person unequal may nevertheless be equal and therefore perfect examples of equality. But Plato does not notice the inconsistency, and accordingly speaks, throughout the passage, as if sensible things necessarily only approximated to equality; and this is the earliest passage (apart from the mystical passage in the *Symposium*) in which this aspect of the Ideas, not as universals manifested in particulars but as ideals, standards, or limits to which invididual things only approximate, is emphasized (ἐκείνου ὀρέγεται τοῦ ὃ ἔστιν ἴσον, καὶ αὐτοῦ ἐνδεέστερά ἐστιν 75 b 1 ; cf. βούλεται 74 d 9, προθυμεῖται 75 b 7). For the first time, the relation of sensible things to Ideas is thought of as imitation (μίμησις) rather than as sharing (μέθεξις), and yet it contains an element of sharing, since the sensible things are throughout spoken of as equals, not as unequals.[1]

Four passages of the *Phaedo* are interesting both as showing very clearly that Plato has reached a generalized theory of Ideas, and as showing the nature of the typical members of his world of Ideas—75 c 10–d 3, 76 d 7–9, 78 d 3–7, 100 b 3–7. Here he refers to 'all the things on which we set the seal of reality in itself' (αὐτὸ ὃ ἔστι),[2] and describes the doctrine as one which 'we are always repeating';[3] and the instances that recur are ideal beauty, goodness, justice, piety, equality, bigness. There have been in earlier dialogues incidental references to the Idea of speed, the Idea of shuttle, the Idea of name,[4] but the first two were introduced only as incidental illustrations, the third only in the interests of a special theory of language. When Plato wishes to refer to typical Ideas, he refers either to moral or aesthetic values or to mathematical qualities or relations such as size or equality. Values and mathematical entities, these remain his dominant interest—values throughout his life and mathematical entities with increasing emphasis as he gets older, until in the end (as Aristotle, at least, says) the theory of Ideas became a theory of numbers. Ideas of substances (like 'animal itself') are not mentioned in the *Phaedo*, and are nowhere prominent except in the *Timaeus*, though they were involved in the theory, since it was the theory that there is an Idea answering to every common name.[5]

It is not by despising the senses and turning to pure contemplation, but by using the senses and finding what they suggest to us, that (in Plato's view) we arrive at knowledge of the Ideas; it is

---

[1] In 100 c 3–6, d 6 particulars are still described as partaking in Ideas; in 100 d 5 the Idea is still described as present in them.
[2] 75 d 1–2.   [3] 76 d 8.
[4] *Laches* 192 a 1, *Crat.* 389 b 5, 390 a 5.
[5] *Rep.* 596 a 6.

our senses that must suggest the thought that all sensible apparent equals both aspire to that which is equal, and fall short of it;[1] and in saying this he describes very truly the co-operation of sense with reason in leading us to knowledge. But the suggestion of Ideas by things of sense can, he maintains, happen only because we knew the Ideas in a previous existence.[2] How did we know them then? If then also we knew them only on the suggestion of things of sense, the reference to a former existence does nothing to explain the process of coming to know them. If the coming to know Ideas on the suggestion of sensible things is not intelligible in itself but presupposes a prior knowledge of Ideas, a previous knowing of Ideas on the suggestion of sensible things would be no more intelligible than such an occurrence now. Thus if recollection is to explain what it is introduced to explain, the previous knowledge of the Ideas must have been a knowledge of them *not* on the suggestion of things of sense, but direct and immediate. And it is thus that Plato conceives us as having known them in a previous life. Thus the doctrine of anamnesis clearly implies the separate existence of Ideas, not as imperfectly embodied in sensible things but as existing apart in their purity. It is in this passage of the *Phaedo* that Plato first expresses a clear belief in the separate existence of Ideas; and that goes naturally with his beginning to adopt the language of resemblance, though he retains the language of participation, to express the relation of sensible things to Ideas.

It would be a mistake to describe Plato as having, either at this or at any stage of his development, made a complete bifurcation of the universe into Ideas and sensible things. For one thing, we have the casual reference to 'equals themselves'[3]—an allusion to mathematical entities which are neither Ideas nor sensible things, an allusion which paves the way for the doctrine of the 'Intermediates'. Plato very likely at this stage did not himself appreciate the significance of his own allusion. But he very certainly recognizes the existence of another type of entity which is neither an Idea nor a sensible thing; for there is a whole section[4] in which he describes soul as akin to the Ideas and not to sensible things

[1] 75 a 5–b 2.   [2] 76 d 7–e 7.   [3] 74 c 1.   [4] 79 b 1–80 b 6.

in respect of unchangeability, and yet nowhere suggests—and indeed how could he?—that souls are themselves Ideas.

The next passage that claims our attention is the famous passage (95 e 7–102 a 2) in which Plato represents Socrates as describing his philosophical development. The early part of the description is not very clear, but the point made seems to be this. Socrates had in his youth busied himself with the physical and physiological problems current in the middle of the fifth century, but the welter of conflicting theories had only produced in him puzzlement about a problem which cut deeper than the theories could penetrate. It seems clear, for instance, that a man grows by eating and drinking, and the theorists had busied themselves with the details of this process; but they had raised in his mind the prior question how a thing that is small can become large, and in general how a thing characterized in one way can come to be characterized in another. In particular, he came to be puzzled by the question of numbers. 'I cannot satisfy myself even that when someone adds one to one, either the one to which it was added has become two,[1] or that which was added and that to which it was added have become two by the addition of the one to the other' (96 e 6–97 a 1). Again, he could not see how it can be true to say both that the addition of one to one makes two and that the division of one makes two, since the cause of two-ness ought to be a single cause (97 a 5–b 3).

Anaxagoras' great saying that mind was the disposer and cause of all seemed to bring light into his darkness. 'If mind is the disposer', he said to himself, 'mind will dispose all for the best, and the explanation of anything's being as it is must be that it is best for it to be in that condition.' But, in fact, Anaxagoras' teleology was no more enlightening than the materialism of the other pre-Socratics; for when it came to details he offered explanations as materialistic as any, assigning, as if they were the causes of things' being as they are, material conditions which are merely the *sine qua non* for the operation of the true cause (98 b 8–99 c 6).

Anaxagoras had failed not by being too teleological but by not being teleological enough, and Socrates' disappointment with

---

[1] Wyttenbach's duplication of ἢ τὸ προστεθέν in 96 e 9 is quite unnecessary.

Anaxagoras did not lead him to abandon the hope of a teleological explanation of the world. But he saw no direct way of reaching it, and therefore fell back on a second-best mode (δεύτερος πλοῦς, 99 d 1) of inquiring into the cause of things. The δεύτερος πλοῦς was originally the use of oars when the wind failed, and the phrase suggests, as Burnet points out, what is not necessarily a less effective but only a slower and more laborious method. Socrates' suggestion is that previous inquiries had failed because they had tried to discover the explanation of things' being as they are, directly by the use of the senses, and had suffered the fate of those who try to look direct at the sun when it is being eclipsed, instead of looking at its reflection in water (99 d 5–e 4). But the comparison is inadequate; he will not altogether admit that his method of studying things is less direct than that of the physicists (99 e 6–100 a 3). His method, at any rate, whether it is to be called direct or indirect, is to study the truth of things ἐν λόγοις, i.e. to assume in each case the λόγος which he judges strongest, to adopt as true whatever agrees with this, and reject whatever disagrees (100 a 3–7).

λόγοι are not here to be understood as definitions; for in the example he gives there is no use of definitions. Nor, though there is use of concepts or universals, is λόγοι to be understood as meaning that; nor yet as meaning arguments. The language of 'agreement', and the fact that what Plato calls the 'strongest λόγος' is the proposition that Ideas exist, show that λόγοι means statements ✻ or propositions. Socrates is hardly fair to his predecessors in contrasting his method with theirs as the study of things ἐν λόγοις as opposed to ἐν ἔργοις. For what they did was not simply, as he suggests, to use their senses and write down what these reported. They also had their λόγοι or ὑποθέσεις, general views which were suggested to them by what their senses reported, and from which they deduced consequences as Socrates did from his own λόγος. The truth is rather that the sort of λόγος they took as their starting-point was one suggested by particular observations, such as Thales' λόγος that all things are water, while Socrates takes as his starting-point something suggested by a much more general reflection. For his 'strongest λόγος' turns out to be 'nothing new'

(100 b 1), but the well-worn thesis (ἐκεῖνα τὰ πολυθρύλητα, ibid. 4) which in this and other dialogues we have often heard him maintain, 'that there is an absolute beauty and goodness and greatness, and the like'. This is the kind of cause that he has studied (100 b 3–4), in distinction from the material and efficient causes studied by most of the pre-Socratics, and from the final cause whose recognition Anaxagoras had preached but not practised.

There are (or rather, under certain circumstances may be) three phases in the proper treatment of a λόγος or ὑπόθεσις. (1) The first is to accept what agrees with it (100 a 3–7)—i.e. the conclusions that follow from it—and to reject what disagrees. (The statement of this element of the method is loose; for the 'agreement' which will justify acceptance of proposition *B* because of the acceptance of proposition *A* must mean logical sequence, while if 'disagreement' is to justify rejection of proposition *C* it must mean not non-sequence, but inconsistency.) But the acceptance must be only provisional. For (2) it may turn out that contradictory conclusions follow from the hypothesis (101 d 5), in which case the hypothesis must itself be abandoned. It has been doubted by some critics whether such contradiction can possibly occur, but it is clear that at least Plato thought it could happen. There is only one way (*a*) in which it could really happen, viz. if *A* is a complex proposition including two inconsistent propositions. But there is also a way (*b*) in which it might *seem* to happen, viz. if *B* is entailed not by *A* alone but by *A* and *C*, and a proposition *D*, inconsistent with *B*, is entailed by *A* and *E*. In case (*a*) it follows, of course, that *A* is false; in case (*b*) it does not. But it is doubtful whether Plato envisaged either of these cases; he speaks as if a single simple proposition could entail contradictory consequences. Thirdly (3), if the hypothesis itself does not commend itself as self-evident, you must proceed backwards among the hypotheses from which successively it would follow, till you come to one that is sufficient (ἱκανός), i.e. that satisfies both you and your opponent. And in all this you must take care not to confuse the different stages of the inquiry.[1]

---

[1] 101 d 3–e 3. For a full and good discussion of the treatment of hypothesis in the *Phaedo*, cf. R. Robinson, *Plato's Earlier Dialectic*, 128–50.

This third element is the procedure already advocated and used in the *Meno*,[1] that of testing the truth of proposition A by searching for some proposition easier to establish, from which the truth of A would follow. In the *Meno* Socrates takes his example from mathematics, and the method is in fact the appropriate method of discovering the proof of mathematical theorems.

The second and third stages do not occur in the case of Socrates' own hypothesis in the *Phaedo*. It is adopted without question by Cebes, the disputant of the moment,[2] and it is not found to entail inconsistent consequences. The only conclusion that Socrates draws from it is that the soul is immortal.[3]

The account Plato gives, then, of Socrates' mental history (though it is probably his own that he is describing) is this: he first tried to explain the facts of the universe by assuming, in the manner of the pre-Socratics, material causes such as hot substance or cold substance, air or fire.[4] Finding no satisfaction there, he tried to explain the facts by a final cause, the good, and by an efficient cause, mind, seeking to produce the good.[5] But here also he failed, and so he fell back on the assumption (which he has already made, on other grounds, in earlier dialogues) of formal causes, the Ideas, to account for things being as they are.

In the statement of the ideal theory here, Plato uses certain important terms in connexion with the relation between the Idea and particulars. From the side of the Idea, it is called presence (παρουσία),[6] from the side of the particulars participation (κοινωνία, μετάσχεσις, μετάληψις).[7] But Socrates adds that he does not insist on any particular name for the relation, but only on the fact that it is by reason of the Ideas that particulars are what they are, that 'by the beautiful all beautiful things are beautiful'.[8] The criticism which Socrates had passed on current accounts of causality was that the cause named was not coextensive with the effect; to say that the addition of two units is the cause of the number 2 must be wrong, because 2 can equally well be produced by the division of 1.[9] There the cause alleged was too narrow.

[1] 86 e 1–87 c 3. [2] 100 c 1. [3] 100 b 7–9. [4] 96 b 2–4.
[5] 97 b 8–d 3. [6] 100 d 5. [7] 100 d 6, 101 c 5, 102 b 2.
[8] 100 d 7. [9] 97 a 5–b 3.

Here he points out that current accounts of causality are some-times too wide. It will not do to say that *A* is taller than *B* by, i.e. by reason of, a head, for *A* may also be smaller than *C* by a head, so that a head is no more the cause of *A*'s being greater than of his being less.[1] The only true explanation is that *A* is greater than *B* by reason of greatness, and less than *C* by reason of small-ness; formal causes alone are coextensive with their effects.

Having pointed out that the same particular thing may share in opposite Ideas, Socrates proceeds to point out that not only cannot an Idea itself be characterized by its opposite, but also the particularization of one Idea in a particular thing cannot be characterized by the opposite Idea; 'the greatness *in us* never admits smallness'.[2] It must do one of two things—either give ground on the approach of its contrary, or be annihilated if its contrary obtains entrance. What greatness cannot do is to accept smallness and become other than what it was.

On the face of it, the stress laid in some earlier passages on the separateness of the Ideas is difficult to reconcile with the language used here of the presence of the Idea in particular things. But the two ways of speaking can be reconciled if we attend to the distinc-tion Plato draws between likeness itself and the likeness in us.[3] We then see that his theory involves not merely the Idea and the particular thing, but also the quality in the particular thing. What is present in the particular thing is not, strictly speaking, the Idea, but an imperfect copy of the Idea. And if we take account of the phrase 'the equals themselves',[4] we see that Plato held that of certain Ideas there are perfect instances. Thus the complete scheme is:

Ideas	imperfectly imitated by	Qualities
exemplified in		exemplified in
Numbers and shapes	imperfectly imitated by	Sensible things.

It is not very clear what Plato means by the two alternatives—giving ground or being annihilated. The phrase is repeated (103 a 1, d 8–11, 104 c 1, 106 a 3–10), and the alternatives are

---

[1] 100 e 8–101 b 2.   [2] 102 d 7.
[3] 102 d 5–8; cf. 103 b 5 and *Parm.* 130 b 1–4.   [4] 74 c 1.

therefore meant to be real alternatives, not merely different ways of saying the same thing. Taylor holds[1] that the melting of snow when exposed to heat is an example of annihilation, and that when a fourth child is born to a man, the fact that the class 'children of so-and-so' ceases to be odd is an example of withdrawal, 'since "oddness" is not, like low or high temperature, a character which can be destroyed'. This can hardly be the real interpretation; for on the one hand neither coldness in general nor oddness in general could be described by Plato as destructible (since both are Ideas), and on the other hand he *could* say that the odd-numberedness of a particular family ceases to be when a fourth child is born, just as much as the coldness of a certain parcel of snow ceases to be when the parcel melts. And in fact he explicitly says that it is 'destruction' that applies in the case of an odd number subjected to the approach of evenness (i.e. which has a unit added to it) (106 b 7–c 3). The distinction may, perhaps, be stated thus: If there is a name N which stands for 'a substance S characterized by a quality Q', then what cannot happen is that the thing should, while retaining the quality Q, also assume the contrary quality Q'. What sometimes happens is that the substance S takes on the contrary quality Q'; in which case the thing called N (which stands for 'S qualified by Q') is annihilated and a new thing, which must be called by a name different from N (e.g. 'water' as against 'snow') comes into being. But in the special case in which the quality Q is the quality of indestructibleness, the thing called N (which stands for the union of a certain substance with indestructibility) is owing to the *special* nature of the attribute incapable of losing the attribute, and instead of being annihilated withdraws in good order (σῶς καὶ ἄτηκτος, 106 a 5; the metaphor, as Taylor points out, is military). This is what Plato believes to happen in the case of soul, which, being the very principle of life (105 c 9–11), is incapable of taking on the attribute of destructibility (106 b 1–4).

Socrates points out that this mutual repulsion of contrary Ideas is quite compatible with what has already been stated in the dialogue, that things come into being out of their contraries.

---

[1] *P.M.W.* 205–6.

A contrary thing (ἐναντίον πρᾶγμα) may come out of its contrary
thing, i.e. a thing characterized by one quality may come to be
characterized by the contrary quality; but one quality cannot
become its contrary (103 a 4–c 2). In this passage we find, perhaps, the origin of Aristotle's doctrine that change is always the
change of a persisting matter from being characterized by one of
two contraries to being characterized by the other. Plato's distinction between τὰ ἐναντία and τὰ ἐναντία πράγματα (or τὰ ἔχοντα τὰ
ἐναντία) is the equivalent of what Aristotle expresses in different
language.

Socrates now proceeds to expound an important development
of the ideal theory. Snow is not identical with coldness; yet snow
can no more, while remaining snow, become hot, than coldness
can become hot (or heat—Plato does not clearly distinguish the
two things). Not only is a Form worthy of its own name eternally,
but there are *things* that have such-and-such a Form so long as
they exist (103 e 2–5). Not only is 'the odd' always odd, but the
number three, the number five, &c., are always odd; i.e., while
there are subjects which can pass from one state to its contrary,
there are other subjects which are so wedded to one state or
quality that they cannot receive its contrary, while remaining
themselves. In other words, there are Forms such that any of
them compels anything which it occupies (κατάσχῃ) not only to
have its own Form (i.e. the Form in question) but also the Form
of a certain contrary.[1] A group occupied by the Form of three
must be odd as well as being a group of three. And while in a
sense it is the Form of three that exercises this compulsion
(104 d 1–3), it may also be said that it is the Form of odd that
exercises it (ibid. 9–12). The principle is restated thus: 'If a Form
introduces one of two contrary Forms into everything into which
it enters, it never receives the contrary of that Form' (105 a 1–5).

This discovery enables Plato to give a new answer to an old
question. To the question, 'by the presence of what in a thing is
that thing made hot?', his 'old, safe, and stupid answer' (105 b 6–
c 1) was 'by the presence of heat', but he can now say with equal

---

[1] Reading in 104 d 3 ἐναντίον ἀεί τινος with Stallbaum; or 'of a contrary to
something' if we read ἐναντίον τῳ ἀεί τινος with Robin.

safety and more insight 'by the presence of fire'. To the question 'by the presence of what in a body is that body made ill?', he will now answer not 'illness' but 'fever'. To the question 'by the presence of what in a number is that number made odd?', he will now say not 'oddness' but 'oneness'.

While something is gained by the new answer, something is also lost. The new answer does not run the risk of being tautologous as the old did, but at the same time it loses the universality of the old answer. For while fever will make sick any body in which it is present, there are other things than fever which will do so. While any class that has but one member is odd, other classes are odd as well. The new answer does not really answer the old question, what is the *necessary* and sufficient cause of *A*'s being *B*-wise characterized. That could only be done not by naming a species of *B* but by naming something coextensive with *B* and such as to entail it. The new answer is an answer only to a new question, viz. what is the *special* form of *B* present in a particular *A* which is *B*-wise characterized; what is the specific Idea that introduces into *A* the generic Idea *B* which *A* is known to be characterized by.

The interest of the passage lies in the fact that in it Plato, apparently for the first time, notices the existence of pairs of Ideas related as genus and species. The passage is thus a prelude to the later problem of διαίρεσις and to the discussion of the κοινωνία εἰδῶν in the *Sophistes*. But it does not take the matter very far. It does not recognize any long train of Ideas related as genus and species, but only pairs of Ideas so related. And that is enough for his immediate purpose, which is that of showing that the Idea of soul introduces the Idea of aliveness and excludes that of deadness. At the same time the passage marks a great logical advance. In its earliest and simplest form, the theory of Ideas embodies the discovery that every empirical judgement, of the form '*A* is *B*' or '*A* is a *B*', includes one universal, as its predicate. In its new form the theory embodies the discovery that there are also non-empirical judgements, of the form '*A* is necessarily *B*' or '*A* necessarily involves *B*', in which both terms are universals.

The passage has also a great historical interest, from the fact that in it we can in all probability find the origin of Aristotle's discovery of the syllogism.[1] In Aristotle's theory, the only figure of syllogism that is recognized as valid in its own right is the first; and in that figure major term, middle term, minor term are respectively property, generic character, and species. Now this is just what we find in the *Phaedo*. The presence of fieriness in a class of things introduces heat into it and excludes coldness. What is this but the syllogism 'Heat belongs to what is fiery, Fieriness belongs to such and such a class of things, Therefore heat belongs to that class', and the syllogism 'Coldness does not belong to what is fiery, Fieriness belongs to such and such a class, Therefore coldness does not belong to that class'—typical syllogisms in Barbara and Celarent? That the connexion between the *Phaedo* and the theory of syllogism is a real one is shown by two facts; not only is παρεῖναι, so often used by Plato to denote the presence of an Idea in its particulars, sometimes used by Aristotle to describe the relation of major to middle or of middle to minor term,[2] but also, as Plato uses ἐπιφέρειν to describe the introduction of the property by the generic character,[3] Aristotle uses συνεπιφέρειν in the same way in the theory of syllogism.[4]

We must ask the question whether the ideal theory, as it appears in the dialogues down to and including the *Phaedo*, implies the 'separate' existence of the Ideas. In the statements directly made about the nature of the Ideas there is little evidence of this; what is emphasized over and over again is that the Ideas are different from particulars, and that they are present in particulars. The passage which most clearly suggests their transcendent existence is the famous passage of the *Symposium*[5] which clearly attributes to the Form of beauty a being apart from its embodiment in any beautiful thing. But this is the language of the wise woman Diotima, not of Socrates, and in the passage of the *Phaedo*[6] which refers to it the more transcendent elements

---

[1] This was clearly pointed out by Shorey in *Class. Philology*, xix (1924), 1–19.
[2] *An. Pr.* 44ᵃ4, 5, 45ᵃ10.   [3] 104 e 10, 105 a 3, 4, d 10.
[4] *An. Pr.* 52ᵇ7.   [5] 210 e 2–211 b 5.   [6] 78 d 5.

disappear, and it is simply self-identity (μονοειδές) and un-changeability that are asserted of the Form. What is said there might be said by anyone who believes in objective universals, whether he does or does not believe in their having any existence otherwise than in particulars.

But we must look not only to what Plato says about the Forms, but also to what he says about our apprehension of them. What he says about our apprehension of them in this life amounts to two things—that it is only by experience of particulars that they are suggested to our minds, but that this suggestion presupposes a prior knowledge of them. If we consider these two assertions, we are driven to the conclusion that the theory of anamnesis logically involves belief in transcendent Forms.[1]

It is a mistake to dismiss the anamnesis theory, as Ritter does,[2] as mere by-play. Socrates expressly says, and Simmias agrees, that the existence of the Ideas and the pre-existence of the soul go together (76 d 7–77 a 5). We are thus left with only two alternatives—either Plato (assuming that we can take what Socrates says, in so serious a vein, as representing Plato's views) failed to realize that the doctrine of anamnesis, if it is to be of any use, implies a previous direct knowledge of disembodied Ideas, or he saw this implication and deliberately accepted it. Between these alternatives it is impossible to decide with cer-tainty; but Aristotle's consistent statement that Plato believed in 'separate' Ideas confirms the latter view; for it is very difficult to suppose that after nineteen years spent in Plato's School Aristotle could have been misinformed about so important a matter.

Gathering together what we have learned so far about Plato's doctrine of Ideas, we may say this: originally the doctrine was simply a belief in the existence of universals as implied by the existence of individuals having qualities. The prevailing language to express the relation of universals to particulars is that of 'presence' of universals in particulars, of 'sharing' by particulars in universals. But in the *Symposium*, and more definitely in the *Phaedo*, another element comes into the theory; the particulars

---

[1] Cf. p. 25 above.   [2] *P.L.S.L.* i. 584–6.

are spoken of as falling short of the Ideas, not only by being particulars and not universals, but by not being genuine examples of the Ideas but only approximate examples of them; the language of imitation begins to creep in, without, however, either displacing the other or being reconciled with it. Further, in the *Phaedo* some of the relations between Ideas themselves begin to be explored. The Ideas Plato has primarily in mind are of two types—(1) the Ideas of goodness (and of the various virtues) and of beauty and (2) mathematical Ideas such as equality, oddness and evenness, twoness, threeness, &c. These are just the two groups of Ideas of whose existence Socrates in the *Parmenides*[1] describes himself as certain. When other Ideas are introduced (e.g. that of the shuttle in the *Cratylus*), it is only by way of illustrating the universality of the doctrine of Ideas, and not because Plato is interested in these particular Ideas. But it would not be true to say that he does not seriously believe in these other Ideas; for they are implied, just as much as moral, aesthetic, and mathematical Ideas, by the recognition that for every set of individuals called by a common name there must be an Idea.

[1] 130 b 1–10.

IV

THE *REPUBLIC* AND THE *PHAEDRUS*

THE early books of the *Republic* contain little that throws light on the theory of Ideas. There has been much discussion about a passage in Book V (476 a 4–7): 'The same holds of justice and injustice, good and bad, and all the essential Forms: each in itself is one; but by reason of the sharing of actions and bodies in them, and of their sharing in one another (τῇ τῶν πράξεων καὶ σωμάτων καὶ ἀλλήλων κοινωνίᾳ) they each of them make their appearance everywhere and appear many.' The sharing of one Idea in another is not, in so many words, discussed earlier than the *Sophistes*; the present sentence has therefore been condemned as an anachronism, and ἀλλήλων has been emended into ἄλλῃ ἄλλων or ἄλλ' ἄλλων. But we have already in the *Phaedo* found Plato saying that the Idea of three imports into particular groups of three the Idea of oddness, and this it can do only because it shares in that Idea itself, so that the notion of the participation of one Idea in another is no new one to Plato.

A passage which follows immediately must, however, be regarded as indicating a development in the theory of Ideas. It is the passage in which Plato correlates three classes of object—that which is, that which is not, and that which is between being and not-being—with three states of mind, knowledge, nescience, and opinion.

The passage starts (476 a 9) by drawing a distinction between two classes of people. One of these is the class of philosophers, defined as those who recognize the existence both of Ideas and of sensible objects and who distinguish between them (476 c 9–d 3). The other is the class of people who are lovers of sounds and sights and do not recognize the existence of Ideas (476 c 2–7). The state of mind of the first class is said to be knowledge, that of the second to be opinion, and Plato proceeds to a discussion of these two states of mind, and of their objects. He begins with a general argument, in which he describes the object of knowledge as being the completely real and the object corresponding to nescience as being the unreal, and infers that the object of opinion must be that which is 'between being and not-being'. The sights and sounds which have already been identified with the objects of opinion are therefore consigned to the status of semi-reality.

Plato shows his insight by drawing a rigid distinction between knowledge and opinion. The one word implies both subjective certainty and infallibility; the other implies the opposites of both. He is much less convincing when he assigns the real as the object of knowledge, and that which is between being and not-being as the object of opinion. And the further argument by which he supports this account of the object of opinion is no more convincing. Some of the instances he takes are instances of things characterized by purely relative terms—double and half, great and small, light and heavy. That a thing A is great as compared with B and small as compared with C has no tendency to show that A is not real; for great and small, which seem to be a pair of contrary predicates and therefore to convict their possessors of unreality, are in fact incomplete predicates, standing for 'greater than certain things', 'smaller than certain things', and between the complete predicates there is no opposition.

The other examples are not of this order. 'Beautiful' does not mean 'more beautiful than', 'ugly' 'more ugly than'. These are genuine contraries, not concealed comparatives. How then can Plato convict particular things of being both beautiful and ugly, or acts of being both just and unjust, or both pious and impious? An individual act which is just is not unjust. Plato must be thinking of what he has shown in one early dialogue after another, that while an act of a certain type (e.g. returning to a man what belongs to him) is right in normal circumstances, another act of the same general type is wrong in abnormal circumstances (e.g. giving back his sword to a man who intends to kill another or himself). But, by this, individual acts are not proved to have contradictory attributes; for a particular act is done in a particular situation, and Plato has said nothing which shows that in this situation it can be both right and wrong. All that is proved is that the generalization 'all acts of returning to a man what is his are right' is not true.

Plato, however, is satisfied by his argument, and draws the momentous conclusion that no particulars are fully real and that only Forms are so.[1] And under this condemnation not only sensible particulars are included, for an act which is just or unjust must be or at least include a mental, non-sensible activity. In earlier dialogues Plato's general tendency has been to treat particulars as real, and indeed it is only on the assumption of their reality that he argues to that of Forms. But from now on he is committed, until in the *Sophistes* he sees a better way, to a false and dangerous disparagement of all particulars, in the supposed interest of Forms.

There follow three connected passages in which the theory of Ideas receives a further elaboration—(1) the passage about the Sun and the Idea of good (504 e 7–509 c 4), (2) the passage about the Divided Line (509 c 5–511 e 5), (3) the simile of the Cave (514 a 1–518 b 5).[2] We should be very chary of introducing in our study of these passages suggestions derived from other (and particularly from later) dialogues. We are studying the *development* of Plato's thought, and what we have to do is to try to discover what was in his mind when he wrote these passages. Other dialogues may be used to help us to choose between rival interpretations that are equally compatible with what he says here, but not to support an interpretation which is the less probable of two in view of the language of the passage, nor to justify us in importing into the *Republic* developments of his thought which, so far as we know, came later in his life.

A. Plato introduces the first passage by remarking that the definitions of the virtues (previously arrived at) in terms of a distinction of three elements in the soul were only a second best— 'that in order to gain the clearest possible view of these qualities

---

[1] 479 b 9–e 9.

[2] These passages, and more particularly the Line and the Cave, have been the subject of much discussion, especially by British scholars. The following may be mentioned: H. Sidgwick in *J. of Philol.* ii (1869), 96–103; H. Jackson, ibid. x. (1882), 132–50; J. Cook Wilson in *Class. Rev.* xviii (1904), 257–60; J. L. Stocks in *Class. Qu.* xv (1921), 73–88; A. S. Ferguson, ibid. 131–52, xvi (1922), 15–28, xxviii (1934), 190–210; H. J. Paton in *Ar. Soc. Proc.* xxii (1922), 69–104; F. M. Cornford in *Mind*, xli (1932), 37–52, 173–90; N. R. Murphy in *Class. Qu.* xxvi (1932), 93–102, xxviii (1934), 211–13; R. Robinson, *Plato's Earlier Dialectic*, 151–213; H. W. B. Joseph, *Knowledge and the Good in Plato's Republic*, 13–60.

we should have to go round a longer way'.[1] Justice and the other
virtues can be completely known only in the light of 'something
greater than themselves' (504 d 4). This 'greatest object of study'
is 'the Idea of good, from which everything that is good and right
receives its value for us' (505 a 2–4). The greatest possessions profit
a man nothing unless what he possesses is good, and knowledge
of anything profits him nothing unless he knows what is good.
The superiority of good to everything else is further evidenced by
the fact that while many people would choose to do and possess
what seems just or noble, even if it is not so, no one is satisfied
to possess what seems good. Every soul pursues what *is* good
and for the sake of it does all that it does, divining that there is
such a thing even though it cannot say what it is. No man will
know adequately, or be a good guardian of, particular instances
of justice or beauty, unless he knows in what respect they are
good.

What Plato has so far vindicated for the good is supremacy in
one particular respect, as an object of desire. Men may desire
things that are not good, but only if they believe them to be good,
and the deeper object of their desire is that which *is* good.

This does not exhaust, for Plato, the supremacy of goodness over
all other Ideas; but to bring out the other aspects of its nature he
adopts an indirect method. He will try to get light on the Idea of
good by studying first its offspring (506 e 3). He starts by equating
particulars with what is seen, and Ideas with what is known
(507 b 9). Here sight stands for sense in general, for a particular
sound is a particular none the less because it is not seen but heard.
But Plato goes on to point out a respect in which sight is distinguished from the other senses—that in order that sight may occur
there must be not only a coloured object and an eye capable of
seeing, but also light playing on the object, and, best of all, the
light of the sun. Just as the eye sees most clearly when its object
is bathed in sunlight, the mind apprehends most clearly when it
views its object in the light of the Idea of good. It is this that 'gives
to objects of knowledge their truth, and to him who knows them
his power of knowing' (508 e 1–3). And as neither light nor sight

[1] 504 b 1.

is the sun, neither truth nor knowledge is the good. The good is something even more to be honoured than they.

After saying what he does of the Idea of good as the source of knowledge and of knowability, the principle of explanation of the world of Ideas, Plato proceeds to exhibit it in a new light, as the source of that world's being. As the sun 'gives to visible objects not only the power of being seen, but also their generation and growth and nourishment',[1] so 'you may say of the objects of knowledge that not only their being known comes from the good, but their existence and being also come from it'.[2] But while the life-giving power of the sun is quite different from its illuminative function, the function of the Idea of good as source of the being of the other Ideas is really the same as its function as source of our understanding of them; for we shall be right in explaining the existence of the other Ideas by reference to the Idea of good, only if it is actually the ground of their being.

If we are to attempt even dimly to understand Plato's meaning, we must first realize that the functions assigned to the Idea of good are assigned to it in relation not to the sensible world, but to the world of Ideas; it plays the part in relation to them that the sun plays in relation to sensible things. In saying what he does of it he is not stating, directly at any rate, a teleological view of the world of nature. What he is saying is that the Ideas themselves exist and are known by virtue of their relation to the Idea of good. What can be the meaning of such a view of the world of universals? It is reasonable to offer a teleological explanation of some or all of the facts of nature, if we believe either in a benevolent Governor of the universe, or in a nisus in natural objects towards the good. But a teleological explanation of the world of Ideas is in a different position. Ideas are not changeable things, plastic to the will of a Governor; they are standards to which a Governor of the universe must conform. Nor on the other hand can we conceive of the Ideas as having a nisus towards good (though a passage in the *Sophistes*[3] has often been misinterpreted as ascribing 'movement' to them); things may have a nisus, but universals cannot. It is, therefore, difficult to see what Plato can

---

[1] 509 b 2-4.   [2] Ibid. 6-8.   [3] 248 a 4-249 d 5. Cf. pp. 108-11 *infra*.

have meant when he says that the Idea of good accounts for the existence and the knowability of the world of Ideas. Nor are we helped by what he says later about the 'unhypothetical first principle', which is undoubtedly to be connected with the Idea of good; the only difference is that while the phrase 'the Idea of good' points to a universal, the other phrase points rather to a proposition, presumably one in which the Idea of good is a term.

We may consider first the relation of the Idea of good to other *ethical* Ideas. What Plato wishes to convey is presumably that the essence of each of the virtues consists in some relation to the good—that it is by virtue of this relation that they exist, and in the light of it that their nature can be understood. There are hints of this view in other dialogues. In the *Laches* Plato had said that knowledge of good and evil is the essence of the several virtues (199 d 4–e 1). In the *Hippias Major* he had said that we pursue φρόνησις and all other fine qualities because their product and offspring, the good, is worthy of pursuit (297 b 2–7). In the *Phaedrus* he defines temperance as the being guided by the desire of the best (237 d 6–e 3). We must suppose that on such lines as these he believed the essence of all the virtues to consist in some definite relation to the Idea of good.

That this is part of Plato's meaning is shown by the introductory passage already referred to.[1] What he has in mind is the possibility of defining the virtues by reference not to parts of the soul, but to the precise relation of each to the *summum bonum* of human life. We may suppose that, as he thought of wisdom as being essentially knowledge of the good,[2] he thought of courage, temperance, and justice as being essentially pursuit of the good in spite of the solicitations of fear, of self-indulgence, and of covetousness. The Ideas of the virtues will then owe their being and their intelligibility to the Idea of the good, and for them the Idea of the good will be 'beyond existence in dignity and power'.[3]

But Plato assigns to the Idea of good, in other words to goodness or excellence, a much wider significance than the ethical significance we have considered. He describes it as 'giving to the objects of knowledge'—to all of them—'their truth, and to him

---

[1] pp. 39–40 *supra*.   [2] 505 b 5–10.   [3] 509 b 6–10.

who knows them his power of knowing'.[1] Here it becomes harder to follow his meaning, and any interpretation must be conjectural.

For Plato ἀρετή, the quality which answers to the adjective 'good', is not limited to human goodness; everything in the world has its own characteristic excellence. In the *Gorgias*[2] he speaks of the goodness of the body, and of the goodness 'of each thing, whether it be an implement or a body or a soul or an animal'. This thought is specially prominent in the *Republic* itself. He speaks there[3] of the goodness of dogs and horses, of eyes, ears, and all other things, of the body, of each implement and animal. In other words he ascribes to everything in the sensible world an ideal excellence which is to it as the end of human life is to men. In these passages there is no direct reference to the Ideas. But in one passage this notion of an ideal excellence is linked with the Ideas. In the *Phaedo*[4] he says that the not quite equal things with which the senses acquaint us aim at or aspire to 'equality itself', the Idea of equality. In this vein of thought—to which also belongs Plato's frequent description of the Idea as a pattern and of the particular as a copy—all the Ideas are thought of as types of excellence, as species (we may perhaps say) of the great generic Idea of excellence itself, and as intelligible only in the light of that Idea.

Many interpreters of Plato have said that in his system God and the Idea of good are identical; but this view cannot be maintained. It would be truer to say two things: First, that while any Idea, and therefore the Idea of good, is for Plato always a universal, a nature, wherever he speaks of God he means a being having a nature, and in particular not goodness but a supremely good being. This is already clear in the *Phaedo*, where, in Socrates' account of his mental history, reason, i.e. the divine reason, is clearly distinguished from the good to which it looks in its government of the world.[5] Again in the early part of the *Republic*, where Plato maintains that the citizens of the ideal state must be taught that God is good (379 b 1), he clearly

---

[1] 508 e 1-3.   [2] 479 b 4, 504 c 9, 506 d 5.
[3] 335 b 8-11, 353 b 2-12, 403 d 2-3, 518 d 9-10, 601 d 4-6.
[4] 75 a 11-b 8.   [5] 97 b 8-c 6.

means that they are to be taught, not that goodness is good, but that the Governor of the universe is good.

But secondly, in the metaphysical section of the *Republic* very little use is made of the conception of God. It is not until we come to the *Sophistes* that we find Plato maintaining that complete reality belongs not only to unchanging Ideas but also to that which lives and thinks, not until we come to the *Timaeus* that we find the functions of the Demiourgos and his relation to the Ideas clearly set forth, and not until we come to the *Laws* that we find the Ideas to have receded from view, and God to hold the central place in Plato's thought. Yet it is worth noting that even in the present passage there is a foreshadowing of the *Timaeus*, when Plato speaks of the artificer (δημιουργός) of the senses (507 c 6).[1]

The view that the Idea of good is, in Plato's thought, identical with God is to a large extent based on a passage in the *Sophistes* in which Plato has often been thought to ascribe 'movement, life, soul, and reason' to the Ideas. But it will be seen later[2] that this is a complete misunderstanding (though a very natural one) of that passage, which concludes with the assertion that reality includes both that which does not change (the Ideas) and that which does (souls divine and human).

In what he says of the Idea of good Plato comes nearer, perhaps, than he does anywhere else to the expression of a transcendental philosophy, and it was largely on this passage that the Neoplatonists based their interpretation of his doctrine. The question naturally arises whether there was any external influence at work on Plato's mind when he wrote the passage. We know that Plato had close connexions with Eucleides,[3] the head of the Socratic-Eleatic school of Megara, who, according to Diogenes Laertius,[4] 'declared that the good was one, though called by many names—sometimes wisdom, sometimes God, sometimes reason, &c. Things opposed to the good he did away with, saying they do not exist.' Burnet suggests[5] that what Plato says of the Idea of good was said by way of going as far as possible with

---

[1] Cf. τῷ τοῦ οὐρανοῦ δημιουργῷ (530 a 6).   [2] pp. 108–11 *infra*.
[3] Diog. Laert. ii. 106, iii. 6 (8).
[4] ii. 106.   [5] *G.P.* 230–3.

Eucleides without accepting his complete monism. The suggestion cannot be verified, but is not improbable.

B. The passage about the Divided Line is continuous with that about the Idea of good and the sun, springs out of it, and is meant to complete it.[1] Accordingly the classes of object to which the two main divisions of the line correspond are called not the sensible and the intelligible, but the visible and the intelligible, and the details of the passage are drawn from the sense of sight alone. 'At any rate you have, in these, two kinds, the visible and the intelligible. Now take them as if they were a line cut into two unequal sections, and again cut each section in the same ratio.'[2]

If we have a line divided in this way

$$A \quad\quad D \quad\quad\quad\quad C \quad\quad\quad\quad E \quad\quad\quad\quad\quad\quad B$$

so that $AC : CB = AD : DC = CE : EB = 1 : n,$

then $CE = \dfrac{1}{n+1} . CB,$ and $CB = n . AC, \therefore CE = \dfrac{n}{n+1} . AC = DC.$

The inference has sometimes been drawn that Plato deliberately means the two middle subsections to be equal, and therefore cannot mean the four subsections to stand for four kinds of object increasing in clearness or reality. But the equality of DC to CE, though it follows from the ratios prescribed, is never mentioned; and on the other hand the passage contains clear indications[3] that the four subsections are meant to stand for four divisions of being of increasing 'clearness' (509 d 9) or 'truth' (510 a 9). The equality of the middle subsections is an unintended, and perhaps by Plato unnoticed, consequence of what he does wish to emphasize, that the subsections of each section, and the sections themselves, stand for objects unequal in reality. If the mathematics of the line had allowed DC to be in the same

---

[1] 509 c 5–d 6.

[2] 509 d 4–8. The readings in d 6 vary: ἄνισα ADM Proclus: ἄν, ἴσα F: ἴσα Ast: ἀν' ἴσα Stallbaum. We may be sure that ἄνισα is right; the difference in respect of 'clearness' between the things symbolized could only be expressed by introducing inequality into the symbol. δίχα is sometimes used, in Plato and elsewhere, in the sense of 'in two *equal* parts', and if it meant that here, we should have either to read ἴσα (or ἀν' ἴσα) τμήματα or to omit ἄνισα τμήματα. But both in Plato (in *Soph.* 221 e 2, 267 a 1, *Pol.* 261 b 4) and elsewhere δίχα can mean simply 'in two'.

[3] See pp. 47–8 *infra*.

ratio to *CE* as *AC* is to *CB*, *AD* to *DC*, and *CE* to *EB*, he would
have had it so; and the fact that this is mathematically impossible
is only an indication of the fact that the line, being but a symbol,
is inadequate to the whole truth which Plato meant to symbolize.

The sections *AC*, *CB* are said to symbolize the visible γένος and
τόπος and the intelligible. The subsection *AD* is said to symbolize
εἰκόνες, i.e. 'shadows, reflections in pools and in close-grained,
smooth, and shiny surfaces, and everything of that kind' (510 a 1–
3). The subsection *DC* symbolizes 'the animals about us and the
whole class of vegetables and that of manufactured things' (ibid.
5–6). It is not easy to say what 'everything of that kind' is meant
to stand for. What would it naturally suggest to a reader? It
would be a mistake to suggest that it is meant to stand for artistic
products. It is true that these, according to Plato in other contexts, imitate real things, as images do their originals. But it does
not seem that a reader would naturally think of them, with no more
clue to guide him than Plato here affords; and it must further
be remembered that the Greeks habitually drew no hard and fast
distinction between artistic products and other manufactured
things. For an ordinary Greek a statue was a manufactured
thing and therefore would be included in the *second* subsection.[1]
We must look for something which a reader would be more likely
to think of as akin to shadows and reflections, and by preference
this should be some object of *sight*. Since the previous words refer
to shadows and reflections, it is most likely that 'everything of the
sort' refers to effects of refraction and to other visual illusions.[2]

The second subsection is evidently meant to stand for physical
objects in general. The things in the first subsection are described
as being like these, and standing to them as copies to patterns
(510 a 5, b 4). And the copies are said to be to the pattern, in
respect to truth, as the object of *opinion* is to the object of *knowledge* (510 a 8–10). Neither of the two main opposites here contrasted is named identically with the two objects with which the
two main sections of the line are correlated. There we heard of
τὸ νοητόν and τὸ ὁρατόν (509 d 1–4); here we hear of τὸ γνωστόν

---

[1] καὶ τὸ σκευαστὸν ὅλον γένος, 510 a 6.
[2] Cf. 602 c 4–d 4, which refers to such illusions.

and τὸ δοξαστόν. This is at first sight embarrassing, but the explanation is simple. Plato is referring back not to 509 d 4, but to the opposition stated earlier[1] between the object of knowledge and that of opinion. γνωστόν is used as a synonym of νοητόν, and though 'opinable' is far from being a synonym of 'visible', Plato means both by 'the objects of sight' and by 'the objects of opinion' the whole world of particulars, as opposed to that of Ideas. Thus in 510 a 8–10 Socrates is asking Glaucon to agree that one sub-section of the visible-opinable (viz. images) falls short of the other (their originals) as the whole system of the visible-opinable does of the knowable.

From the subsections of the visible Plato proceeds to the sub-sections of the knowable. But what he in fact points out is not a difference of nature between two kinds of knowable, but a differ-ence, or rather two differences, of procedure between two ways of knowing. One difference is that in coming to know things in the third subsection the mind has to use as images the objects in the second subsection, while in coming to know things in the fourth subsection it needs no such aid but deals only with the contents of the subsection—Ideas themselves. The other is that in coming to know things in the third subsection the mind proceeds from hypo-theses to a conclusion, while in knowing things in the fourth it proceeds from an hypothesis to an unhypothetical first principle.

In the phrase 'using as images the things which formerly were imitated',[2] which tells us that the contents of the second sub-section are images of those of the third, as those of the first were images of those of the second, I find the clearest evidence that the equality of the two middle subsections of the line, which follows from the ratios Plato states, is something unintended; that if (compatibly with the ratios he states) Plato could have had *DC* standing in the same ratio to *CE* as *AD* does to *DC*, and *CE* to *EB*, he would have had it so; that the visible and its subsections are not (as Prof. Ferguson holds) introduced *merely* as an illustra-tion to bring out the relations between the two subsections of the intelligible, but that there is a continuity between all four subsections of what is symbolized, as there is between all four

[1] 477 a 9–b 9.   [2] 510 b 4.

subsections of the symbol (the line); that in the series εἰκασία, πίστις, διάνοια, νόησις each term is thought of as being of higher worth than that which precedes. This point is evidently fundamental to Plato's meaning; for it is explicitly mentioned twice again—in 510 e 1–3 and in 511 a 6–8.

Finally, that Plato was all along thinking of the third kind of apprehension as intermediate in value between the second and the fourth—in other words, was thinking of the two lower not as merely illustrative of the two higher, but as forming a series with them—is shown by the remark in 511 d 4 that διάνοια, the third state of mind, is intermediate between δόξα (the summary name for the first two) and νοῦς (the fourth), and by the remark in the passage of summary (533 d 5) that it is clearer than opinion, but dimmer than knowledge.

It is not to be supposed that Plato thought of the four states of mind as differing only in degree. They differ in kind, and in the Cave passage the difference in kind is symbolized by saying that in passing from their first stage to their second the prisoners are slewed right round, and that at a later stage they are led from the dim fire-lit cave to what is its very antithesis, the sun-lit upper air. But while there is a difference of nature between the four states, they are states of which each is clearer than the previous one, and not merely the second clearer than the first, and the fourth than the third. In that sense there is continuity through that which the line symbolizes, just as the line itself is continuous, containing sections but no gaps and no changes of direction.

The examples in 510 c 1–511 a 1 show that it is mathematics that Plato has in mind in his description of the third subsection. It is not on *a priori* grounds but on the basis of a study of mathematical method that he insists on the necessity of diagrams for the study of geometry. It is his conviction that geometry consists not in deducing, by pure logic alone, conclusions from propositions taken as starting-points, but in apprehending the implications of figures which we draw. The drawn 'square' is not that which the geometer is reasoning about, but a mere image of or approximation to it; yet he would not be able to deduce the properties of the genuine square if he did not see the way in which the elements of a seen or imagined square fit together. He needs an intuition of spatial figures, as well as his axioms, definitions, and postulates. Aristotle gives the same account of geometrical procedure when he says (*Met.* 1051^{a}22) that it is only by 'dividing figures' that the geometer makes his discoveries; and that was undoubtedly the procedure of the Greek geometers. The general enunciation of the theorem to be proved or of the problem to be solved is always followed by a particular enunciation—'let *ABC* be a triangle', &c.—and the proof is reached by such methods as dividing the triangle by joining one point with the middle of the opposite side or by bisecting one of the angles.

Thus Plato opposes in advance two theories which have found favour in modern times—the empirical theory represented by Mill,[1] which holds that geometry is an inductive science reasoning from observation of sensible figures and reaching approximately true generalizations about them, and the rationalistic or logistic theory which regards geometry as proceeding by pure reasoning alone from axioms, definitions, and postulates relating to perfect geometrical figures, without any need for spatial intuition. The question which of the three views is true is one of great importance, but would need a separate treatise for its discussion, and belongs rather to epistemology than to metaphysics. This much seems clear, that it is by following the method described by Plato and Aristotle that geometry has actually progressed.

Plato is at fault, no doubt, when he describes the geometer as necessarily drawing or modelling his particulars; he overlooks the fact that anyone with a lively visual imagination can make do with imaginary figures. But the recognition of this does not invalidate his general thesis, that it is by the use of particulars that the geometer gains his knowledge; for an imaginary figure is as particular as one that is drawn and seen.

He assumes that the method of arithmetic is in this respect the same as that of geometry (510 c 2). No doubt in the early stages it is by the use of particular numbered groups—groups of balls on wires, of dots on paper, &c.—that the truths of arithmetic are

---

[1] *System of Logic*, Bk. ii, ch. 6, § 1.

learned. But when a very early stage has been passed, arithmetic and algebra proceed without any such necessity. They use symbols, indeed—the names of the numbers, and symbols such as a, b, x, y. But the relation of these to the numbers the arithmetician is thinking about is quite different from the relation of the particular figures of the geometer to the perfect figures he is studying. They are not individual sensible things used to help us to concentrate our attention on invisible things to which they approximate; they are arbitrary symbols each of which stands for any one of a number of genuinely mathematical entities—'2' for any group that has two members, and so on. Plato is probably too much influenced here by the Greek habit of representing each number by a group of dots arranged in a certain way, as we still do on dice and dominoes. He may have thought that the arithmetician in dealing with numbers always has before him such particular representations of them, seen or imagined. But it is clear that in dealing with large numbers this is impossible; the artificial symbols alone are enough to direct our attention to and concentrate it on our real object.

I have assumed, as one has every right to do, that Plato meant this characteristic of the third subsection, as well as its hypothetical character, to apply to arithmetic as well as to geometry; but it is worth noting that, while in speaking of the hypothetical character he mentions, and gives instances from, both sciences (510 c 3–5), in speaking of the use of symbols he gives instances only from geometry (510 d 7–e 1). If he had tried to find instances in arithmetic he might have been led to notice the essential difference between the two sciences in this respect.

The second characteristic of this subsection is that in it the mind proceeds from unexamined hypotheses. It is important to try to form a definite conception of the nature of the hypotheses with which Plato supposes mathematics to start. To begin with, there is nothing hypothetical, in the ordinary sense, about the hypotheses; they are not assumptions entertained merely in order to see what consequences can be drawn from them. They are accepted unquestioningly as true and as obvious to anyone (510 c 6–d 1). Next, as to what it is that is thus assumed, we must rely for information on the instances Plato gives. Mathematics, he says, assumes 'the odd and the even, the figures, and three kinds of angles'. It is natural to suppose that the assumptions are assumptions of the existence of these things, not assumptions of their definitions;[1] and this view derives some confirmation from the fact that Aristotle, who was probably following the Platonic tradition, uses the word ὑποθέσεις expressly (in *An. Post.* 72ᵃ18–24) to mean the assumptions of existence which are basic to the sciences, as distinguished from the ὁρισμοί or definitions which are equally basic.

How, then, should we interpret these instances? The first we should naturally interpret as meaning 'the assumption that there are odd and even numbers', perhaps with the addition 'and that there are no others'. The second we should naturally interpret as meaning the assumption of the existence of triangles and of their kinds; of quadrilaterals and their kinds; of circles and their sectors and segments. The third we should naturally interpret as the assumption of the existence of right angles, acute angles, and obtuse angles.

The attitude of the practising mathematician towards the subjects of his science, so long as he does not philosophize about its foundations, is one of assumption. It seems to him self-evident that every whole number must be either odd or even, that there are figures such as the triangle and the circle, that there are right angles, acute angles, and obtuse angles; and he is interested not in the ultimate nature of number or of space but in tracing the conclusions that follow from such assumptions. Plato's account of the procedure of mathematics in this respect is certainly correct; we shall presently have to consider his account of the supplementation which he thinks this procedure requires, and receives, from philosophy.

Jackson[2] suggested a logical connexion between the two distinctive features of mathematics mentioned by Plato. 'The inferior method then starts from λόγοι, which (1) are hypothetical in the

---

[1] Similarly in the *Phaedo* the hypothesis is εἶναί τι καλὸν αὐτὸ καθ' αὑτό (100 b 5), and in the *Parmenides* also the hypotheses are existential; cf. pp. 92–3 *infra*.

[2] *J. of Philol.* x (1882), 145.

sense that they have not been shown to be correct and complete accounts of ideas, and (2) *for that reason*[1] are still dependent upon the particulars or "many" from which they were originally derived.' The suggestion is an interesting one, but it cannot be said to be based on anything that Plato actually says. His language would suggest, if anything, that he made the first of these characteristics depend on the second; he says[2] 'using as images the things that formerly were imitated, the soul is compelled to start its search from hypotheses', where 'using' may mean 'because it uses'. His meaning may be that the mathematician is so much tied to the use of visible diagrams that he is prevented from apprehending in their purity the real objects of his study.

Plato conceives the state of mind which deals with the third subsection as including something more than the study of geometry and arithmetic—'students of geometry, arithmetic, and the like',[3] 'the procedure of geometry and of the kindred arts'.[4] By this he meant the branches of applied mathematics, such as astronomy and harmonics. There is no evidence that he thought of anything beyond these, and it was natural that he should not, since mathematics pure and applied was the only study which in his day had been pursued in a systematic way. But in principle his account (so far as the use of hypotheses is concerned) is applicable to all sciences which study a particular subject without raising ultimate questions about the status in reality of the subject-matter, and its relation to other subject-matters.

In contrast with the third subsection, he describes the fourth as that which is studied without the use of sensible images, and not by progress from hypotheses to conclusions but by regress from hypotheses to a single unhypothetical first principle.[5]

It is of course true that philosophy works without sensible images. But geometry also can work without sensible images (being able to use imaginary figures instead), and arithmetic habitually works without sensible images of the universals it studies, its only imagery being that of language and of other arbitrary symbols. Now philosophy also must use language, just as much as arithmetic does; and further, though it is possible for

---

[1] Italics mine.   [2] 510 b 4.   [3] 510 c 2.   [4] 511 b 1.   [5] 511 b 6–c 2.

philosophy to work at times without imagining examples of the universals it studies, we find over and over again that it has to check its results by imagining such examples and considering how the relations it asserts to exist between universals would work out in examples of these universals. It may be questioned, therefore, whether the distinction Plato draws between philosophy and the sciences in this respect can really be maintained as a hard and fast distinction. What we can say is that philosophy never uses sensible images, and that it is less dependent than geometry on imaginary examples.

The second distinction Plato draws between science and philosophy can be accepted with less reserve. We can at any rate say that there is a complete distinction between two ways of thinking, one that accepts without inquiry hypotheses which are *prima facie* apparent, and another which tests, or aims at testing, all hypotheses until it does one of three things—finds them to follow from first principles that cannot be doubted, finds them to conflict with such principles, or fails to find either logical sequence or contradiction between them and clear first principles.

The division of labour Plato here assigns to science and dialectic (or philosophy) reminds us of the stages in the treatment of hypothesis outlined in the *Phaedo*, viz. (1) acceptance of what appear to be well-founded hypotheses, and the descent from them to conclusions, (2) the rejection of those from which contradictory conclusions follow, (3) the ascent from hypothesis to hypothesis till 'something sufficient' is reached. It is impossible not to see the affinity of the first of these stages with the method ascribed to the sciences in the *Republic*, and of the third stage with the method ascribed to dialectic. In fact Plato in the *Republic* makes more explicit the final warning expressed in the *Phaedo*,[1] that one must at all costs not confuse the various stages with each other. He now marks off the first stage definitely from the third and assigns them respectively to science and to philosophy.

There can be no question that the third stage—the testing of the hypotheses by seeing whether there are indubitable principles from which they follow—is necessary with regard to the hypotheses

[1] 101 e 1–3.

of the sciences. The history of science is rich in examples of
hypotheses long accepted as self-evident and later discovered
neither to be self-evident nor to be capable of deduction from
anything that is so. In later days, science itself has to a large extent
undertaken the revision of its own premisses; the attention of
many mathematicians is largely devoted to the examination of
the assumptions of mathematics itself, and a very important
purification of its assumptions has been achieved. And though
the two processes—of deduction from assumptions and of
examination of the assumptions—are quite different, there is no
reason why they should not be done by the same persons—no
reason except that many people have great talent for one of the
two processes and little for the other.

Plato, however, in two respects goes farther in his description
of the work of philosophy than has yet been indicated.

1. In the first place, he apparently contemplates the derivation
of all the hypotheses of science (or rather of such of them as survive the test) from a single first principle. The idea of Good is not
mentioned as such in the Line passage, but we can hardly doubt
that 'the first principle of the universe'[1] is an allusion to it. For
the whole Line passage is introduced in order to complete the
account of the Idea of Good; the Idea of Good has already been
described as the ultimate principle of explanation;[2] the prisoners
released from the cave see the sun last of all, and the sun stands
for the Idea of Good; and in 532 a 5–b 2 Plato says 'the summit
of the intelligible world is reached in discussion by one who
aspires, through the discourse of reason unaided by any of the
senses, to make his way in every case to the essential reality, and
perseveres until he has grasped by pure intelligence the very
nature of Goodness itself'.

Cornford put forward[3] the view that Plato had in mind two
'unhypothetical first principles'—the Idea of Good, from which
the moral Ideas were to be derived, and the Idea of One, from
which the Ideas of the numbers and then, through them, the
Ideas of the spatial figures were to be derived. What Aristotle

[1] 511 b 7.   [2] 508 e 1–509 a 5.
[3] In *Mind*, xli (1932), 176–85.

tells us about the theory of Idea-numbers shows that Plato did ultimately attempt such a derivation of the mathematical Ideas; but there is nothing to support the view that in the *Republic* Plato has this in mind. There is no mention of the Idea of unity, and no suggestion that there are two ultimate principles of explanation.

It is a stimulating ideal, that of the deduction of the whole fabric of science from a single principle; but this ideal can be criticized from two points of view. On the one hand it may be argued that it is entirely beyond the power of the human mind to deduce the whole structure of the system of Ideas from one principle. What concrete meaning, for instance, can be assigned to the suggestion that the division of numbers into odd and even can be shown to be necessary because it is 'good' that they should be so divided? On the other hand it may be said that no such deduction is necessary—that the division of numbers into odd and even follows from the very meanings we attach to the words number, odd, and even. The best that can be said in defence of Plato is that he only goes too far by asserting in an exaggerated way the sound principle, that the assumptions we accept as axioms should be reduced to the smallest possible number.

2. Plato makes an even stronger statement about the relation of philosophy to the sciences. In 533 c 7 he says that dialectic proceeds by doing away with (ἀναιροῦσα) their hypotheses. The expression is so strong and at first sight so surprising that other readings have been suggested. One suggested reading, τὰς ὑποθέσεις ἀναίρουσα ἐπ' αὐτὴν τὴν ἀρχήν, would give no good meaning; if you deduce hypotheses from a higher principle, you do not raise them to that principle. ἀνάγουσα, which occurs in a corrected manuscript of Stobaeus, gives a good sense, but is too remote from ἀναιροῦσα, and gives too easy a sense, to be likely to have been corrupted into ἀναιροῦσα. ἀναφέρουσα, ἀνιοῦσα, ἀνάπτουσα are open to the same objections. ἀνείρουσα is nearer to the manuscript reading, and would give a good sense. But it appears better to accept ἀναιροῦσα and to try to find a good sense for it.

Taking the word to mean 'denying the truth of', Taylor made[1] an interesting suggestion about the three examples of mathematical

[1] In *Mind*, xliii (1934), 81–4.

hypothesis that Plato gives.[1] The first example is 'the odd and the even'. Taylor suggests that Plato had in view a widening of the whole notion of number so as to include irrationals, which are neither odd nor even. But there is no evidence in Plato, up to the probable date of the *Republic*, of a special interest in irrationals (that seems to begin with the *Theaetetus*), nor evidence anywhere before the *Epinomis*[2] (which, if he wrote it, was his last work) that he would have called the irrationals numbers.[3]

The second example is 'the figures'. Taylor thinks that what is referred to is some assumption made by mathematicians of Plato's time which involved consequences that are contradicted by the fact that there are only five regular solids that can be inscribed in the circle. But it is unlikely that the assumption of 'the figures' which Plato ascribes to the mathematicians of his time was an assumption relative to solid geometry, since in Book vii[4] he speaks of this as a science to be created, not as one already in existence.

The third example is 'three kinds of angles'. Taylor thinks this is the assumption that there are angles formed by straight lines, angles formed by curves, and angles formed by a straight line and a curve, which assumption was found to lead to difficulties with regard to the angle formed by a circle and its tangent. But it is unlikely that Plato would describe the assumption of the latter two kinds of angle as one of the basic assumptions of geometry, since it is only in fairly advanced geometry that such angles come into the reckoning.

We know comparatively little as to what were the basic assumptions of geometry in Plato's time, but some light is thrown on them by the definitions which stand at the beginning of Euclid; for Euclid's *Elements* were based on *Elements* already existing in Plato's time.[5] Now Euclid, at the beginning of Book I, offers definitions of, and by implication assumes the existence of, right, obtuse, and acute angles, the circle, the semicircle, triangles, quadrilaterals, and polygons, equilateral, isosceles, and scalene

---

[1] In 510 c 3-5.   [2] 990 d 1-e 1.
[3] Cf. Van der Wielen, *I.P.* 13-17.
[4] 528 a 9-c 8.   [5] Cf. Heath, *History of Greek Mathematics*, i. 319-21.

triangles, right-angled, obtuse-angled, and acute-angled triangles, squares, rectangles, rhombuses, rhomboids, and trapeziums; and he offers nothing answering to Taylor's suggestions. It is reasonable to suppose that the assumptions Euclid names are the sort of thing that Plato had in view. We must look elsewhere for an interpretation of ἀναιροῦσα.

It should be interpreted in the light of the phrase which just precedes it, in 533 b 6–c 3, where Plato says that 'the sciences are only dreaming so long as they use the hypotheses and leave them unmoved, not being able to give an account of them', i.e. to deduce them. This points to a cancelling of the hypotheses, not in the sense of rejecting them as untrue, but in the sense of ceasing to regard them as sure bases for deduction, until they have themselves been deduced. So interpreted, ἀναιροῦσα merely says in a heightened way what he has already said in the Line passage. An example of cancellation of hypotheses in this sense will be found in his later derivation of odd and even numbers from the One and the great and small.[1]

The second stage of the treatment of hypotheses in the *Phaedo* is not mentioned in the *Republic*, but it is unlikely that Plato had forgotten it; and a further, though probably secondary, significance for ἀναιροῦσα may be found if we suppose that, while he thought all the hypotheses to need deduction from a self-evident first principle, he thought that some of them should be actually rejected as untrue because they led to self-contradictory conclusions. That he was prepared to reject some assumptions of contemporary mathematics is shown by his rejection of the point as a 'geometrical dogma'.[2] Finally, the third stage of the treatment of hypotheses may yield two further justifications of ἀναιροῦσα, as applied to some though not to all the presuppositions of science. For in the attempt to justify them by search for more certain principles lying behind them, dialectic may find that some of them are incompatible with more certain principles, and that others cannot be deduced from any such; and in either case the hypothesis might justly be said to be cancelled.

But if we regard Plato's treatment of hypotheses here as carrying

[1] Cf. pp. 176–205 *infra*.   [2] *Met.* 992ª19–22.

out the principles laid down in the *Phaedo*, we must recognize that in one point Plato goes beyond the *Phaedo*. There the search ended as soon as τι ἱκανόν,[1] a sufficient principle, was reached, and any principle to which all the parties in a discussion were ready to agree could be called sufficient. In the *Phaedo* such a principle was found in the theory of Ideas, simply because all the disputants accepted it. But now Plato is no longer content with general agreement; only a principle that is absolutely self-luminous will satisfy him.

A word must be added on the latter half of the work of dialectic, the downward progress from the unhypothetical first principle (511 b 7–c 2). The upward progress is not a process of proof, but the search for a principle which does not need nor admit of proof, a process that terminates in the direct vision of such a principle. The downward process is that in which the consequences of this principle are exhibited in their due order, right down to those hypotheses which have survived examination and to those new ones which have taken the place of any that have been discarded. It will not be a mere reduplication of the upward process, because the upward process has been tentative, with (in all probability) many false starts, while before the downward process begins all such errors will have been purged away, and the process will be through a chain of propositions in their due order of dependence, *ordine geometrico demonstrata*. It will be related to the earlier stage as the exposition of the proof of a mathematical theorem is related to the original search for its proof; but both search and exposition will reach a higher level in the hierarchy of Ideas than scientific search and exposition do.[2]

A further question now awaits us. The four divisions of the line are said to stand for the two divisions of the visible and the two divisions of the intelligible. We naturally suppose that they are meant to symbolize not different mental activities or states, but different objects; and as regards the divisions of the visible this was true. But as regards the two later divisions, while Plato has

---

[1] 101 e 1.
[2] For a full and lucid discussion of 'hypothesis' in the *Republic* cf. R. Robinson, *Plato's Earlier Dialectic*, 151–91.

indicated magnificently the difference between science and philosophy, he has said little or nothing of a difference between their objects. Now there is a doctrine which we know that at some period of his life he held, which would exactly fit the needs of the passage. In *Met.* 987ᵇ14–8 Aristotle tells us that Plato distinguished between Ideas and τὰ μαθηματικά, which were also called τὰ μεταξύ because they were intermediate between Ideas and sense-particulars, unchanging like the Ideas but plural like the particulars that fall under one Idea. A little reflection shows that when a mathematician speaks of two triangles on the same base, or of two intersecting circles, he is not speaking of Ideas of triangle or of Ideas of circle, since there is only one Idea of triangle (viz. triangularity) and one Idea of circle (viz. circularity). On the other hand he is not speaking of sensible triangles or circles, since these have only approximately the attributes which the geometer proves to belong, not approximately but precisely, to the entities he is speaking of. He is in fact speaking of divisions of space bounded by three straight lines or by one circular line. And Plato seems to have persuaded himself that similarly when the arithmetician says 2 and 2 make 4, he is speaking not of twoness, nor yet of sensible twos, but of numbers having an intermediate status between these.

The view[1] that τὰ μαθηματικά and Ideas are the objects symbolized by the two later subsections is very attractive; but it is difficult to accept it. For one thing, the discovery of the μαθηματικά was a great innovation. It meant the replacing of the dualism, which has reigned in the dialogues up to this point, of Ideas and sense-particulars, by a triple classification of the contents of the universe. Now anyone who is familiar with Plato's writings knows that he is nothing if not explicit. The point which he wishes to make, he makes very clearly and usually with a certain amount of repetition to drive it home. There is no attempt in the Line passage to bring out the difference between Ideas and τὰ μαθηματικά; no hint of the central difference between them, that to each Idea many μαθηματικά correspond. Indeed the objects of διάνοια are spoken of in a way which implies that they *are*

---

[1] Which goes back to Proclus (*in Euc.* 4. 14–5. 10 (ed. Friedlein)).

Ideas. They are spoken of in the singular, not in the plural, and with the qualification αὐτό, which is the very hall-mark of an Idea—τοῦ τετραγώνου αὐτοῦ ἔνεκα τοὺς λόγους ποιούμενοι καὶ διαμέτρου αὐτῆς (510 d 7). Further, he says of them (511 d 1) νοῦν οὐκ ἴσχειν περὶ αὐτὰ δοκοῦσί σοι, καίτοι νοητῶν ὄντων μετὰ ἀρχῆς. νοητός, it is true, is ambiguous. The two subsections together form τὸ νοητόν, yet only the higher of the two is the object of νοῦς; the lower is the object of διάνοια. But in the passage quoted, logic requires νοητός to have its more specific sense: 'scientists have not νοῦς about their objects, although these are νοητά when viewed in connexion with a first principle.' Here the very objects of διάνοια are said to become objects of νοῦς when treated differently. Further, the whole Line is based on the dichotomy 'visible-intelligible', and in the 'Sun-Idea of Good' passage the intelligible has been identified with the Ideas (507 b 9–10). It follows from this that each of the two upper subsections of the Line stands for a part of the world of Ideas, as each of the two lower stands for a subdivision of the sensible world.

We must look to see what evidence there is elsewhere in Plato of his holding a belief in the 'intermediates'.

(*a*) The first passage to be noticed is *Phaedo* 74 c 1, where we find the question 'Did the equals themselves ever seem to you unequal, or equality to be inequality?' Here the 'equals themselves' are undoubtedly distinguished from the Idea of equality. But no use is made of the distinction; for 'these equals' in 74 c 4 means not 'the equals themselves' but sensible equals (or rather, approximately equal sensible things), and it is these alone whose difference from the Idea of equality is stressed. The passage does not necessarily imply a belief in the existence of perfect equals; Plato may only mean that no pair of things known to be perfectly equal has ever appeared to be unequal. If he had, when he wrote the *Phaedo*, already come to believe in the intermediates, he could hardly have failed to stress their existence, in this passage.

(*b*) In *Republic* 526 a 1 Plato says of mathematicians: 'If they are asked what are these numbers they are talking about, in which every unit, as they claim, is exactly equal to every other and contains no parts, what would be their answer? This, I should say, that the numbers they mean can only be conceived by thought.' Here Plato describes mathematicians as recognizing units which exist in the plural number and yet are distinct from sensible things (because they are exactly equal). Now units which exist in the plural must of course be different from the Idea of unity, so that the distinction between the Ideas, the objects of mathematics, and sensible things is implicit in the passage; but it is not explicitly brought out.

(*c*) In *Tim.* 50 c 4 'the things that go into and come out of' space have sometimes been supposed to be perfect geometrical shapes; but that is negatived by the fact that they are described as 'imitations of the things that exist for ever' (the Ideas), and are therefore implied not to be eternal themselves, as the intermediates (according to Aristotle's account of Plato's doctrine) are. At this stage of the argument in the *Timaeus*, too, there is not yet anything to show that they are shapes at all. They are characteristics of any kind whatever, making their appearance in and disappearing from the 'receptacle of becoming'; they are, in fact, sensible qualities.

(*d*) In *Tim.* 53 a 7–b 5 we read that it was 'by shapes and numbers' that the Demiourgos shaped into genuine fire, air, water, and earth the rudimentary fire, air, water, and earth which alone existed before he began his fashioning work. But this reference is too general to amount to a definite recognition of shapes and numbers intermediate in character between the Ideas and sensible things.

(*e*) It has sometimes been supposed that the element of limit which occurs in the fourfold division of existing things, in *Phil.* 23 c 4–d 8, is to be identified with the intermediates. Undoubtedly 'limit' stands for numerical and metrical definiteness, but it cannot be said with any plausibility that Plato in that passage distinguishes the intermediates from the Ideas.

(*f*) *Phil.* 56 d 4–e 3 is more to the point. Plato there says 'Is not arithmetic of two kinds, one of which is popular, and the other philosophical? . . . Some arithmeticians reckon unequal units; as for example, two armies, two oxen, two very small things or two very large things. The party who are opposed to them would not agree; they insist that every unit in ten thousand must be without difference from every other unit'; and presently he draws a similar distinction between practical mensuration and 'philosophical' geometry. This passage makes exactly the same point as passage (*b*).

(*g*) In *Ep.* 7. 342 a 7–c 4 Plato distinguishes, with regard to 'each existing thing', three means to the knowledge of it, and he takes the circle as his example. The three are (1) the name 'circle', (2) the definition of it, (3) the circle 'that is drawn and rubbed out, or turned on the lathe and destroyed'. There are also (4) the knowledge of the thing, and (5) the thing itself. There is no mention of the individual perfect circles recognized in the theory of 'the intermediates'. Now the Seventh Letter was probably written some twenty-five years after the *Republic*, and it would be very surprising if a theory held by Plato when he wrote the *Republic* was ignored in a much later passage where the mention of it would have been so appropriate.

Of these passages the two which come nearest to a definite recognition of the intermediates are the second and the sixth. But these, when set against the evidence in the Divided Line passage itself, do not justify the view that the doctrine is to be found in that passage; and the passage from the Seventh Letter suggests that it was not till very near the end of his life that Plato formulated the doctrine, though he had long been on the point of formulating it.

It is worth while to examine more thoroughly the thesis that the logic of the Line requires Plato to have already in mind a clear distinction between Ideas and the 'intermediates'. It is sometimes emphasized that he starts with a division of objects and only later distinguishes and supplies names for the corresponding states of mind. And it is true that the passage distinguishes between images and their originals long before it supplies names for the corresponding states of mind—εἰκασία and πίστις. But at the very beginning the division, though nominally a distinction of objects, really rests on a distinction between mental faculties. The two main sections are described as standing, not for Ideas and physical particulars, but for the objects of intelligence and the objects of sight (509 d 1–4). It is true that when Plato comes to subdivide the lower section he describes the contents of its subsections by reference to their own nature, as images and as animals, vegetables, &c. But by referring to the main sections as the visible and the intelligible he has already in principle said that one legitimate way of distinguishing two classes of object is to distinguish them as objects of mental state *a* and objects of mental state *b*. And this, and not the method of distinguishing objects by reference to their own nature, is the method which he actually follows when he comes to divide the intelligible. How are we to divide the intelligible? he asks (510 b 2) ; and he does not answer 'by the fact that some intelligibles are eternal but plural, while others are eternal and unique', as he could easily have done if he had had the doctrine of the mathematicals in his mind. He says 'in respect of the fact that one of them is studied by the aid of images and hypotheses, the other without images and hypotheses'; he recurs to the principle involved in his original opposition of the visible to the intelligible, the principle of dividing objects by reference to the mental activities of which they are objects. Not one word is said of any other distinction between the objects of διάνοια and those of νόησις.

What this points to is a division among *Ideas*, and a division which he thinks of only in terms of the way they are studied. But if one method of study is appropriate to one set of Ideas and another to another, it must be because of some objective difference between the two sets. How would Plato have stated this, if he had asked himself the question? Each of the two characteristics by which the two states of mind are described throws some light on the question. The reference to the use of images shows that the objects of διάνοια are mathematical Ideas, for whose understanding a sensuous or imaginative intuition of the structure of spatial figures or (according to Plato) of numbers is needed, as against moral and aesthetic Ideas, for which there is no corresponding necessity; and it may be pointed out that these are the two main kinds of Idea that are familiar in the early dialogues and that are emphasized again in the *Parmenides* (130 b 1–10). On the other hand, the opposition drawn between the procedure which proceeds downwards from hypotheses and that which proceeds upwards from them points to a division of Ideas into those that come high and those that come low in the hierarchy of Ideas. The suggestion would seem to be this, that if you start with Ideas low down in the hierarchy, the possibility of deriving them from something self-evident seems so remote that you almost inevitably resign the attempt and simply take the Ideas for granted and proceed to draw out what consequences you can;[1] while on the other hand if you start high up in the hierarchy, the possibility of connecting the high Ideas from which you start with others higher still, and ultimately with the Idea of good, naturally occurs to you, and you move upward rather than downward.

Further, it seems not unlikely that Plato thought of these two ways of dividing the ideal world as actually producing the same division, between mathematical Ideas as coming low in the hierarchy and ethical Ideas as coming high. For ethical Ideas are much more closely and obviously connected with the Idea of good than mathematical Ideas are.

Plato twice (510 b 5, 511 a 4) speaks of mathematics as 'compelled' to use the method it does, that of employing images and assuming hypotheses; he implies that something in the nature of the Ideas studied dictates the method in use. Yet undoubtedly it was his view, implied in the Sun and Idea of good passage, that ultimately the whole world of Ideas is capable of being illuminated by the Idea of good, and studied by the method of dialectic; this is further implied by the words καίτοι νοητῶν ὄντων μετὰ ἀρχῆς (511 d 2). He thinks, then, of the two parts of the ideal world as sufficiently different to suggest, at the start, different methods of study, and yet sufficiently alike and connected to be ultimately studied by the one method of dialectic.

Yet Plato must have meant to draw some distinction between the objects of διάνοια and those of νοῦς, as well as between those activities themselves. The conclusion to be drawn surely is that he thought of Ideas as falling into two divisions, a lower division consisting of Ideas involving number or space, and a higher division not involving these. When philosophy has done its work, the

---

[1] ὡς οὐ δυναμένην τῶν ὑποθέσεων ἀνωτέρω ἐκβαίνειν (511 a 5).

Ideas which hitherto were only διανοητά have become νοητά by derivation from the unhypothetical first principle; yet they remain different Ideas from those which were from the start objects of νοῦς.

I conclude that the objects of διάνοια are not the 'intermediates' but are simply the mathematical Ideas, and those of νοῦς the other Ideas. Plato divides Ideas into these two classes because he has found by experience that geometry has this peculiarity, that it is only by the use of constructions that it can progress. If we want to see a specimen of the method he here assigns to νοῦς in contrast to διάνοια, that of progress from Ideas to Ideas without any use of images, we can look to the discussion of the 'greatest classes' in the *Sophistes*.

The chief interest of the section on διάνοια lies, perhaps, in the advance it marks from earlier dialogues in which reason and sense-perception had been simply opposed to one another as the fallible to the infallible. Plato has come to see that in geometry, at least, the two are partners indispensable to each other.

If, as I believe, those are mistaken who find the doctrine of the 'intermediates' in the *Republic*, Prof. Cherniss goes too far in the opposite direction when he denies[1] that Plato ever believed in them at all. His evidences are these:

1. In *Met.* 991^{b}27–30 Aristotle says: 'They must set up a second kind of number, with which arithmetic deals, and all the objects which are called intermediates by some thinkers; how do these exist or from what principles do they proceed?' and in 1090^{b}32–5 he repeats the complaint that the believers in 'intermediates' do not explain their genesis. Plato may well, however, have believed in intermediates without explaining their genesis. It was the *Ideas* of number he was interested in, and he may well have left the other question to mathematicians.

2. In 991^{a}2–5 (repeated in 1079^{a}32–6) Aristotle says: 'If the Ideas and the particulars that share in them have the same form, there will be something common to these; for why should 2 be one and the same in the perishable 2's and in those that are many but eternal, and not the same in the 2-itself as in the particular 2?' This points to an identification by some unnamed Platonist of the

[1] *R.E.A.* 75–8.

2'ness in sensible and in mathematical 2's, but cannot be used to support the view that Plato did not distinguish between them, as Aristotle emphatically says elsewhere that he did.

3. In 990^{a}29–32 Aristotle says: 'Even Plato thinks that both bodies and their causes are numbers, but that the intelligible numbers are causes, while the others are sensible.' But the main difference, for Plato, was that between the Ideas and sensible things, and neither he, nor Aristotle in reporting him, is bound always to mention the intermediates when he mentions the Ideas and the sensible numbers.

4. The writer of the *Epinomis*, whether he be Plato or another, says in 990 c 5–8: 'There is need of courses of study. The most important and the first of these is also the one which deals with numbers by themselves, and not corporealized, with the whole generation of the odd and even, and with all the character which it imparts to nature.' What has been said about the previous quotation applies here too.

5. Alexander *in Met.* 78.16–17 quotes, apparently from Aristotle's early work *De Ideis*, an academic proof of the existence of the Ideas: 'Number is the number of something real, but the things in this world are not real; so it must be the number of the Forms; therefore the Forms exist.' And in 79.13–15 he quotes another argument for the existence of Ideas: 'If geometry is not about this particular equal and this particular commensurate but about what is simply equal and what is simply commensurate, there must be an equal-itself and a commensurate-itself, and these are the Ideas.' But these may well be arguments used not by Plato but by Xenocrates, who identified mathematical entities with the Ideas.

These arguments, used to show that Plato never distinguished the 'intermediates' from the Ideas, cannot outweigh two facts: (1) that the distinction is, as we have seen, below the surface in dialogue after dialogue, only waiting to be made explicit, and (2) that the whole basis of Aristotle's discussion of Academic views in Books M and N of the *Metaphysics* is a distinction between the view (which he distinctly states to be Plato's) which recognizes both kinds of number, the view (which can be assigned to Speusippus) which refused to recognize the ideal numbers, and the view (which can be assigned to Xenocrates) which identified the mathematical with the ideal numbers.[1] Is it likely that Aristotle would without good reason have committed himself to a distinction which if it had been erroneous could so easily have been repudiated by the members of any of the three divisions of the school?

The Line passage concludes with a section[2] in which Plato supplies names for the states of mind answering to the four kinds of object—εἰκασία, πίστις, διάνοια, νόησις. εἰκασία means here 'apprehension of images' (εἰκόνες), i.e. of shadows and reflections. Yet there is, between εἰκασία and πίστις as Plato uses the terms, a distinction analogous to that between the words in the most relevant of their ordinary senses. εἰκασία in its ordinary sense (= 'conjecture') is a consciously insecure attitude towards its objects, πίστις an attitude which, whether well or ill grounded is free from hesitation. εἰκασία and πίστις as used here by Plato are distinguished not by a smaller or greater feeling of security, but by a smaller or greater actual security in their grasp of reality; for the one is a less clear apprehension and an apprehension of objects which are less real,[3] being merely images of the objects of the other.

The distinction between νόησις and διάνοια is not, as it is in Aristotle, a distinction between immediate and mediate apprehension. The work of philosophy no less than that of science was for Plato one of reasoning, the deduction of less general from more general propositions. Only it includes a 'moment' of direct apprehension—the apprehension of the unhypothetical first principle, which cannot be deduced from any other because it is higher than all others.

Looking back on the whole passage, we must admit that there is some truth both in the traditional interpretation and in that offered by Prof. Ferguson. The older interpretation seems to be right in maintaining that Plato is not using the distinction between εἰκασία and πίστις merely as illustrating at a lower level that between διάνοια and νοῦς. If that were the whole of Plato's mean-

[1] Cf. pp. 151–3 *infra*.   [2] 511 d 6–e 5.   [3] 511 e 2–4.

ing, he would have expressed it better not by taking one continuous line but by taking two lines, each divided in the ratio
which they bear to each other; and further, the objects of πίστις
are said to be images of the objects of διάνοια just as those of
εἰκασία are images of those of πίστις (510 b 4, e 1–3, 511 a 6–8).
There is therefore justification for the view that Plato thought of
the four states of mind as forming a series, gaining in clarity as it
proceeds. On the other hand Prof. Ferguson is right in pointing
out the close connexion of the passage with that on the Idea of
good and the sun, and also in calling attention to the facts that,
since the passage is introduced to throw light on the Idea of
good, it is νόησις and not any other state of mind that is the *main*
object of Plato's interest, and that the distinction of πίστις from
εἰκασία is introduced *mainly* as an illustration of the difference
between νόησις and διάνοια. It follows from this that we are not
bound to hold that Plato thought of εἰκασία as an important phase
of our apprehension of the world. The looking at shadows and
reflections is only a rather occasional interlude in the life of the
ordinary man, whose habitual state of mind is that of πίστις; and
attempts to find a substantially wider range for εἰκασία than Plato
distinctly assigns to it are mistaken. πίστις, διάνοια, νόησις on the
other hand are for him the characteristic states of three different
kinds of men—the plain man, the mathematician, the philosopher; and from this in due course followed his final classification of the contents of the universe (other than souls) into three
main kinds corresponding to the three states of mind—sensible
particulars, mathematical objects, Ideas.

This general interpretation of the passage is confirmed if we
take note of the space assigned to the different types dealt with
in it. The first main section and its subsections are dismissed in
12 lines (509 d 9–510 b 1). The second main section and its subsections have 56 assigned to them (510 b 2–511 d 5). Clearly the
main object of interest is the second section, and the first is meant
mainly to throw light on the distinction between νόησις and
διάνοια, by a comparison with two states of mind similarly related
at a lower level. Again, in the treatment of the second main section, the whole emphasis is laid on the difference between the

methods of διάνοια and of νόησις, and nothing whatever is actually said of the difference between their objects. Must we not conclude that the main purpose of the passage is to throw light on the nature of philosophy in contrast with science, as a preliminary to the detailed study in Book VII of the mathematical studies and the philosophic study which is to succeed them; and that while the passage begins by referring to a difference of objects, its real purpose is better indicated by its close, which is a division of states of mind (511 d 6–e 5)? This is confirmed by the passage of recapitulation (533 e 7–534 a 8), where he carefully states the proportion between the four states of mind but excuses himself from going into the 'proportion and division' of their objects. As regards the objects, only the broad distinction between the two main sections, the δοξαστόν and the νοητόν, is considered important enough to be worth repeating.

C. We now come to the third connected passage, that about the Cave. In this, six successive phases of man's state 'in respect of education and its opposite' (514 a 2) are depicted. (*a*) A company of men is imprisoned in an underground cave, with their heads fixed so that they can look only at the back wall of the cave. Behind them across the cave runs a wall behind which men pass, carrying all manner of vessels and statues which overtop the wall. Behind these again is a fire. The prisoners can only see the shadows of themselves, of one another, and of the things carried behind the wall, and must take these to be the only realities (514 a 2–515 c 3). (*b*) They are freed and forced to turn their heads towards the fire and the objects passing by, but can see neither clearly, owing to dazzle (515 c 4–e 5). (*c*) They are dragged into the open, but cannot face the light of the sun, nor see any of the natural objects round them. They therefore look first at the shadows and reflections of these objects (515 e 6–516 a 7); then (*d*) at the objects themselves (516 a 8), (*e*) at the stars and the moon (516 a 8–b 3), and (*f*) at the sun, and come to infer that 'it is the sun that produces the seasons and years, and controls everything in the sphere of the visible, and is in a way the cause of all these things which the prisoners used to see' (516 b 4–c 2).

There are two passages in which Plato interprets for his readers the meaning of the cave. The first is 517 a 8–c 5:

☆ (Every feature in this parable . . . must be linked on to our earlier account (προσαπτέον ἅπασαν τοῖς ἔμπροσθεν λεγομένοις). The prison dwelling corresponds to the region revealed to us through the sense of sight, and the firelight within it to the power of the Sun. The ascent to see the things in the upper world you may take as standing for the upward journey of the soul into the region of the intelligible; then you will be in possession of what I surmise, since that is what you wish to be told. Heaven knows whether it is true; but this, at any rate, is how it appears to me. In the world of knowledge, the last thing to be perceived, and only with great difficulty, is the essential Form of Goodness. Once it is perceived, the conclusion must follow that, for all things, this is the cause of whatever is right and good; in the visible world it gives birth to light and to the lord of light, while it is itself sovereign in the intelligible world and the parent of intelligence and truth. Without having had a vision of this Form no one can act with wisdom, either in his own life or in matters of state.)

Here two preliminary questions arise. (a) What does τοῖς ἔμπροσθεν λεγομένοις mean? (b) What does προσαπτέον mean? (a) τοῖς ἔμπροσθεν λεγομένοις has usually been taken to mean the Line passage. But Prof. Ferguson points out that the 'power of the sun' (517 b 3) has not been mentioned in the Line passage (though it has of course been implied, in the reference to shadows and reflections which it causes). The first two sentences (in the translation) (517 a 8–b 4) tell us, then, that the cave and the fire stand for the visible world and the sun, *in the Sun and Idea of Good passage*. The remainder of the passage is harder to interpret. It begins 'The ascent to see the things in the upper world you may take as standing for the upward journey of the soul into the region of the intelligible.' Now in the Sun passage nothing has been said of an ascent from the sensible to the intelligible, so that it is difficult to find here a reference to that passage. Commentators have usually taken the reference to be to the Line, because there an upward movement *has* been described. But it will not meet the case. The only upward journey there described was an ascent not to but in the intelligible world, from hypotheses to an unhypothetical first principle (511 d 1); nothing was said of an ascent from objects of sight to objects of intelligence. It might seem, then, that these words in our present context refer neither to the Sun nor to the Line—that they are simply interpretations of the Cave passage itself, telling us that the ascent from the cave to the upper air is to be taken to typify the ascent from the sensible to the intelligible. Yet this view is not wholly satisfactory. It would imply that only the second sentence (517 b 1–4) carries out the πρόσαψις of the Cave to 'what was said before', what follows being not an inter-pretation of the cave in the light of what was said before but simply an interpretation of the symbolism of the cave itself. This is not satisfactory, because, while Plato bids us connect the Cave as a whole (ἄπασαν, 517 b 1) with 'what was said before', he would in fact be so connecting only the life in the cave, and not that in the upper air (for in the second sentence nothing is said of the latter). We must suppose that the third sentence (b 4–6) continues the πρόσαψις. This it does by saying that the ascent to the upper air stands for the ascent to the intelligible region, but in saying this Plato brings in, by a trick of memory, a reference to an ascent which was not actually mentioned either in the Sun passage or in the Line passage, though implicit in Plato's thought in both, and hinted at when he describes νόησις as answering to the 'highest' subsection of the line (511 d 8).

That the passage of summary on the whole refers back to the Sun passage and not to the Line passage is confirmed by what Plato goes on to say in the fifth and sixth sentences (517 b 8–c 4), where he refers back to the Idea of good, to its being the cause of all that is right and beautiful, to its giving birth to light and the lord of light (the sun) in the visible world and to truth and intelligence in the intelligible—all of them matters men-tioned in the Sun passage and not in the Line passage, while no reference is made to any of the distinctive features of the Line passage.

Although in this passage of summary there is no distinct reference to the line, yet of course in identifying the cave with the visible world, and the upper air with the intelligible, Plato is indirectly identifying the cave with the lower main section of the line, and the upper air with the higher, for the lower and the higher section are expressly said to stand for the visible and the intelligible (509 d 8).

(*b*) Believing that a direct comparison of the Cave with the Line was what Plato intended in this passage of summary, most scholars have taken προσαπτέον to mean 'should be applied', i.e. superimposed, in the sense of establishing a one-to-one correspondence between the stages in the Cave allegory and those in the Line. Now προσάπτειν apparently never occurs in Greek mathematical writers in this sense,[1] and Prof. Ferguson is justified in saying that it should not be so translated here. He pleads for a wider interpretation, and prefers 'attach' to 'apply'; and he quotes passages from the *Frogs* (1216, 1231, 1234) in which it is used of 'tacking on or rounding out'. None of the passages quoted by Liddell and Scott or by Ast is like enough to the present passage to throw light on its precise meaning here; some such translation as 'linked on to' probably comes nearest to the truth.

Plato has perplexed his readers by saying too much. The use of the sun as a symbol of the Idea of the good, and of the visible as a symbol of the intelligible, was clear and satisfactory enough. Here in the Cave passage, things are complicated by a further symbolism. The sun is itself symbolized by the fire in the cave, and the sunlit sensible world by the firelit cave.

Prof. Ferguson will not have this interpretation. 'On the face of it', he says,[2] 'this is a contrast between two systems of light; yet the current interpretations ignore the point on which the comparison lays most stress. The point of attachment is, in fact, the visible region outside the cave.' The cave is thought by him to be related to the line in this way: The life in the cave represents a life as far removed from the ordinary sensuous life (symbolized by the first main section of the line) as that is removed from the intellectual life (symbolized by the second main section of the line). Plato tells us that the cave is meant to illustrate our state 'in respect of education and the lack of it' (514 a 2), and Prof. Ferguson interprets 'lack of education' as meaning not the untutored life but a deeper depth, in which we are deceived by man-made sophistries.

[1] Plato's word for it is παρατείνειν (*Meno* 87 a 5); Euclid's is παραβάλλειν (6.27).
[2] *Class. Quart.* xv (1921), 139–40.

This view involves Prof. Ferguson in great difficulties. τὴν μὲν δι' ὄψεως φαινομένην ἕδραν τῇ τοῦ δεσμωτηρίου οἰκήσει ἀφομοιοῦντα[1] he interprets[2] by saying 'the visible region, held together by sunlight, is compared *and contrasted*[3] with a wretched place, where the light is a fire and the place a prison'; but it is impossible to interpret ἀφομοιοῦντα so. What Plato says is that we must take the firelit life within the cave as standing for the whole sensuous life, for which the first main section of the line also stands.

'Further,' says Prof. Ferguson,[4] 'on the current view it seemed inexplicable that Plato should specify only the lower line (with which he dealt so summarily in Book VI), and the cave with such particularity, and remain silent about the vitally important application of the upper "world" outside the cave to the upper line.' But that is just what Plato does speak about, in the same sentence in which he bids us liken the visible region to the cave. 'The ascent to see the things in the upper world you may take as standing for the upward journey of the soul into the region of the intelligible.'[5])

Again, in interpreting the cave life as that in which we are deluded by man-made sophistries, Prof. Ferguson seems to overemphasize the fact that the prisoners look at shadows and reflections of man-made objects,[6] and to forget that they also look at shadows of themselves and of one another,[7] who are God-made beings.

The second passage in which Plato interprets the cave is 532 a 1–d 1:

(Here at last, then, we come to the main theme, to be developed in philosophic discussion. It falls within the domain of the intelligible world; but its progress is like that of the power of vision in the released prisoner of our parable. When he had reached the stage of trying to look at the living creatures outside the Cave, then at the stars, and lastly at the Sun himself, he arrived at the highest object in the visible world. So here, the summit of the intelligible world is reached in philosophic discussion by one who aspires, through the discourse of reason unaided by any of the senses, to make his way in every case to the essential reality, and perseveres until he has grasped by pure

---

[1] 517 b 1–3.   [2] p. 140.   [3] My italics.   [4] p. 140.
[5] 517 b 4–6.   [6] 514 c 1.   [7] 515 a 6.

intelligence the very nature of Goodness itself. This journey is what we call dialectic. . . . There was also that earlier stage when the prisoner, set free from his chains, turned from the shadows to the images which cast them and to the firelight, and climbed up out of the cavern into the sunshine. When there, he was still unable to look at the animals and plants and the sunlight; he could only see the shadows of things and their reflections in water, though these, it is true, are works of divine creation and come from real things, not mere shadows of images thrown by the light of the fire, which was itself only an image as compared with the Sun. Now the whole course of study in the arts we have reviewed has the corresponding effect of leading up the noblest faculty of the soul towards the contemplation of the highest of all realities, just as in our allegory the bodily organ which has the clearest perceptions was led up towards the brightest of visible things in the material world.)

Here the reference to looking to the animals, the stars, and the sun itself clearly refers to the Cave passage, and we are told plainly that the last step of the post-cave life is meant to symbolize the procedure of dialectic (i.e. the same thing which the last subsection of the line represents). The turning from shadows to the images that cast them (i.e. the statues, &c., of 515 a 1) and to the firelight, the ascent to the sunlight, and the looking at reflections and shadows of things in the sunlit world, are said to symbolize the study of the mathematical arts (i.e. the same thing which the third subsection of the line symbolizes).

There is thus a slight misfit between Plato's first interpretation of the Cave[1] and his second.[2]

First passage

The visible, symbolized by the cave-world.

The intelligible, symbolized by the outer world.

Presumably, therefore,

εἰκόνες (objects of εἰκασία), symbolized by shadows and reflections in the cave.

Physical things (objects of πίστις), symbolized by solid objects in the cave.

Mathematical Ideas (objects of διάνοια), symbolized by images (of animals, stars, moon, sun) in the outer world.

[1] 517 a 8–b 6.   [2] 532 a 1–d 1.

Higher Ideas (objects of νόησις), symbolized by animals, stars, moon, sun, in the outer world.

Second passage

διάνοια, symbolized by looking at σκευαστά (εἴδωλα) in the cave and at images of animals, stars, moon, and sun.

νόησις, symbolized by looking at animals, stars, moon, and sun.

Therefore presumably εἰκασία and πίστις, symbolized by looking at shadows of σκευαστά.

The interpretation of the Cave seems, as it were, to have shifted a stage upwards. The second stage within the cave stands no longer for the plain man's observation of sensible things, but for the beginning of the life of science, whose later stages are symbolized by the first stage of the life in the upper air.

In Plato's final interpretation, then, there is no distinction in the cave symbol answering to the distinction between εἰκασία and πίστις. Both together are symbolized by the earliest stage in the life of the prisoners. This should perhaps act as a warning against any attempt to take the distinction too seriously, by supposing that Plato thought of εἰκασία as an important substantive phase of our mental life. The difference between εἰκασία and πίστις was introduced to serve as an illustration of the difference between two stages in the life of intelligence, and once it has served its turn it is tacitly dropped as unimportant.

Plato's final interpretation negatives Prof. Ferguson's view that the life outside the cave is meant to stand for the ordinary sensuous life, and the life within the cave to stand for a deeper depth, in which people are deceived by man-made errors. For Plato tells us expressly here that the later stage of the life in the cave, and the earlier stage of the life outside it, stand for the pursuit of science, and the later stage in the life outside the cave for the pursuit of philosophy; so that all that is left of the cave-symbol to stand for the ordinary sensuous or pre-scientific life is just the earlier stage of the life in the cave, and there is no room within the cave-symbol for the representation of a deeper depth of error.

At the same time we must not interpret Plato too simply or tie

him down to a single set of ideas. The whole tone of the Cave is
different from that of the Line. The distinctions for which the
Line stands are epistemological distinctions, and ethical considerations do not come in at all. While the Line is meant to foreshadow the account given in Book VII of science and philosophy
as intellectual pursuits, the Cave is meant to bring out their
ethical significance, as leading men not only from the life of sense
to that of intelligence, but also from the life of acquiescence in
half-truths and human conventions to the direct apprehension of
moral truth (517 d 4–e 2, 520 c 1–d 4).

It must have struck many readers as surprising that the distinction between νόησις and διάνοια is, in the Line, treated simply as
a distinction between philosophy and *mathematics*. The reason is
that Plato already has in his mind the conception of two stages
in the higher education of the Guardians, the study of mathematics and the study of dialectic,[1] and that he is preparing the
way for these. But it is obvious that in other studies also there is
a distinction between the critical and the uncritical attitude
towards hypotheses, and between a way of thinking which studies
universals alone and one which studies them by the help of
approximate examples. This defect in the Line is to some extent
remedied in the Cave. For here we find him saying:[2]

Nor, again, is it at all strange that one who comes from the contemplation of living things to the miseries of human life should appear awk-
ward and ridiculous when, with eyes still dazed and not accustomed
to the darkness, he is compelled, in a law-court or elsewhere, to dis-
pute about the shadows of justice or the images that cast those
shadows, and to wrangle over the notions of what is right in the minds
of men who have never beheld Justice itself.

And later he says:[3]

You must go down, then, each in his turn, to live with the rest and let
your eyes grow accustomed to the darkness. You will then see a thousand times better than those who live there always; you will always
recognize every image for what it is and know what it represents,
because you have seen justice, beauty, and goodness in their reality.

---

[1] Dealt with in 521 c 1–531 c 8 and in 531 c 9–535 a 2 respectively.
[2] 517 d 4–e 2.   [3] 520 c 1–6.

We have seen what the four possible attitudes towards, say, triangles and triangularity are:

1. looking at images (shadows or reflections) of sensible approximate triangles;
2. looking at sensible approximate triangles;
3. studying triangles with the help of sensible approximate triangles;
4. studying triangularity in the light of higher Ideas and ultimately of the Idea of good.

What will be the corresponding attitudes towards, say, just acts and justice? We may conjecture that they will be:

1. contemplating shadows of εἴδωλα of justice, i.e. actions or institutions that are counterfeits of justice;
2. contemplating εἴδωλα of justice, i.e. particular approximately just acts;
3. contemplating the Idea of justice, but without seeing its logical dependence on the Idea of good;
4. contemplating the Idea of justice in its place in the whole hierarchy of Ideas and in its connexion with the Idea of good.

Many interpreters of the Divided Line have thought that the scope of εἰκασία must extend beyond the instances which Plato gives—the looking at shadows and reflections. Probably the insistence on giving a wider significance to εἰκασία in the Line passage is a mistake, due to failure to notice that the distinction between εἰκασία and πίστις is introduced not for its own sake but to throw light on that between διάνοια and νόησις; when we notice that, we need no longer assume that εἰκασία stands for some far-reaching state which can fitly be regarded as the first stage in all mental development. But we may now consider a passage which may indicate a widening of the conception of εἰκασία in Plato's mind. Shadows and reflections are images of natural things, which in turn are images of Ideas, and in the discussion of painting and poetry in *Rep.* 595 a 1–608 b 2 paintings and poems are similarly described as copies of natural things, which in turn are copies of Ideas. Even a closer parallelism is suggested by one passage (596 b 12–e 11), where the painter (and by implication the poet)

is said to be doing in principle the same as one who 'makes all
things' by turning a mirror round and round, and producing 'sun
and stars and earth and himself and all the other animals and
plants and lifeless objects'. The creations of art are thus placed
on the same level of reality as the shadows and reflections which
are the objects of εἰκασία. It is true that Plato nowhere in this
context uses the word εἰκασία, but we can hardly doubt that he
means to tell us that the contemplation of artistic objects is a
form of εἰκασία; and this betokens a considerable extension of the
meaning of the term. Further, there is emphasized a feature of
εἰκασία which was not emphasized in the Line passage, viz. that
those who are in this state are not merely apprehending images,
but are constantly supposing the images to be originals (598 c 1–
4). And further, the faculty to which art appeals is identified with
that in virtue of which we fall into sensuous illusions, such as
that by which a large body looks small when seen at a distance,
or a straight line looks crooked in water, or a convex body looks
concave (602 c 7–d 4). Plato is no doubt in error in supposing that the purpose of art is to produce illusion; and Charles
Lamb was nearer the truth when he described the condition of
spectators at a play not as illusion but as *willing* suspension of
disbelief.

Plato's theory of art is no part of our subject; but one other
feature of the passage calls for comment. It is that in which Plato
describes the Idea of bed as having been made by God (597 b 6).
The relation said to exist between the Ideas and God is surprising,
and indeed impossible to reconcile with the eternity and independence which are consistently ascribed to the Ideas. The truth
is that at this stage of his thought (in distinction from that which
we find in the *Timaeus* and the *Laws*) Plato does not seem to have
thought out the relation between God and the Ideas. In 597 b 6
the Ideas owe their being to God, but in 509 b 6–10 they owe it
to the Idea of good, which is by no means to be identified with
God; and that passage represents more truly than the present one
the metaphysics of the *Republic*. Further, when (in the *Timaeus*)
Plato has come to assign a serious significance to God, as the
Artificer of the universe, the Ideas are not subordinated to God,

but are represented as forming an order which exists independently of God and which God has to respect.

That we are justified in not taking seriously Plato's description of God as making the Ideas is indicated by the fact that while he says (597 c 1) that God 'whether by choice or because he was under some necessity' made only one Idea of bed, he proceeds to say that God could not have made more than one, because if there had been two there would have had to be one Idea whose form they both had, which would have been the true Idea. In other words, uniqueness is involved in the very nature of an Idea; the reference to God's wish cannot be serious, and if not it, then presumably not the whole reference to God. God is introduced merely to give the ideal bed some maker, answering to the carpenter and the painter who are the makers of the physical bed and of its likeness.

One more passage in the *Republic* calls for some comment. This is the famous passage in 596 a 5-7—'Shall we proceed as usual and begin by assuming the existence of a single essential nature or Form for every set of things which we call by the same name?' Plato goes on to assume the existence of an Idea of bed and one of table. Some interpreters have found a difficulty in this, because of Aristotle's statement[1] that Plato recognized Ideas only of things that exist by nature, and because there is very little reference in Plato to Ideas other than Ideas of value and mathematical Ideas. The truth is that these are the Ideas he is most interested in, and of whose existence he is instinctively most sure—as is made clear in a well-known passage of the *Parmenides*.[2] But there is enough evidence elsewhere that he did in truth believe in an Idea answering to every common name,[3] and there is no reason why he should have insisted more often than he does that this is so. The problem arising from Aristotle's statement will be considered in its place.[4]

Looking back on the *Republic* as a whole, we can see in it a notable advance on Plato's earlier presentation of the theory of Ideas. Hitherto he had maintained simply a complete opposition

---

[1] *Met.* 1070ᵃ18.   [2] 130 b 1-10.

[3] The evidence may be seen at length in Zeller, *Phil. d. Gr.* ii. 1⁴. 701 n. *Ep.* 7. 342 d 3-e 2 may be added as evidence that Plato held the belief very near the end of his life.   [4] pp. 171-5 *infra.*

between the eternal, unchanging world of Forms and the temporal, changing world of individual things. He now still maintains that opposition, but he recognizes degrees within each of these worlds. Within the world of individual things he distinguishes between those that are direct copies of Forms and those that are copies of these copies. Within the world of Forms he distinguishes between those which are, as it were, earth-bound—those that are studied with the aid of sensible examples—and those for whose study we need no such aid. Furthermore, within this last kind he recognized a hierarchy reaching from the narrowest of the Forms to the highest and widest of them, the Form of good. We thus find in him a tendency to what may be called scalarism, a recognition of the complexity of the universe, and of the intermediaries that exist between the highest and the lowest —the same tendency which finds expression in a passage of the *Philebus*.[1]

The same tendency is at work in his commendation, in the *Phaedrus*, of the joint method of συναγωγή and διαίρεσις, and in his exposition of that method in the *Sophistes* and the *Politicus*. This tendency is the very reverse of Eleaticism, which makes an abrupt distinction between reality and the completely unreal and recognizes no gradations within either. How are we to reconcile this fact with Plato's growing interest in Eleaticism, which becomes so visible in the *Parmenides* and the *Sophistes*? May it not be that the more Plato's interest was drawn to Eleaticism and the more he recognized Parmenides' greatness[2] as the protagonist of the intellect against the senses, the more he also saw the barrenness of his system and his failure to account for the facts of sense-perception? As he says in the *Sophistes*,[3] 'It strikes me that Parmenides and everyone else who has set out to determine how many real things there are and what they are like, have discoursed to us in rather an off-hand fashion.'

The *Phaedrus* is occupied in the main with matters far removed from the theory of Ideas; but it contains one famous passage in

[1] 16 c 5–17 a 5. Cf. pp. 130–2 *infra*.   [2] *Tht.* 183 e 5–184 a 1.
[3] 242 c 4–6.

which the 'intelligible region' of the *Republic*[1] appears, in language appropriate to the myth in which it occurs, as the supracelestial region (ὑπερουράνιος τόπος), and the Ideas appear as 'the colourless, figureless, intangible, truly real reality, seen only by the steersman of the soul, reason'. In that region the soul in due season 'sees justice itself, temperance itself, knowledge itself, not the knowledge that comes into being nor that which differs according as it is concerned with different so-called realities, but the real knowledge that is concerned with real reality'.[2] ὑπερουράνιος is not to be taken in its literal sense; yet the passage does stand for an extreme separation of the Ideas from sensible things. But while in this, and in its doctrine of ἀνάμνησις, the *Phaedrus* recalls the *Phaedo*, in another respect it points forward. For in it the method of dialectic, i.e. of philosophy, is described not (as in the *Republic*) as the passage from hypotheses to the unhypothetical first principle and down again, but as that of συναγωγή or generalization (εἰς μίαν τε ἰδέαν συνορῶντα ἄγειν τὰ πολλαχῇ διεσπαρμένα), followed by διαίρεσις, 'dividing according to kinds, at the joints indicated by nature, and not breaking up any part of the flesh as a bad cook does'[3]—the method which is illustrated at length in the *Sophistes* and the *Politicus*. It is thus possible to understand, though not to accept, the reasoning which led Schleiermacher to regard the *Phaedrus* as the earliest of the dialogues, since (in his view) it contains in brief the whole of Plato's philosophy. It would be truer to describe it as standing at a transition point of Plato's thought, in which he is passing from the assertion of the existence of Ideas to study the structure of the hierarchy which they form.

There is something rather paradoxical in Plato's new description of dialectic. It is a method consisting of 'collection' followed by 'division'. What this seems to imply is that we start by knowing certain Ideas, and that the first step in the method is to grasp a wider Idea which embraces these, and the second step is to divide this wider Idea into its species—so that we seem to end just where we began, with the specific Ideas. The second step in

---

[1] 508 c 1.   [2] 247 c 3–e 2.
[3] 266 b 3–c 1, 265 d 3–e 3; cf. 273 d 7–e 4, 277 b 5–8.

the method seems a needless repetition of the first; we first see that *A* is the genus to which *B*, *C*, and *D* belong, and then that *B*, *C*, *D* are species into which *A* is divided. Plato cannot have meant anything so stupid as this; what is needed, to make sense of the passage, is to notice the stress he lays on dividing 'at the joints'. In the process of 'collection' what we do is to recognize an affinity between certain universals recognized in ordinary language. But these universals may not form a true system; they may overlap one another, they may be loosely conceived; what we do in the process of 'division' is to recognize the true and accurate lines of demarcation within the genus. In other words, if we are to make sense of the passage we must suppose that Plato already has at the back of his mind the distinction he draws in the *Politicus*[1] between the haphazard 'parts' which fall within a genus and the genuine species into which it falls.

There is no suggestion in the *Phaedrus* that the whole world of Ideas forms a vast hierarchy culminating in one *summum genus*; Plato's point is that the true understanding of a single generic Form requires us not only to see that somehow it embraces a number of specific Forms, but also to see precisely what the articulations within it are.

[1] 262 a 5–263 b 11.

V

THE *PARMENIDES* AND THE *THEAETETUS*

WE now come to a group of dialogues[1] which display an interest in Eleaticism that has hitherto been absent. But Plato was no convert to Eleaticism. With its insistence that reason is reliable and the senses unreliable he was in complete agreement; but he found the doctrine that there is but a single reality, and that an unchanging one, quite unsatisfactory. The study, in the second part of the *Parmenides*, of the implications of this doctrine is undertaken mainly as a training in philosophical thinking, but there are hints of the attitude Plato was adopting towards the doctrine, and in the *Sophistes* he pronounces definitely in favour of a view which assigns reality both to that which changes not—the world of Ideas—and to minds which are subject to change.

At the meeting which Plato feigns to have taken place between Parmenides, Zeno, and Socrates, Zeno read aloud part of a discourse of his own which developed the conclusions that follow from various hypotheses. The first hypothesis was that 'things are a many', and the conclusion drawn was that then they must be both like and unlike, which Zeno denounced as impossible.[2] The purpose of his discourse was, in fact, to defend Parmenides' thesis that things are not a many but an undifferentiated unity, by drawing out the consequences of the opposite view.[3]

Taking up the conclusion to which Zeno has driven his opponents, that the many, if there were a many, would be both like and unlike, Socrates says, in effect: 'Why not? If there is a Form of likeness, and a Form of unlikeness, there is no reason why some things should not partake of both—though of course that which is "just like" could not become unlike, or *vice versa*.'[4] In other words, he puts forward the doctrine of participation in Forms as an answer to Zeno's refutation of pluralism. What would be sur-

---

[1] On the relations between these dialogues cf. pp. 6–9.
[2] *Parm.* 127 d 6–e 4.
[3] 128 a 4–b 6.   [4] 128 e 5–130 a 2.

prising, he maintains, would be if the Forms themselves had opposite attributes. Zeno has argued manfully, he admits, for the thesis that on the pluralistic view an individual thing will have opposite attributes, but he has not proved what alone would be fatal to that view—that on it a Form itself would have opposite attributes.

That of which Plato here says that it would be surprising is, it may be remarked, just what he sets himself to show in the *Sophistes*, where he argues that being, for instance, is both the same and different—the same as itself and different from everything else. And even in the *Parmenides* his language betrays a certain attraction to the problem.[1]

Parmenides asks whether this doctrine of Forms is Socrates' own, and Socrates answers that it is his very own. Parmenides proceeds to criticize it. His first question is, what things have, on Socrates' view, Forms corresponding to them.[2] The first group of Forms in which Socrates professes undoubting belief consists of Forms such as likeness, unity, plurality. A second group is that of value-Forms—justice, beauty, goodness, and the like. When Parmenides asks whether he believes in Ideas of man, fire, water, and the like (i.e. of natural kinds), Socrates confesses to doubt. And when Parmenides asks whether he believes in Ideas of hair, mud, or dirt, or 'any other trivial and undignified objects', Socrates answers that this seems absurd, but that nevertheless he has had doubts whether he should not believe in such Ideas too. Parmenides replies that Socrates' hesitation to admit such Ideas is due to youth, to philosophy not having exercised its full power on him, and to deference to general opinion.

This passage offers an accurate summary of the trend of Plato's thought as expressed in earlier dialogues. The two classes of Ideas of whose existence Socrates says he is certain are the mathematical Ideas of unity and plurality (with which he couples other very abstract Ideas such as that of likeness), and the Ideas of value. The latter had predominated in the earliest dialogues, in which Plato had followed most faithfully in the footsteps of Socrates, and in the *Symposium* and the *Phaedrus*. The former had

---

[1] ἀγαίμην ἂν θαυμαστῶς 129 e 3, ἀγασθείην ibid. 5.   [2] 130 b 1–e 4.

come into prominence in the *Phaedo* and the *Republic*. Socrates expresses doubt about the existence of Ideas of biological species and of the four elements, and still more about Ideas of such things as hair, mud, and dirt, which he no doubt thinks of as by-products of natural processes, not part of the settled plan of nature; and this answers to the fact that, while he has in the *Republic*[1] said that there is an Idea answering to every common name, he has never asserted in particular the existence of Ideas such as these. The effect of Parmenides' remarks at the end of the passage is to express Plato's conviction that such doubts should be discarded and the principle stated in the *Republic* maintained.

Ideas of the four elements and of biological species play a dominant part in the *Timaeus*, but if value-Ideas are absent there it is not because Plato has ceased to believe in them, but because his subject is not, as in most of the early dialogues, human life, but cosmology. The most catholic list of classes of Ideas Plato anywhere gives is in one of his latest writings,[2] where he recognizes Ideas of shapes and surfaces, of the good, the beautiful, and the just, of all bodies, artificial and natural, of fire and water and the like, of every animal, of every quality of character, of all actions and passivities. What conclusions he finally reached about the population of the world of Ideas is a question which will be considered later in the light of what Aristotle says on the subject.[3]

While Parmenides both here and later in the dialogue[4] encourages Socrates to go on believing in an Idea answering to every common name, he has much to say in criticism of Plato's view of the relation of the Ideas to particulars; and that in all probability reflects a second set of doubts that had sprung up in Plato's mind. Parmenides fastens first[5] on the word μεταλαμβάνειν ('come to partake'), which Socrates has used to express the relation of particulars to the corresponding Idea. Does the particular share in the whole Idea or in part of it? Socrates at first sees no difficulty in the whole Idea's being present in each particular. But Parmenides argues that if the whole Idea were present in separate individuals, it would be separate from itself; and further, that

[1] 596 a 6.   [2] *Ep.* vii. 342 d 3–8.   [3] pp. 165–75 *infra.*
[4] 135 b 5–c 3.   [5] 130 e 4–131 e 7.

though we talk of spreading a sail over several men, it is only a part that is over each, and that it must similarly be a part of the Idea that is present in each particular. But we cannot really say (he maintains) that each particular large thing is large by virtue of containing a part of largeness less than largeness itself, and that each thing that is equal to another is equal to it by containing a part of equality less than equality itself. Absurdity reaches its height with the Idea of smallness. If each small thing has only a part of smallness, the 'small itself' will be larger than that part; and if a small thing acquires that part of smallness which at first it lacked, it will become smaller instead of larger by the addition.

This passage, like the previous passage on the population of the world of Ideas, is clearly the expression of a more reflective attitude towards the theory of Ideas than anything we have found in earlier dialogues. It does not express doubt about the theory itself, but it does express doubt about Plato's earlier formulation of the theory. Must it not express a dawning sense that to speak of an Idea by such a phrase as 'the large itself' is a mistake, since it treats the Idea of largeness as just another large thing, something more perfectly large than particular large things? It is only if we so think of the Idea that the question 'Does the individual possess the whole or a part of it?' presents a difficulty. The cure is to realize that the Idea is not another thing, but an attribute, to which the distinction of whole and part does not apply. Plato does not here draw this moral, but it is to this that the passage points and for this that we must look in his later references to the Ideas, to see whether he anywhere takes up the hint and distinguishes clearly between the Form and the perfect particular. In one department the answer is to be found in his distinction between the Forms and the mathematical entities—perfect particulars—that intervene between the Ideas and sensible particulars.[1]

Parmenides now[2] passes to a fresh point. It is by noticing many large things that Socrates has been led to form the notion that there is a 'large itself' common to them all. But then must there not be a further Form of 'large' (C) common to the 'large itself' (B) and the many large things (A_1, A_2, &c.), and yet another (D)

---

[1] *Met.* 987^{b}14–18.   [2] 131 e 8.

common to all of these, and so *ad infinitum*? The argument which Parmenides here brings against the view that particulars share in the Idea, he repeats in 132 d 5–133 a 3 against the view that they are imitations of the Idea. In two other places Plato uses a somewhat similar argument, but to quite a different purpose. In *Rep.* 597 c 1–d 3 he argues that there can only be one Form of bed because if there were two there would necessarily be a third, which would be the real Form of bed. And in *Tim.* 31 a 2–b 3 he argues that if there were two Ideas of universe they would be merely parts of the true Idea of universe, on which the visible universe had been modelled. Apelt[1] and Cornford[2] have suggested that these arguments effectively answer the arguments he puts into the mouth of Parmenides; but that they do not do. To show that if there were two Ideas of bed there would have to be a third does nothing to disprove the contention that if there is one Idea of bed, related to particulars as Plato supposes, there must be a second.

In none of the four passages referred to does Plato use the example of the Idea of man. But clearly either he or some member of his school must have used that example; for Aristotle refers to the argument, under the name of 'the third man', as one of the 'more precise arguments' current in the Academy.[3] Alexander in his commentary on the *Metaphysics*[4] describes two other forms of 'third man' argument, one of which he assigns to 'the sophists', and the other (on the authority of Phanias) to 'Polyxenus the sophist'. Whether either of these forms was earlier than that used in the *Parmenides* we do not know, nor does it matter. They are entirely different from Plato's form, and in particular they do not lead to an *infinite* regress; so far as we know, Plato was the inventor of the 'infinite regress' argument.

Plato nowhere answers Parmenides' argument, but he continued to hold the theory of Ideas, and therefore plainly thought the argument not fatal to the theory. It is in fact fatal, not to the

---

[1] *Beitr. z. Gesch. d. Gr. Phil.* 53. [2] *P.P.* 90.

[3] *Met.* 990b17 (= 1079a13). He uses the phrase also in 1039a2 and in *Soph. El.* 178b36–179a10, and uses the argument, without using the phrase, in *Met.* 991a2–5 and 1032a2–4. He uses the phrase, but with quite a different meaning, in 1059b8.

[4] 84. 7–21.

theory of Ideas, but to the language in which Plato has formulated it. The expressions 'share' and 'imitate', against which the arguments are directed, are alike metaphors inadequate to express the relation of particulars to an Idea, because they both treat the Idea as if it were a thing, instead of being a characteristic of things. Plato's use of the phrase 'the x-itself' (αὐτὸ τό) is open to the same objection; for it treats the Idea of x as one x among others, and implies an x-ness common to it with others. The mistake occurs in its crudest form in *Prot.* 330 c 2–e 2, where justice is said to be just and piety to be pious.

Socrates does not draw the moral, but makes another suggestion,[1] that each Idea is a thought, found only in souls, and thus saves its singleness and escapes the objection that has been brought against it. But to this Parmenides answers that a thought is always a thought of something, and of something which exists and is recognized as common to a number of things, and that it is this objective nature, and not the thought of it, that is a Form; so that we are left with objective Forms still on our hands. To this argument against a conceptualistic interpretation of the Forms he adds a further point:[2] 'If in saying that all things share in Forms you mean that they share in thoughts, you must mean that all things are composed of thoughts and either themselves think or are thoughts that do not think.' The conceptualist interpretation of universals is thus dismissed very summarily, and Plato never recurs to it. There is nothing in Plato to justify the view sometimes expressed by scholars, both ancient and modern, that the Ideas are simply thoughts, in the divine or in the human mind.

He passes[3] to an interpretation much more typical of his general attitude to the Ideas. He suggests that the participation of particular things in them is to be taken to mean that the Forms are patterns established in nature and the particulars are copies of them. Against this view Parmenides brings the fatal objection that if a particular is a copy of a Form, it must be in virtue of their sharing in a common nature, which will be the real Form, and so there will be Form above Form *ad infinitum*; we once more have a vicious infinite regress.

---

[1] 132 b 3.   [2] 132 c 9–11.   [3] Ibid. 12.

An attempt has been made[1] to show that Parmenides' argument is unsound, on the ground that the relation of copy to original is not one of likeness, since if *A* is like *B*, *B* is like *A*, but if *A* is a copy of *B*, *B* is not a copy of *A*. But the defence itself fails. Grant that the relation is not merely one of likeness; it still involves likeness, and likeness between two things involves some Form, some character, that they have in common. Cornford urges that Plato must have seen the criticism to be unsound, since in the *Timaeus* he still describes the relation as one of copying. But the fact remains that neither here nor elsewhere does Plato attempt to meet the criticism; and we may infer that he accepted it, as Socrates does in the dialogue, and realized that 'copying' was only a metaphorical way of describing the relation. It is, of course, the plain truth that a good thing is not like, and therefore not a copy of, goodness.

Thus two ways in which Plato has habitually spoken of the Ideas—the description of the Idea as 'the x-itself' and the description of the particulars as resembling it—have been effectively refuted. But while Parmenides rejects completely these descriptions, he does not reject the alternative description of the relation as 'sharing'. What he says is that we must find another account of the 'sharing'.[2] The true answer to both criticisms is to insist that the relation of particulars to the universal is a unique relation, and that both 'resembling' and 'sharing' are inadequate metaphors for it.

Parmenides now turns[3] to what he describes as a still greater objection to Socrates' theory, viz. that the Forms, if there are Forms, must be unknowable to us. The argument by which he reaches this result is as follows: 'Any Form that is essentially relative must be relative to another Form, not to any of the things in this world, and any particular thing that is relative must be relative to another particular thing; e.g. if any of us is a master, he is master of a slave who is also one of us, and on the other hand mastery itself is relative to slavery itself. It follows that knowledge that is really knowledge is relative to that which is really truth,

---

[1] e.g. by Taylor, *P.M.W.* 358, and by Cornford, *P.P.* 93–5.
[2] 133 a 5.   [3] Ibid. 11.

and any particular kind of knowledge that is really knowledge is relative to something that really exists; and on the other hand *our* knowledge is relative to truth in our world, and any particular knowledge we have is relative to some particular thing in our world. Thus, since we do not possess what is really knowledge, we do not and cannot know the Forms—"the beautiful itself, the good itself, and the other Ideas".'

But there is, Parmenides adds,[1] a still stranger consequence. To no one can true knowledge be more fittingly assigned than to God. But just as our knowledge is relative to things in our world, true knowledge is relative only to things in the world of Forms. Thus God's knowledge will not be knowledge of anything in our world, nor God's mastery mastery of anything in our world. This, Socrates admits, is a very strange consequence of his theory; and he admits further the force of Parmenides' whole argument.[2]

The argument cannot be dismissed as merely dialectical, but it is quite unconvincing. It turns upon a confusion—obviously present in such statements as 'Presumably the Forms, just as they are in themselves, are known by the Form of knowledge itself',[3] and 'You will grant, I suppose, that if there is such a thing as a Form, knowledge itself, it is much more perfect than the knowledge in our world'[4]—between the Form of knowledge, i.e. its essence, and perfect knowledge. Socrates does not point out the fallacy, and that may mean that Plato did not detect it. Yet Parmenides does not claim that his refutation is complete; he only says that it is difficult to meet,[5] and that suggests that Plato hoped by recasting his theory to preserve its essential core. Parmenides' last words[6] about the theory are not words of triumph over it: 'If, in view of all these difficulties and others like them, a man refuses to admit that Forms of things exist or to distinguish a definite Form in every case, he will have nothing on which to fix his thought, so long as he will not allow that each thing has a character which is always the same; and in so doing he will completely destroy the significance of all discourse.' Socrates is not necessarily in the wrong. His impulse to reasoning

---

[1] 134 c 4.   [2] 134 e 7–8, 135 b 3–4.   [3] 134 b 6–7.   [4] 134 c 6–8.
[5] 134 e 9–135 b 2; cf. 133 b 4–c 1.   [6] 135 b 5–c 3.

is noble and divine;[1] his mistake is that he has followed it without first undergoing a training in the often despised practice of disputation, such as has been exhibited by Zeno. Parmenides commends a proviso that Socrates has suggested, viz. that the method of hypothesis should be applied not to visible examples, but to Forms themselves; and Parmenides himself makes an addition— that one should explore not only the consequences of a particular hypothesis, but also those of the opposite hypothesis.[2]

What, we may ask, is the general upshot of this 'first part' of the *Parmenides*? Burnet[3] and Taylor[4] hold that Parmenides' arguments are directed not against the reality of the Ideas, but against that of sensible things. The only substantial argument that can be urged in favour of this view is that it would seem more natural to make Parmenides, a monist and an intellectualist, the mouthpiece of an attack on the reality of sensible things, rather than on that of intelligible Forms. But the fact is that from start to finish it is the doctrine of Forms and nothing else that is made the subject of criticism. It is the fact, too, that there is nothing specifically monistic in the standpoint from which Parmenides' criticisms are brought forward; nor is his final admission, that without something like Forms thought could not go on, consistent with Parmenides' own thoroughgoing monism. Parmenides is treated, in fact, not in his capacity of monist. He is chosen as the mouthpiece of Plato's reflections on his own theory of Ideas because they are too far removed from Socrates' way of thinking to be put in *his* mouth, and because Parmenides represents the reflective wisdom of age in contrast with the enthusiasm of youth. Two features stand out in Plato's presentation of him. One is his magnanimity—his readiness to consider with an open mind the novel theory of a younger man, and to admit that, when pruned of certain defects, it represents the truth. The other is his insistence—proper to an intellectualist—on rigour of thought. What he says of the theory of Ideas is that it is fundamentally true, but that it has been proclaimed without that regard to precision of thought which only a training in dialectic can give. The object of the 'second part'

[1] 135 d 2.   [2] Ibid. 8–136 a 2.
[3] *Gk. Phil.* i. 254.   [4] *P.S.* 41–2.

of the dialogue is to furnish an example of such training. It may
be added that in the *Sophistes* and the *Politicus* the Eleatic Stranger
is similarly treated—not as a monist but as a representative of
precise reasoning, and that to him is assigned the very un-
monistic contention that change must find a place in reality, not
less than unchangingness.

Parmenides' preliminary exposition of the dialectical method[1]
makes it quite clear that only two hypotheses are to be examined
—that a One exists, and that it does not exist. It also makes it
clear that two questions are to be considered, on the basis of each
of these hypotheses, viz. what then can be said about the One,
and what can be said about 'the others'. Thus we are led to
expect four arguments; but we find in fact eight (not nine, for
the section 155 e 4–157 b 5, though it is described as the third,
is plainly only an appendix to the second). How does this arise,
and how do pairs of arguments starting from the same hypothesis
and asking the same question—(1) and (2), (3) and (4), (5) and
(6), (7) and (8)—arrive in each case at exactly opposite results?
The answer is that when the same hypothesis is twice made and
the same question twice asked, different implications of the hypothesis are from the start taken account of. In (1) only the oneness
of the One is taken account of, it is regarded as being a unit and
nothing else, and from that it is deduced that nothing further can
be said about it. In (2) its existence as well as its oneness is taken
account of, and from this initial duality it is inferred that various
attributes can be asserted of it. If (3) be compared with (4), (5)
with (6), and (7) with (8), similar diversities of twists given to the
assumption can be detected from the start, and account for the
oppositeness of the conclusions.

In considering the hypotheses, we may begin by noting the
forms in which the various protases appear. They are as follows,
in Burnet's text:

1. 137 c 4–142 a 8   εἰ ἕν ἐστιν 137 c 4
2. 142 b 1–157 b 5   ἓν εἰ ἔστιν 142 b 3, 5, c 8, 155 e 4
                      εἰ ἓν ἔστιν 142 c 3
3. 157 b 6–159 b 1   ἓν εἰ ἔστιν 157 b 6, 7

[1] 136 e 8–137 b 4.

4. 159 b 2–160 b 4   ἓν εἰ ἔστιν 159 b 3, 5
5. 160 b 5–163 b 6   εἰ μὴ ἔστι τὸ ἕν 160 b 5
                 εἰ ἓν μὴ ἔστιν 160 b 7, c 1
                 ἓν εἰ μὴ ἔστι 160 c 6, d 3, 6
6. 163 b 7–164 b 4   ἓν εἰ μὴ ἔστι 163 c 1
7. 164 b 5–165 e 1   ἓν εἰ μὴ ἔστι 164 b 5
                 ἓν εἰ μὴ ἔστιν, τἆλλα δὲ τοῦ ἑνός 165 c 5
8. 165 e 2–166 c 2   ἓν εἰ μὴ ἔστι, τἆλλα δὲ τοῦ ἑνός 165 e 2

The variations under (2) and (5) show that there is no significance in the difference of order of the words, and that in particular it is unjustifiable to distinguish the protasis in (1) from that in (2) by supposing that the first is the hypothesis that the universe is one and the second the hypothesis that a One exists. Further, we must remember that in all there were to be only two hypotheses, one the contradictory of the other. Now the form εἰ μὴ ἔστι τὸ ἕν under (5) and the form ἓν εἰ μὴ ἔστιν, τἆλλα δὲ τοῦ ἑνός under (7) and (8) show that in these the hypothesis is existential, that a One does not exist. From these two facts it follows that in (1) to (4) the hypothesis is that a One exists; i.e. that there exists one all-embracing unity, and that in (5) to (8) the opposite assumption is made. The accents in our text have no authority, since they date from a time centuries later than Plato; but it may be noted that in (1) we should read ἔστιν, to conform with our conclusion that all (or rather both) the hypotheses are existential.

The conclusions of the arguments may be summed up as follows:

1. If a One exists, it admits of neither member of many pairs of opposite predicates, does not exist, cannot be named, spoken of, known, perceived, or judged about.

2. If a One exists, it admits of both members of the same pairs of opposite predicates, exists, can be named and spoken about, known, perceived, and judged about.

3. If a One exists, the others are like and unlike one another, the same as and different from one another, and admit of both members of many pairs of opposite predicates.

4. If a One exists, the others are neither like nor unlike, neither the same nor different, and admit of neither member of the same pairs of opposite predicates.

5. If a One does not exist, it admits of each member of many pairs of opposite predicates.

6. If a One does not exist, it admits of neither member of the same pairs of opposite predicates.

7. If a One does not exist, the others admit of each member of many pairs of opposite predicates.

8. If a One does not exist, the others admit of neither member of the same pairs of opposite predicates.

Thus, while the same hypothesis is made in the first four arguments, by dwelling on different implications of that hypothesis (1) and (4) arrive at indiscriminate negation, (2) and (3) at indiscriminate assertion. And while the opposite assumption is made in the last four arguments, by dwelling on different implications of that assumption (5) and (7) arrive at indiscriminate assertion, and (6) and (8) at indiscriminate negation. The result of the whole set of arguments is summed up[1] by saying that 'whether there is or is not a One, both that One and the others alike are and are not, and appear and do not appear to be, all manner of things in all manner of ways, with respect to themselves and to one another'.

Many interpretations of these arguments have been put forward by scholars, and Proclus' commentary shows that several were offered even in antiquity. It would be tedious to attempt to review them all; I will content myself by considering four of the most recent, three of which are discussed by Mr. Hardie in his *Study in Plato*,[2] but I will take them in a different order.

1. I begin with the 'idealist' interpretation put forward by Taylor in his articles in *Mind*.[3] According to this (I use Mr. Hardie's language[4]) the first of the eight arguments is 'the refutation of an abstract and merely eristic view of "The One". Extreme monism is reduced to absurdity by identifying it with that denial of the possibility of predication which arises from a failure to recognize the intercommunication of forms. But the second and kindred hypotheses[5] contrast with this false view a true and concrete notion of unity as a significantly differentiated whole.'

---

[1] 166 c 2–5.
[2] Chap. 10.
[3] v (1896), 297–326, 483–507, vi (1897), 9–39.
[4] p. 103.
[5] i.e. the third, fifth, and seventh.

This view need not be examined at length, since it was later discarded by its author; it may be enough to point to one or two serious objections to it. (*a*) There is the point which Mr. Hardie makes very effectively, that a refutation of abstract monism is one of the last things we should expect Plato to put into the mouth of Parmenides. (*b*) The indiscriminate ascription of opposite attributes to the One and to the Many which the second and the kindred arguments lead to is really no more satisfactory than the indiscriminate negation which the first and kindred arguments lead to. (*c*) There is no real indication that Plato means us to be more impressed by the second argument than by the first. He does indeed reject the conclusions to which the first argument leads, and therewith the abstractly monistic assumption from which these follow: 'Now can this possibly be the case with the One? I do not think so.'[1] But there is nothing to show that the conclusion of the second argument is more acceptable to Plato than that of the first, or that of the third more acceptable than that of the fourth. The reasoning in all eight arguments is of the same order, very ingenious, in places convincing, in others pervaded by fallacies that seem obvious to us, and some of which must have been obvious to Plato. (*d*) In the final conclusion[2] he treats all the arguments as forming one single argument leading to completely contradictory conclusions.

2. Secondly, there is the 'eristic' interpretation (a variant of the first) which Mr. Hardie[3] describes as holding that the hypothetical arguments 'are nothing but a logical exercise with the object of showing how, with the aid of certain logical fallacies supposed to be characteristic of Eleatics, the Eleatic hypothesis itself can be refuted. Both hypotheses[4] are *reductiones ad absurdum*.' This is the view adopted by Taylor in *Plato, the Man and his Work*, and in the introduction to his translation of the *Parmenides*. The most serious objections to this interpretation are the following: (*a*) It would surely be very curious if Plato had put into the mouth of Parmenides arguments of which the main purpose was to refute Eleaticism by parodying its methods. (*b*) This interpretation

[1] 142 a 6–8. [2] 166 c 2–5.
[3] pp. 102–3. [4] i.e. the first and second.

makes the same sort of mistake as the first. That took the second argument and the others leading to positive results as more seriously meant by Plato than the first and the other 'negative' arguments. The present interpretation stresses only the first four arguments, which show the paradoxical consequences of belief in the One, and ignores the last four, which show the paradoxical consequences of denying its existence. But it is clear that Plato is impartial as between all eight arguments. (*c*) Another feature of Taylor's later view is his interpretation of the second part of the *Parmenides* as 'a highly enjoyable philosophical jest'.[1] Most readers will be inclined to say, 'We are not amused.' Enjoyment we may receive from the arguments, but it is enjoyment not of humour but of virtuosity, and a little of it goes a long way.

3. Thirdly, there is the 'transcendentalist' interpretation, which (again I use Mr. Hardie's language[2])

finds a positive metaphysical suggestion even in the first hypothesis. It takes the hypothesis to refer to a 'One beyond being' which can be characterized only negatively, an ultimate principle of unity 'beyond' other forms, like the 'Idea of the Good' in the *Republic*. The second hypothesis deals with a 'One' which is differentiated but derivative, and regards unity and existence as connected aspects of an intelligible world. But the sphere of the existent is not ultimate or self-explanatory; it points 'beyond being'.

There is this in favour of this interpretation, that the first argument, which stresses the unity of the One and not its existence, is that which antecedently we might expect Plato to put into the mouth of Parmenides. But in considering the 'first part' of the dialogue we have been led to the view that Parmenides appears there not in the character of a monist, but simply in that of a great and honoured philosopher; and in consistency that is how he should appear in the 'second part' also. Further, it is Parmenides himself who at the end of the first argument describes its conclusions as quite unacceptable.[3]

Against this interpretation the following objections must be considered: (*a*) It appears to make the same mistake which the previous interpretations made, that of singling out one set of

[1] *P.M.W.* 370.   [2] p. 103.   [3] 142 a 6–8.

arguments (those that lead to negative results)—or at least the first of them—as stating a deeper truth than the other. If anything is clear, it is clear that Plato makes no such distinction. Not only is the first 'hypothesis' that at the end of which Plato says definitely 'this will not do', but in the last sentence of the dialogue he expressly puts all the 'hypotheses' on the same level of validity.

(b) Taylor has little difficulty in showing[1] that Plotinus' interpretation of the 'hypotheses' (from which the transcendentalist interpretation is derivable) is in many of its details completely unwarranted; the question remains whether Plotinus may not be right in holding that Plato meant to set up as that which is most completely real a completely unknowable One, and as derivable from it a One which is an object of knowledge. Perhaps in all his works the passage which comes nearest to corresponding to this view is that in the *Republic*[2] in which the Idea of the good is said to be more exalted than knowledge; but it seems to me that what Plato meant by that is not that it is unknowable but that it is a presupposition of knowledge, and that it can be known only in part; that in part it can be known is said in the *Republic* itself.[3] It may be added that the One that Parmenides speaks of in the first 'hypothesis' is a completely abstract unity to which goodness and all other value-attributes are inappropriate and of which they are never asserted.

(c) In the fourth argument Plato reaches with regard to the 'others' conclusions corresponding to those which in the first argument he reaches with regard to the One. Can we really suppose him to be unfolding or hinting at a mystical theory of 'the others', as Plotinus supposes him to be unfolding in the first argument a mystical theory of an ineffable and unknowable One? And can we suppose him to be unfolding a mystical doctrine in the sixth and eighth arguments, which (like the first and fourth) arrive at indiscriminate negation—in the sixth a mystical doctrine about the One on the hypothesis that there is no One, and in the eighth a mystical doctrine about 'the others' on the same hypothesis? It is surely clear that in the fourth, sixth, and eighth argu-

---

[1] Trans. of *Parmenides*, 145–59.   [2] 508 e 1–509 a 5.
[3] ἡ τοῦ ἀγαθοῦ ἰδέα μέγιστον μάθημα, 505 a 2.

ments Plato is not expressing a philosophy of the ineffable, but dispassionately working out the results of a certain type of reasoning applied to certain assumptions; and if so, it is most improbable that in the first he is doing anything else.

(*d*) In the *Sophistes*,[1] a dialogue probably not very much later than the *Parmenides*, we find a criticism of extreme monism in which Plato reproduces in brief the argument of the 'second hypothesis'; he points out that to assert that only one thing exists is to assert that both reality and oneness exist, and therefore that not only one thing exists; in other words, that extreme monism refutes itself. No one, I think, doubts that the argument in the *Sophistes* expresses Plato's own view; and that is difficult to reconcile with the theory that in the *Parmenides* he holds extreme monism to represent the deepest truth about the world.

4. We may consider next an interpretation put forward since Mr. Hardie wrote. This is that of Cornford. His main interpretation is thus summarized by Mr. Robinson:[2] 'the second part of the *Parmenides* is not parody or sophistry, but a serious and very subtle analysis. Nearly all the conclusions of all the hypotheses are true and important. What Plato here analyses is the logic of Parmenides, which he shows to be incorrect. The fifth hypothesis, for example, "is a brilliant refutation of the Eleatic dogma that nothing can be said about 'what is not'"'.

This view is open to the following objections. (*a*) There is the difficulty of supposing that Plato puts into the mouth of Parmenides an anti-Eleatic polemic. (*b*) There is the difficulty that the last four arguments, which start by supposing the *opposite* of the Eleatic dogma, lead by the same sort of logic to the same sort of paradoxical conclusions as the first four, which start from the Eleatic dogma. (*c*) There is the objection that, since there are many obvious fallacies in the arguments, Cornford has to eke out his main view by imputing to Plato a secondary object, that of furnishing his readers with practice in the detection of fallacies. Mr. Robinson shows effectively[3] that this secondary object would interfere most seriously with the main object. In proportion as

---

[1] 244 b 6–245 e 5.
[2] Plato's *Parmenides*, in *Class. Philol.* xxxvii (1942), 181.   [3] pp. 181–6.

the reader detects the fallacies, he will be less impressed by the anti-Eleatic argument; in proportion as he fails to detect them, the attempt to educate him in the detection of fallacies will have failed.

All these attempts to treat the inculcation of doctrine as the main, or only, object of the hypothetical arguments have failed; and it would seem that, in view of Plato's position of impartiality between arguments that lead to opposite conclusions, they are bound to fail. The only cure is to suppose that that is not the main purpose. The real clue to the interpretation is Parmenides' five-times-repeated[1] description of the arguments as affording γυμνασία, training in argument. He nowhere suggests that they will directly enlighten Socrates on the difficulties Parmenides has pointed out in the theory of Ideas, or on any other philosophical problem. We may note that in the *Politicus*,[2] written not so very long after the *Parmenides*, Plato expressly says that the discussion of the definition of the statesman is valuable less as throwing light on that particular problem than as making those who take part in it better dialecticians.

To other considerations which support this view we may add one piece of evidence which, while far from decisive, has some weight. The one important dialogue to which, it appears, Aristotle never refers is the *Parmenides*. If it were a serious exposition of Plato's views, and particularly if the first 'hypothesis' were the expression of his deepest views about ultimate reality, it would be strange that Aristotle never refers to it; if it is essentially a piece of logical gymnastic, his silence is much more intelligible.

This interpretation was put forward long ago by George Grote,[3] and it has been very powerfully defended by Mr. Robinson. This view avoids the objections we have seen to the four other interpretations we have considered; it does justice to what Parmenides says about the arguments, when he describes their purpose as essentially gymnastic, not the inculcation of philosophical doctrine but the giving of an example of a training which will fit Socrates better for the ultimate grasping of philosophical truth. It makes a unity of the dialogue; for while the first part convicts

[1] 135 c 8, d 4, 7, 136 a 2, c 5. [2] 285 d 4–7. [3] *P.C.S.* ii. 263.

Socrates of failure to see the weak points in his own view, the second part gives him an example of the sort of intellectual exercise which will make him more alive to such defects.

Only less illuminating than Plato's five-times-repeated description of the 'second part' as gymnastic is his description of it as a 'strenuous game'.[1] Strenuous it certainly is; the ingenuity and variety of the arguments in it are very striking. But it is a game, a game in which the arguer will do anything to score his point. He will use sound and sometimes profound argument when that helps him; but he will also when it suits him use unblushing sophistry; only so can he achieve the *tour de force* of deriving from apparently identical premisses contrary conclusions, and from apparently contrary premisses identical conclusions.

To treat the 'second part' as primarily a gymnastic exercise does not exclude the possibility that in the course of it Plato may hit on positive ideas that will fructify in his later thought. Cornford *may* be right in thinking that the poverty-stricken result of the first 'hypothesis' forms a *reductio ad absurdum* of Socrates' conviction[2] that what is simply unity itself cannot be many, and paves the way for the doctrine of the intercommunion of kinds in the *Sophistes*, and that the same point is reinforced in 144 a 5–145 a 3; that 144 e 8–145 a 3 and 158 b 5–159 a 4 foreshadow Plato's later analysis (known to us from Aristotle) of the Ideas into the One and the great and small; that 149 d 8–150 e 5 is meant as a recantation of the theory of the *Phaedo* which treats greatness and smallness as properties inherent in their possessors;[3] that the fourth hypothesis is meant, among other things, as a criticism of Socrates' insistence, in the *Phaedo* and the early part of the *Parmenides*, on the separateness of the Forms. Every student must judge for himself, but it is at least doubtful whether these supposed allusions to the theory of Ideas are really there. What Parmenides promises Socrates from the study of the hypotheses is not direct development or emendation of his theory, but a gain in dialectical skill which may ultimately produce that result; and that, I believe, is the whole purpose of the 'second part'. It was

---

[1] πραγματειώδης παιδιά, 137 b 2.   [2] 129 d 6–130 a 2, 131 c 9–11.
[3] 102 b 8–c 9.

not the theory of Ideas, but the implications of Parmenides' own hypothesis 'there is a One', and of its opposite, that were to be examined, in the hope that practice in the detection of implications and of ambiguities would ultimately enable Socrates to reach a more completely thought-out theory than that which in youthful enthusiasm he had embraced. It seems to me a mistake to try to trace grains of positive teaching in the wilderness of paradox which the 'hypotheses' present.

In the *Theaetetus* there is no direct reference to the Ideas, and it is possible to conjecture the reason for this. The dialogue was written, as we saw reason to believe,[1] after at least the 'first part' of the *Parmenides*, and not long after it. In that dialogue Parmenides had made important criticisms of the theory of Ideas, but had admitted that without such a theory to account for it discourse would be impossible. We may fairly suppose that it is in view of this situation that Plato leaves the theory of Ideas alone in the *Theaetetus*,[2] and turns to examine the soundness of the foundation on which he had built it—the assumption that knowledge exists, and is something quite different from sensation and from opinion. Reading between the lines, we can see certain advances in his views.[3]

1. In the *Phaedo*[4] Plato had lighted on the problem of relative size. Simmias is taller than Socrates, and shorter than Phaedo. He is taller than Socrates because Socrates has shortness relatively to Simmias' tallness, and shorter than Phaedo because Phaedo has tallness relatively to Simmias' shortness. Plato is content with pointing out that in all this neither is tallness itself, nor tallness in us, at the same time tall and short. Tallness either retires before shortness when shortness approaches, or is destroyed by its approach. He is satisfied to vindicate the Form against the charge of having contradictory attributes. In the *Theaetetus*[5] he lights on the same problem, and lays down three propositions. (*a*) Nothing can become greater or less in size so long as it remains equal to

[1] pp. 6-9.
[2] 175 c 2-3 and 203 e 2-5 come the nearest to being references to the theory.
[3] These were clearly pointed out by Jackson in *J. of Philol.* xiii (1885), 267-72.
[4] 102 a 11-103 a 3.   [5] 154 c 7-155 c 10.

itself. (*b*) That to which nothing is added and from which nothing is taken away remains equal to itself. (*c*) A thing that was not at an earlier time cannot be at a later without coming into being. He then points out that he, being at the time taller than Theaetetus, may within a year become shorter than Theaetetus without having himself become shorter; i.e. by comparing the relation between two people at one time with the relation between them at another he becomes aware of a difficulty which he had not realized when he was merely comparing the relation of *A* to *B* with the relation of *A* to *C* at the same time. Even in the earlier passage he showed some awareness of the relativity of the terms 'tall' and 'short'; but he has now become aware of a new difficulty about them, and come nearer to awareness of their complete relativity. He does not offer any direct solution of the difficulty, but hints that a doctrine which he proceeds to expound may throw light on it.[1] This is the doctrine which he ascribes to certain thinkers 'subtler than the uninitiated' (κομψότεροι)—the doctrine that in perception neither the perceived object nor the perceiving organ exists except in potentiality, until they meet.[2] The theory throws no direct light on the problem he has been considering, but he seems to be hinting that *similarly* tallness and smallness imply two things coming into comparison with each other; in other words, that they are out and out relative, not inherent in either of the things compared, as in the *Phaedo* they were supposed to be.

2. This doctrine of sense-perception is itself an earnest of something that is to follow, in the *Sophistes*. In the *Theaetetus* Plato maintains, under the guise of the κομψότεροι, that the universe (i.e the universe of perceiving souls and perceived objects) is motion and nothing else, that one kind of motion has the power of acting, the other that of being acted on, and that sensible qualities and the perception of them are produced simultaneously, the former in the object and the latter in the sense-organ, by the active motion in the one acting on the passive motion in the other. He does not specify whether the object acts on the sense-organ or *vice versa*, but it is natural to suppose that he means the former. There is here a clear resemblance to the passage of the *Sophistes*[3] where

---

[1] 155 d 5–e 1.   [2] 155 e 3–157 c 2.   [3] 247 d 8–e 4.

he tentatively treats the power of acting or being acted on as a sure sign of reality. And just as in the *Theaetetus* he presumably makes the object act and the sense-organ be acted on, in the *Sophistes*[1] he makes the Forms act and the souls be acted on, and argues that souls subject to change are real, as well as the Forms which in his earlier period he had identified with all that is truly real.

3. In 184 b 4–186 e 12 he distinguishes between objects like sound and colour, which are the objects of one sense only, and characteristics that we recognize as common to the objects of more than one sense—existence and non-existence, difference and sameness, twoness and oneness, unlikeness and likeness, evenness and oddness, beauty and ugliness, goodness and badness, 'and all that kind of thing'. Further, he insists that these are apprehended not by sense but by thought. Though he does not describe these as Forms, they correspond to the first two classes of Forms recognized in the *Parmenides*[2] (likeness, unity, and plurality; rightness, beauty, and goodness), and to the 'greatest of the kinds' recognized in the *Sophistes*[3] (being, sameness and difference, motion and rest). Thus from two angles of approach—from theory of knowledge in the *Theaetetus*, from metaphysics in the *Sophistes*—Plato arrives at the isolation of a class of very wide-ranging attributes, which later thought was to recognize as the *transcendentalia*.

Finally, it is in the *Theaetetus* that Plato most fully states the grounds on which his theory of Ideas in fact rests. For it rests on the belief that there is a complete difference between sensation and knowledge, and that knowledge demands as its objects entities not perceived by sense, and it is in the *Theaetetus*[4] that he gives his final and most elaborate proof of the difference between sensation and knowledge. His theory rests, again, as he says explicitly in the *Timaeus*,[5] on the belief that there is a complete difference between knowledge and true opinion, and of that also his most elaborate proof is given in the *Theaetetus*.[6] Thus, while the dialogue is concerned not with metaphysics but with epistemology, it furnishes the strongest argument Plato gives anywhere for the foundation of his metaphysical theory.

---

[1] If we interpret him aright; cf. pp. 108–11 *infra*.   [2] 130 b 1–10.
[3] 254 b 7–258 c 5.   [4] 151 d 7–186 e 12.   [5] 51 d 3–e 6.   [6] 187 a 1–210 b 3.

VI

THE *SOPHISTES* AND THE *POLITICUS*

THE *Sophistes* is the earliest dialogue in which Socrates plays an entirely subordinate part, appearing only in the first few opening pages; the chief part is played by an 'Eleatic stranger'. If we ask the reason for this change, the most probable answer is that Plato has come to realize more than he had previously done the importance of Parmenides. He has hitherto placed the theory of Ideas in the mouth of Socrates, since he has thought of it as essentially based on Socrates' insistence on the problem of definition. In reading the earlier dialogues we might almost suppose that for Plato there had been no philosopher, or no philosopher worth considering, before Socrates. In some of the dialogues of the early and middle periods—the *Protagoras*, the *Cratylus*, the *Theaetetus*—Plato has crossed swords with this or that other thinker. In the *Sophistes* he takes a much wider sweep. In the section 242 b 6–251 a 4 he passes under review the whole range of previous Greek philosophy. In his choice of an Eleatic stranger as his mouthpiece he hints that he is himself in some sense an heir to the philosophy of Parmenides, with its insistence on the supreme reality of that which cannot be perceived but only known, over against the objects of the senses. But while he is attracted by Parmenides' intellectualism, he is just as much repelled by his monism; and accordingly he takes as his spokesman not Parmenides, not a thoroughgoing monist like Zeno, but an enlightened Eleatic[1] who can criticize his father Parmenides[2] as well as he does other philosophers, and can say,[3]

It strikes me that Parmenides and everyone else who has set out to determine how many real things there are and what they are like, have discoursed to us in rather an offhand fashion. . . . They each and all seem to treat us as children to whom they are telling a story. . . . They have shown too little consideration for ordinary people like ourselves, in talking over our heads. Each school pursues its own argument to the conclusion without caring whether we follow what they say or get left behind.

[1] 216 b 3–8.   [2] 241 d 5–7.   [3] 242 c 4–243 b 1.

He distinguishes[1] three schools of philosophy—the pluralists, who recognize three, or it may be two, principles (and by these he probably means early cosmologists like Pherecydes), the monists, whom he calls the 'Eleatic race' and links with Xenophanes, and finally those who say that reality is both many and one, and are referred to as 'certain Ionian and Sicilian Muses'; i.e. Heraclitus and Empedocles. Of these groups the one which he criticizes most carefully is the Eleatic. In the first two 'hypotheses' of the *Parmenides* he had distinguished two senses in which Parmenides' saying 'One thing is' may be taken—that in which its unity is affirmed to the exclusion of everything else, and that in which its existence is also emphasized and therefore two Forms are recognized from the start and an indefinite number of others can be deduced. The 'second part' of the *Parmenides* is essentially an object-lesson in method, and Plato does little there to show where his preference lies. But he gives a hint, when at the end of the first 'hypothesis',[2] in which unity is assumed to the exclusion of everything else, Parmenides says 'Now can this possibly be the case with the One?' and Aristoteles replies, 'I do not think so.' The argument, in the second 'hypothesis' of the *Parmenides*, that monism entails its own opposite, is reproduced with little alteration in *Soph.* 244 b 6–245 e 5. Plato in effect, while retaining Parmenides' intellectualism, renounces extreme monism.

He proceeds[3] to consider other philosophers who are described as being less precise in their statements. Among these, too, there is a difference of opinion. They are divided into materialists, who say that only that which is tangible is real, and the 'Friends of Forms', who say that only Forms are real. Different views have been held about the identity of these 'Friends of Forms'. It has been held (1) that they were Megarians;[4] (2) that they were Italian Pythagoreans;[5] (3) that they were Platonists 'who, resting in their imperfect realization of an earlier phase of his own teaching and reverting to Pythagorean and Eleatic elements, held the doctrine of ideas in the form in which it is often controverted by Aristotle';[6]

[1] 242 c 4–243 a 2.   [2] 142 a 6–8.   [3] 245 e 6.
[4] So Schleiermacher, Zeller, Bonitz.
[5] Proclus *in Parm.* 5 a 2, Stallbaum, Burnet, Taylor.
[6] Campbell, Ed. of *Soph.* and *Pol.* lxxv.

(4) that Plato is referring to himself in an earlier phase.[1] There is virtually nothing to be said for the first view; we know very little about the Megarian school, and we have no independent knowledge of their having held such views as are here ascribed to the Friends of Forms. For the second view as against the third and fourth Taylor argues that the relegation of particular things to the realm of mere becoming, which is ascribed to these persons, is not the teaching of the *Phaedo*, which by its doctrine of participation assigns a modest place in reality to sensible things, and by its doctrine of anamnesis assigns to sense-perception a modest contribution to knowledge. He points, further, to the remark of the Eleatic stranger[2] that he knows the views of the Friends of Forms better than Theaetetus διὰ συνήθειαν, which (Taylor argues) in the mouth of a man of Elea can only mean that they are men of Italy. Taylor regards their doctrine as having developed naturally from the Pythagorean view that 'things are numbers'.

Ritter[3] thinks that Plato *may* be criticizing his own earlier self. He points out that the view Plato describes[4] seems to be precisely that of the *Phaedo* and the *Republic*, and that the phrase used of the perfectly real—that it 'stands immutable in solemn aloofness, devoid of intelligence'[5]—recalls the language of the famous passage of the *Phaedrus*[6]: 'There abides the very being with which true knowledge is concerned; the colourless, formless, intangible essence, visible only to mind, the pilot of the soul. . . . In the revolution she beholds justice, and temperance, and knowledge absolute, not in the form of generation or of relation, which men call existence, but knowledge absolute in existence absolute.' But he prefers to think that Plato never held at all definitely the doctrine of the immortality of the soul, and that he is rebuking the *Schwärmerei* of disciples who took the language of the *Phaedo* too seriously. He holds that in the pre-*Phaedo* dialogues there is no suggestion of 'separation' of the Idea from sensible things, and that Plato was led to it by his conjectural entertainment of the doctrines of immortality and anamnesis, since the Forms which the

---

[1] Grote, Ueberweg, Jackson, Cornford.   [2] 248 b 6–8.   [3] *P.L.S.L.* 2. 131–4.
[4] In 246 b 6–c 2 and 248 a 4–13, 248 c 7–d 3.   [5] 249 a 1.   [6] 247 c 6–e 2.

soul was aware of before it had a bodily existence, with sense-organs at its command, could only be Forms existing apart from any sensible examples.

It is noteworthy, however, that it is not the immortality of the soul that Plato rejects in the *Sophistes*, but the treatment of reality as *not* including life and soul. In fact the *Sophistes* ranks soul more definitely as included in the truly real than the *Phaedo* does, which only describes it as akin to the truly real. It looks, therefore, as if Plato was now criticizing himself for *not* having sufficiently recognized the complete reality of life and soul. We need not be surprised if he should here be criticizing his earlier self; for he has already done so in the first part of the *Parmenides*, where he has used the same device, that of putting the criticism in the mouth of one who was not himself a Platonist. And indeed the criticism is of the same kind as the last of the criticisms put into the mouth of Parmenides, that the earlier Platonic view severs the world of becoming too completely from that of being.

It is not altogether easy to choose between the second and the fourth view. But one must hesitate before accepting the view that there was in Italy a school of the type that Taylor presupposes, a school that is not mentioned in any ancient writer other than Proclus. And his interpretation of διὰ συνήθειαν is not the only possible one. συνήθεια may mean 'acquaintance', and it may be on that understanding of it that Proclus based his interpretation. But in several passages[1] it means 'habituation', and if that be what it means here, it can be explained by supposing the Stranger to be saying that he, a professed philosopher, is more used to the sort of discussion in question than Theaetetus, a new-comer from mathematics to philosophy. On the whole, then, the other interpretation is more probable;[2] the 'Friends of Forms' are Plato's earlier self and those who had accepted his earlier view.

The Stranger first turns his attention to the materialists, and drives them to admit that there are things which without being tangible manifest their reality by their power of affecting or being

[1] *Rep.* 516 a 5, 517 a 2, 620 a 2; *Tht.* 157 b 2, 168 b 7; *Laws* 655 e 6, 656 d 8, 865 e 3.
[2] For a detailed defence of it cf. Jackson, *J. of Philol.* xiv (1885), 200–2, and Cornford, *P.T.K.* 242–4.

affected by something else—souls, justice and injustice, wisdom and folly, goodness and badness.[1] He now turns to the Friends of Forms,[2] who assign reality only to Forms and relegate everything else to the realm of becoming. In what follows there is a passage which has often been supposed to imply that Plato so far changes his view about Ideas as to ascribe to them change, life, soul, and reason. This would be a most surprising, and indeed an incredible, development, since his main reason for believing in Ideas is his conviction that knowledge must have an unchanging object. The whole passage must be studied, to see whether he really abandons that view:

[248 c 4] *Str.* 'We propose as a sufficient mark of real things the presence in a thing of the power of being acted on or of acting in relation to however insignificant a thing.'—*Tht.* 'Yes.'

Str. 'Well, to that they reply that a power of acting and being acted upon belongs to Becoming, but neither of these powers is compatible with Real Being.'—*Tht.* 'And there is something in that answer?'

[11] *Str.* 'Something to which we must reply by a request for more enlightenment. Do they acknowledge further that the soul knows and Real Being is known?'—*Tht.* 'Certainly they agree to that.'

Str. 'Well, do you agree that knowing or being known is an action, or is it a being acted on, or both? Or is one of them a being acted on, the other an action? Or does neither of them come under either of these heads at all?'—*Tht.* 'Evidently neither; otherwise our friends would be contradicting what they said earlier.'

Str. 'I see what you mean. I suppose they would say this: If knowledge is to be acting on something, it follows that what is known must be acted upon by it; and so, on this showing, reality when it is being known by the act of knowledge must, in so far as it is known, be changed owing to being so acted upon; and that, we may say, cannot happen to the changeless.'—*Tht.* 'Exactly.'

[e 6] *Str.* 'But tell me, in heaven's name: are we really to be so easily convinced that change, life, soul, understanding have no

---

[1] 246 e 2–248 a 3.   [2] 248 a 4.

place in that which is perfectly real—that it has neither life nor thought, but stands immutable in solemn aloofness, devoid of intelligence?'—*Tht.* 'That, sir, would be a strange doctrine to accept.'

[249 a 4] *Str.* 'But can we say it has intelligence without having life?'—*Tht.* 'Surely not.'

Str. 'But if we say it contains both, can we deny that it has soul in which they reside?'—*Tht.* 'Surely not. How else could it possess them?'

Str. 'But then, if it has intelligence, life, and soul, can we say that a living thing remains at rest in complete changelessness?'—*Tht.* 'All that seems to me unreasonable.'

Str. 'In that case we must admit that what changes and change itself are real things.'—*Tht.* 'Certainly.'

[b 5] *Str.* 'From this, however, it follows, Theaetetus, first, that, if all things[1] are unchangeable, no intelligence can really exist anywhere in anything with regard to any object.'—*Tht.* 'Quite so.'

Str. 'And, on the other hand, if we allow that all things are moving and changing, on that view equally we shall be excluding intelligence from the class of real things.'—*Tht.* 'How so?'

[b 12] *Str.* 'Do you think that, without rest, there could ever be things[2] that abide constant in the same condition and in the same respect?'—*Tht.* 'Certainly not.'

Str. 'And without such objects can you make out that intelligence exists or could ever exist anywhere?—*Tht.* 'It would be quite impossible.'

Str. 'Well, then, all the force of reasoning must be enlisted to oppose anyone who tries to maintain any assertion about anything at the same time that he suppresses knowledge or understanding or intelligence.'—*Tht.* 'Most certainly.'

Str. 'On these grounds, then, it seems that only one course is open to the philosopher who values knowledge and the rest above all else. He must refuse to accept from the champions either of the One or of the many Forms the doctrine that all Reality is changeless; and he must turn a deaf ear to the other party who

---

[1] Reading ὄντων ⟨πάντων⟩, with Badham.
[2] Reading τὰ κατὰ ταὐτά, with Jackson.

represent Reality as everywhere changing. Like a child begging for "both", he must declare that Reality or the sum of things is both at once—all that is unchangeable and all that is in change.' —*Tht.* 'Perfectly true.'

Those who suppose Plato to be here abandoning his belief in the unchangeability of Ideas, and assigning soul to them, think (*a*) that in 248 c 11–e 4 he argues that being known is a form of being acted on, and that being acted on is incompatible with being an unchanging nature; and (*b*) that in 248 e 6–249 a 2 he affirms that what is perfectly real must have movement, life, soul, and reason. Both of these interpretations are mistaken. (*a*) In the first passage there is no admission that knowing is an action and being known a passivity; it is simply pointed out that *if* this were admitted it would lead to a contradiction of the belief of the Friends of Forms in the unchangeability of the real. The supposition that knowing is an action and being known a passivity, which is only one of several suggestions put forward in 248 d 4–7, is simply dropped. (*b*) It is only by a complete, though very natural, misunderstanding that the second passage is supposed to say that whatever is perfectly real must have movement, life, soul, and reason. What Plato is saying is that (though the attempt to prove that the object of knowledge is in movement has failed) we should find it difficult to believe that what is perfectly real cannot have movement, life, and the rest. He does not say that whatever is perfectly real must have these things; he simply denies that it cannot. His real meaning becomes clear in 249 b 5– 10, where he says, in effect, that knowledge implies minds that are real and subject to change, and objects (the Ideas) that are real and not subject to change. He has not given up his belief in unchanging Ideas (which he expresses in later dialogues),[1] but he adds that minds subject to change must also be accepted as completely real. And when he says that to the question whether reality is changeable or unchangeable we must answer 'it is both', he does not mean that the same reality in some mysterious way manages to be both, but that both unchanging Ideas and changing minds are perfectly real.

[1] e.g. in *Tim.* 28 a 1–2, 51 e 6–52 a 2; *Phil.* 59 a 7, c 2–5.

What, then, becomes of the suggestion that knowing is a form of acting, and being known a form of being acted on? It is silently dropped when the consequence of accepting it has been pointed out.[1] And if Plato means to stick to his suggestion that only that which has the power either of acting or of being acted on is real, he must be supposed to adopt the other alternative, that in knowledge the object acts on the mind; which would be at least more reasonable than the view that the mind acts on the object, and would correspond better with the account he gives of sensation in the *Theaetetus*.[2]

As Plato has forced the materialists who were open to conviction to admit that there are non-sensible realities as well as sensible, he has now forced the idealists to admit that reality includes living, thinking beings as well as the Ideas. Now in the *Phaedo* and the *Republic* he has often described the Forms as alone completely real; but the conclusion he here reaches is one which was already foreshadowed in the *Phaedo*, where he says[3] that soul is more akin to the unseen and eternal than to the seen and temporal; and indeed the same thing is implied in the doctrine of immortality, in the *Phaedo*, the *Republic*, and the *Phaedrus*. What he does in the *Sophistes* is to recognize, more explicitly than ever before, two elements in reality—universal Forms and individual souls. Finally, summing up the argument, he says that reality must include all things immovable and movable;[4] the immovable Forms which alone the Friends of Forms admit to be real, the movable bodies which alone the materialists admit to be real, and the souls which have 'movements of their own'.[5]

Plato has come, then, to recognize two attributes—rest and motion—each of which is consistent with reality, and the scene changes to a consideration of the question of the κοινωνία γενῶν,[6] the intercommunion of kinds, of which this is an example.

---

[1] In 248 d 10–e 4.   [2] cf. pp. 102–3 *supra*.
[3] 79 b 1–c 1.   [4] 249 c 10–d 4.
[5] For the 'movements of the soul'—learning, practising, wish, consideration, &c., cf. *Tht.* 153 b 9–c 1, *Laws* 896 e 8–897 a 3.

[6] Plato uses κοινωνία, κοινωνεῖν, ἐπικοινωνεῖν, ἐπικοινωνία, προσκοινωνεῖν in two different constructions—with the genitive (250 b 9, 252 a 2, b 9, 254 c 5, 256 b 2, 260 e 2) and with the dative (251 d 9, e 8, 252 d 3, 253 a 8, 254 b 8, c 1, 257 a 9, 260 e 5). In the former usage the verbs mean 'share in'; in the latter

Plato dismisses with contempt[1] the theory—usually and no doubt rightly attributed to Antisthenes—that a thing cannot have an attribute distinct from itself, that it cannot be true to say of a man that he is good, but only to say that a good is a good and a man is a man. Plato's problem is not the question whether that is true (he assumes that it is not), but the question how one Form, such as being, can be predicated of two or more other Forms, such as motion and rest—the question at which he has already hinted in the *Parmenides*.[2] He had there said that, while there is no difficulty in seeing that one *thing* can share in different and even in opposite Ideas, what he would be really astonished at would be if any one could, after distinguishing the Forms, such as likeness and unlikeness, plurality and unity, rest and motion, then exhibit *them* as being 'mixed together and severed from each other'. The conclusion he will presently reach is that, while no Form can be 'mixed' with another in the sense of being identified with it, there are three Forms—Being, Sameness, Difference— that can be predicated of all Forms, certain pairs of Forms of which one can be predicated of the other, and other pairs of Forms of which neither can be predicated of the other. His problem is that of the organization of the system of Forms themselves. He first[3] considers the statement that no Form can combine with any other. This is dismissed, as being inconsistent with any theory of the nature of the real; for any such theory holds that things having some special character —moving bodies, or motionless unities, or unchanging Forms—exist, or in other words share in the Form of existence. Indeed the theory is self-refuting; for in saying of each Form that it is apart from all others and that it exists by itself, such thinkers are asserting a connexion between it and existence apart from all other things, and between it and existence by itself. It is equally impossible to say[4] that all Forms blend with each other; for that would imply, e.g., that movement

they mean 'combine with' or 'communicate with'. The 'sharing' of one Form in another has some affinity with the sharing of a particular thing in a Form, with the important difference that the Form which shares in another is a perfect specification of the other, while a particular which shares in a Form is only an imperfect example of it. Though Plato uses the two different constructions, he does not seem to attach any importance to the difference between them.

[1] 251 a 8–c 6.   [2] 129 d 6–130 a 2.   [3] 251 e 7–252 d 1.   [4] 252 d 2–e 8.

is at rest and rest is in movement. The truth is[1] that some Forms blend and some do not, and our problem is to discover which do and which do not. Plato adds that we must ask ourselves whether there are certain kinds (or Forms) which run through all Forms and connect them, and whether there are other Forms which run through all Forms and separate them. He does not tell us here what the connecting Forms are, or what the separating Forms are. But the sequel makes it clear that the connecting Forms are being, sameness, and difference, which are predicable of all Forms and, simply by being so, connect them, and that the most general separating Form is difference, which is predicable of all Forms and by its *special* nature separates them.[2] The science which discovers these uniting Forms and these separating Forms is dialectic, and its exponent is the true philosopher. In other words philosophy is the discovery of the organization of the system of Forms, the connecting of Forms that are really connectible and the disconnecting of Forms that are really unconnectible.[3]

The Stranger turns[4] to consider some of the 'greatest of the kinds' with a view to discovering the nature of each and their relations to each other. The greatest of the kinds are those we have already discussed in the passage on the Friends of Forms[5]— being, motion, and rest.[6] Of these, motion and rest will not 'mix', but being mixes with both. Further, each of the two is other than the other and the same as itself, so that we must recognize two other great Forms, sameness and difference. Plato has little difficulty in showing that both sameness and difference are different alike from motion, rest, and being. His proof that difference is

---

[1] 252 e 9–253 c 5.
[2] 254 d 10–255 e 7.   [3] 253 c 6–254 b 6.
[4] 254 b 7.   [5] 248 a 4–249 d 5.
[6] Cornford insists that Plato only says that being, motion, and rest are very great kinds, not that they are the greatest, since sameness and difference are presently added to their company, and are in fact greater kinds than motion and rest, being predicable of everything while motion and rest are not predicable of each other. This might be accepted if the Stranger had described being, motion, and rest simply as μέγιστα γένη, but he says they are μέγιστα τῶν γενῶν, and Theaetetus answers πολύ (254 d 4–6). 'Much very great' will hardly do, while πολὺ μέγιστα is ordinary Greek for 'much the greatest'. Motion and rest are in fact less 'great' than sameness and difference; but it is natural that Plato should at this stage mention only those greatest kinds which have already been discovered.

different from being is interesting because it introduces[1] the distinction between terms that are absolute (αὐτὰ καθ' αὑτά) and those that are relative (πρὸς ἀλλά). Difference must be different from being because it is always relative while being may be absolute or relative.[2]

Thus we have five 'greatest kinds'. Plato proceeds to sum up their mutual relations:[3]

1. Motion is completely different from rest (i.e. neither identical with nor predicable of it).

2. It shares in existence.

3. It is different from sameness; yet it shares in sameness, being the same as itself.

4. It is different from difference; yet it shares in difference, being different from sameness and from rest.

Plato now asks[4] whether motion stands in a second relation to existence, as well as that of sharing in it, and answers that (5) it is different from existence. Similarly[5] it must be true of each of the kinds other than existence that (*a*) it is not existence, being kept apart from it by difference, but (*b*) it is existent, by sharing in existence. And we may say of every kind (not merely of the greatest kinds) that there is much that it is (i.e. that there are many kinds predicable of it) and an infinity of things that it is not (since it is not identical with any other kind).

6. It is true of being, in respect of any other kind, that it *is not* (is not identical with) any of them; yet it *is* one thing, namely itself.[6]

Adding to what Plato says what he might easily have added by parity of reasoning, we can now state the mutual relations of the greatest kinds:

1. Each of them is different from every other.

2. Being, sameness, difference are predicable of each other, and of motion and of rest.

3. Motion and rest are not predicable of each other.

At an earlier stage of the dialogue,[7] the Stranger has said that the existence of falsehood implies that that which is not has,

---

[1] 255 c 12. [2] 255 d 3-7. [3] 255 e 8-256 d 10.
[4] 256 c 11. [5] 256 d 11. [6] 257 a 1-6. [7] 237 a 3-9.

nevertheless, some being, and thus runs counter to Parmenides' saying, 'Never shall this be proved, that things that are not are.' He now[1] recurs to the problem of τὸ μὴ ὄν, that which is not, and begins by saying that by this phrase we do not mean something contrary to what exists, but only something different. He justifies this by pointing out that 'not great' (which, since 'great' is a comparative term, means 'not greater') is just as applicable to what is equal as to what is small (i.e. smaller). Thus that which is denied to be *x* is not said to be the contrary of *x*, but only to be other than *x*. Further, as knowledge is parcelled out into the sciences, so 'the other' is parcelled out into the not-beautiful, the not-great, &c. And the things denoted by these negative terms are just as real as the things denoted by the corresponding positive terms. Thus not-being is established as one among the many kinds;[2] but it is not a sixth 'greatest kind', because it is simply difference under another name.

Finally, we must note the very ingenious use Plato makes of the account he has given of 'that which is not' as being not the non-existent but that which is different—the context determining what it is different from. The whole discussion of the communion of kinds started from an attempt to give an account of false statement and false opinion. It seems natural to say that false statement asserts, and false opinion thinks, that which is not; and to say this seems, *prima facie*, to be implying that that which is not is; and against this is invoked the great authority of Parmenides—'never shall this be proved, that that which is not is'. The Stranger now attacks the problem of false statement and false opinion in the light of his discussion of 'that which is not'. He begins[3] with the proposition that all discourse depends on the weaving together of Forms by the speaker or thinker. This is in fact an over-statement, since a sentence may have a proper name for subject, and a proper name does not stand for a Form or universal. But the *predicate* of a sentence normally stands for a Form, and all subjects of statements except proper names stand either for Forms or for things described by means of Forms.

[1] 257 b 1.　　　　　[2] 258 c 3.　　　　　[3] 259 e 5.

The Stranger proceeds to say[1] that every statement asserts or denies a verb (standing for an action) of a noun (standing for the doer of the action); and he takes an example which illustrates this (though it does not illustrate his thesis that every statement is a weaving together of Forms), viz. the statement 'Theaetetus flies'.[2] Theaetetus' flying is something that does not exist, and the statement seems therefore on the face of it to say that which is not; but the Stranger points out[3] that while Theaetetus' flying does not exist, Theaetetus exists and flying (the Form or universal of flying) exists, so that in saying Theaetetus flies we are not asserting of him something that does not exist, but simply something that does not belong to him, something 'other', i.e. other than all the things that do belong to him.

The result of Plato's examination of the communion of classes may seem rather meagre—the discovery of certain very obvious relations between five terms. But we must remember two things; first, that this whole examination is only incidental to the examination of the possibility of false statement and false opinion, starts from this and returns to this; and secondly, that what is important is the establishment of the *principle* that the Forms are neither a collection of entities standing in no positive relations to each other, nor yet are capable of entering into all sorts of relations to one another—that they form, indeed, a system. The discussion is only the first instalment of a process that may be carried much farther—to the establishment of one or other of two relations, predicability or non-predicability, between each pair of Forms, and thus to a map—a rather abstract map, it must be admitted—of the world of Forms.

Plato has in the *Phaedrus*[4] described dialectic as consisting in a joint use of collection and division. Of these operations, the first seems to be merely preliminary to the second. In the attempt to reach the definition of a specific term, the first stage—the 'collection'—is the tentative choice of a wide genus under which the term to be defined seems to fall. In the *Sophistes* and the *Politicus*,

---

[1] 262 c 2-7.   [2] 263 a 8.   [3] 263 b 7-d 5.
[4] 265 d 3-266 c 1, 273 d 7-e 4, 277 b 5-8.

'collection' is never treated as a separate part of the process, the word συναγωγή does not occur, and though the word συνάγω often occurs,[1] it is only once[2] used of the collection of species into a genus. The whole stress falls on the process of division. In the attempt to define the angler, which is preliminary to the attempt to define the sophist, it is assumed without discussion that the angler is a species of craftsman,[3] and the stress falls on the attempt to divide the genus 'craftsman'. In the first attempt to define the sophist, the sophist is assumed, without discussion, to belong to the genus 'craftsman',[4] and in each successive attempt the genus is similarly assumed, and the stress falls on the subdivision of the genus into species. And when Plato comes to describe the nature of dialectic in general, he defines it not, as in the *Phaedrus*, as a joint process of collection and division, but simply as a process of 'dividing according to kinds, not taking the same Form for a different one or a different one for the same'.[5] But in the same passage dialectic is described in yet another way. In the *Parmenides*[6] Socrates had said that, while there is nothing surprising in the fact that a stick or a stone is many—has many parts—as well as being one, what would surprise him would be if anyone could show that Forms themselves—unity and plurality, or likeness and unlikeness, or rest and motion—can be combined. And now in the *Sophistes* he defines dialectic as 'knowing how to distinguish, kind by kind, in what ways the several kinds can or cannot combine'.[7] What this points to is not the construction of a hierarchy of the Ideas ranging from a *summum genus* down to *infimae species*, but rather a study of the relations of consistency, inconsistency, and implication that exist between Forms.

The *Politicus* is mainly occupied with a discussion of the nature of statesmanship, but it contains one passage which is germane to the study of the doctrine of Ideas. Here, too, the stress falls not on collection but on division. Plato takes a point which he has not explicitly made in the *Phaedrus* or in the *Sophistes*, namely that not every possible division of a genus by the use of dichotomy is

[1] *Soph.* 224 c 9, 230 b 6, 251 d 8. *Pol.* 267 b 6, 278 c 5, 308 c 6, 311 a 1, c 1.
[2] *Soph.* 267 b 1.   [3] 219 a 4-7.   [4] 221 c 5-d 6.
[5] 253 d 1-4.   [6] 129 c 1-130 a 2.   [7] 253 d 9-e 6.

likely to conform to the true structure of the genus. By successive uses of dichotomy, the Stranger reaches the conclusion that statesmanship falls under the heading of 'the tending of many animals together',[1] and the 'younger Socrates' proceeds to identify it with the management of many men together.[2] To this the Stranger objects that 'we had better not cut off one small portion, against portions that are great and many, nor a portion without a Form; let the part have a Form . . . it is not safe, my friend, to chop small; it is safer to proceed by cutting through the middle—one is more likely to hit on real Ideas.'[3] Socrates has made the same mistake as one would who divided men into Hellenes and *barbarians*, or number into the number ten thousand and *the other numbers*; he is supposing that he has found a single class because he has given to a mere collection a common name. He would have done much better if he had divided numbers into odd and even, or men into male and female. 'A class is necessarily a part, but there is no similar necessity that a part should be a class.'[4] There are 'two ways to that part which the argument aims at reaching —the one a speedier way, which cuts off a small portion and leaves a large, the other a way which as we prescribed divides as nearly as possible in the middle, but is longer.'[5]

Two important principles with regard to the world of Ideas are here recognized. One is that its structure is a stratified structure. The division of mankind into Greeks and barbarians is bad because it ignores this principle; the Greeks are 'too small a chip' of the whole, not on the same level of generality as the class with which they are contrasted. In dividing, we should not pass direct from 'man' to 'Greek', but recognize the intervening classes. The second principle is that the absence of a positive characteristic does not in itself constitute a class. A barbarian, for a Greek, was simply one who was not a Greek; 'barbarian' was as negative a term as 'not-ten-thousand' would be.

It will be seen that the conception of dialectic, i.e. of philosophy, put forward in the *Phaedrus*, the *Sophistes*, and the *Politicus* is quite different from that put forward in the *Republic*. The

---

[1] 261 d 7–9.   [2] 262 a 3–4.   [3] 262 a 5–c 1.
[4] 263 b 7–9.   [5] 265 a 1–5.

objective of dialectic is no longer to deduce all truth from a single transcendent truth. It is a more modest and a more realizable one—one with which Plato at least succeeds in making a beginning—that of tracing the relations of assertability and deniability that exist between Ideas, and the relations of genus and species that exist between them. It is typical of Aristotle's good sense that, while he completely rejected the ideal of deducing all truth from a single truth, he accepted from Plato the notions of genus, species, and differentia, and by adding to them the natural corollaries, property and accident, established his doctrine of predicables.

VII

THE *TIMAEUS* AND THE *PHILEBUS*

THE discourse of Timaeus[1] is divided by Plato himself into three main sections. There is first[2] the section in which he describes the operation of reason in the construction of the world; secondly[3] the section which describes 'the things that happen of necessity, i.e. those features of the world that are due to the pre-existing conditions of which reason has to take account and which it cannot alter; and thirdly[4] the section in which Plato returns 'to the beginning' and takes account of both the elements that have been treated separately in the first two parts. The third section, being concerned with the details of that combination of body and soul which we call a man, throws no light on the theory of Ideas; nor do many of the details of the first two sections. But the more general parts of these sections are very relevant to our theme.

Plato begins[5] with his familiar distinction between 'that which is always real and has no becoming' and is 'apprehensible by thought with a rational account', and 'that which is always becoming and is never real' and is 'the object of belief together with unreasoning sensation'. Thus the distinction between Forms and sensible things is placed in the forefront of the discourse.

The world, being apprehensible by the senses (he continues),[6] must have come into being, and have done so by some agency; and its maker must have looked to an unchanging model, i.e. to a Form; for only so will the product be good. The framer of the universe was good, and desired that all things should come as near as possible to being like himself.[7] He therefore 'took over all that was visible—not at rest but in discordant and unordered motion—and brought it from disorder into order'.[8] Since nothing that is without intelligence can be better than that which has intelligence, and since intelligence cannot be present without soul,

---

[1] 27 c 1 to the end of the dialogue.   [2] 27 c 1-47 e 2.
[3] 47 e 3-69 a 5.   [4] 69 a 6-end.   [5] 27 d 5-28 a 4.
[6] 28 b 2-29 b 2.   [7] 29 e 1-3.   [8] 30 a 3-6.

in framing the universe 'he fashioned reason within soul, and soul within body'.[1] The model used by the divine craftsman could not be any particular living creature; it must be that which embraces them all, 'for that embraces and contains within itself all the intelligible living creatures, just as this world contains ourselves and all other creatures that have been formed as things visible'.[2] In other words, the model must have been the generic Form of living creature, together with all its species and sub-species.

After describing in general terms the nature of the sensible world modelled after the ideal living creature, Plato proceeds[3] to speak of the world-soul, which like the sensible world itself is described as having been made by the Demiourgos. This he made 'prior to body and more venerable in birth and excellence, to be the body's mistress and governor'.[4] Thus Plato at once assigns to soul a place in reality lower than the eternal Forms, and higher than bodily things; and this intermediate position is maintained in the passage which immediately follows, about the composition of the world-soul. It will be remembered that in the *Sophistes* existence, sameness, and difference were singled out as the widest of the Forms, predicable of one another and of all other Forms since every Form exists, and is the same as itself and different from every other Form. With reference to these three Forms Plato assigns the following stages to the composition of the world-soul :[5]

(1) Between the indivisible Existence that is ever in the same state and the divisible Existence that becomes in bodies, he compounded a third form of Existence composed of both. (2) Again, in the case of Sameness and that of Difference, and on the same principle, he made a compound intermediate between that kind of them which is indivisible and the kind that is divisible in bodies. (3) Then, taking the three, he blended them all into a unity, forcing the nature of Difference, hard as it was to mingle, into union with Sameness, and mixing them together with Existence.

1. The existence assigned to Forms is here doubly characterized —it is indivisible and unchanging; that assigned to bodies is

divisible and changing; that ascribed to the world-soul is in both respects intermediate. Plato does not elucidate his meaning, but it is possible to do so, conjecturally. (*a*) Every Form is indivisible; it may have elements, a generic element and a differential one, but these are indivisibly united. Every body can always be divided into smaller bodies. The world-soul extends throughout the world-body,[1] and we may conjecture that Plato means that it is therefore notionally divisible, while yet it is actually indivisible.

(*b*) Again, a Form is eternal and unchanging; a body comes into being and changes. Plato does not explain how the world-soul is intermediate in this respect, but we can get a clue to his meaning by looking to what he says in 37 d 3–7 about the world-body. 'The nature of that Living Being' (the Idea of Living Being) 'was eternal, and this character it was impossible to confer in full completeness on the generated thing' (the world-body). 'But he took thought to make, as it were, a moving likeness of eternity; and, at the same time that he ordered the Heaven, he made, of eternity that abides in unity, an everlasting likeness moving according to number—that to which we have given the name Time.' To the world-soul also, we must suppose, Plato assigns an existence intermediate between that of Forms and that of sensible things, in that, while not eternal—it has been created by the Demiourgos—it lasts throughout time.

The language here used of the world-soul echoes what Plato had written long before, in the *Phaedo*:[2] 'The soul is most like that which is divine, immortal, intelligible, uniform, indissoluble, and unchanging; whereas the body is most like the human, mortal, multiform, unintelligible, dissoluble, and perpetually changing.' What Plato there said of soul in general he here says of the world-soul. But while he says little in the *Timaeus* about the immortality of individual souls, there is evidence that he had not changed his mind about this.

2. By the sameness proper to Forms Plato means the complete singleness and self-identity that characterizes every Form. By the difference proper to Forms he means the clean-cut difference that

---

[1] 34 b 3, 36 e 2.   [2] 80 a 10–b 5.

separates every Form from every other. By the sameness and the difference proper to bodies he means partial sameness, partial difference, the likeness in some respects, unlikeness in others, that every body has in relation to every other. To the world-soul he ascribes an intermediate type of sameness and of difference, as well as of existence, in order (on the principle that like knows like) to account for its power both of knowing Forms and of forming judgements about bodies.[1]

The first section of Timaeus' discourse contains nothing more that is directly relevant to our theme. But in the second section he says that besides the two things he has named in 27 d 5-29 b 2 —the pattern and the copy—we must recognize a third thing which is 'difficult and obscure', 'the receptacle and as it were the nurse of all becoming'.[2] Before we consider it further, he continues, we must consider the things that come to be in it—the elements recognized by Empedocles, fire, air, water, and earth. Water when it is compressed becomes earth, and when it is dissolved, air; air when inflamed becomes fire; fire when compressed becomes air, and when further condensed, water, and when still further condensed, earth. The four elements 'slip away and do not wait to be called "this" or "that", or referred to by any expression that indicates that they are permanent'.[3] Only that in which each of them appears from time to time and from which it vanishes should be referred to as 'that' or 'this'.[4] In other words, the four so-called elements are not ultimate elements, but four states of one thing.

Timaeus attempts to elucidate his meaning still further by an analogy.[5] 'If one were to mould all sorts of shapes out of gold and never to cease remoulding each into all the rest, and were then shown one of them and asked what it is, far the safest answer, with a view to truth, would be that it is gold. We should never speak of the triangle or the other shapes that were coming to be in it, which change in the very moment of our assuming their existence, as being, but be content if they can with any safety be referred to as "that which has such and such a character". So,

---

[1] 37 a 2–b 3.   [2] 48 e 2–49 a 6.   [3] 49 e 2–4.
[4] Ibid. 7–50 a 2.   [5] 50 a 4–d 2.

too, the nature that receives all bodies should be described as always the same; for it never departs from its own capacity; it receives from time to time all things, and never takes a shape in any way like any of the things that pass into it; it remains by nature a plastic material (ἐκμαγεῖον)[1] for everything, changed and diversified by the things that pass into it, and because of them appears now of one kind, now of another; while the things that pass into and out of it (τὰ εἰσιόντα καὶ ἐξιόντα)[2] are copies of the eternal things, modelled after them in a way that is hard to express and marvellous, which we shall pursue later. But for the present we must recognize three kinds of thing, that which comes into being, that in which it comes into being, that in whose likeness that which comes into being is born.' Timaeus goes on to say[3] that, in order to be able to accommodate all sorts of qualities (such as heat and cold), the receptacle is necessarily not itself characterized by any of these. It is neither earth nor air nor fire nor water, but is 'invisible and formless, all-receptive, partaking in a most obscure way of the intelligible, and most difficult to grasp'.

Timaeus now[4] asks whether there is such a thing as fire-itself, air-itself, and so on, or only the fire, air, &c., that we apprehend by the senses, i.e. whether the ideal patterns he has assumed need be assumed. His answer is this: 'If reason and opinion are different things, then Forms imperceptible by us, objects of thought alone, must exist by themselves; but if true opinion differs in no wise from reason, the things we perceive by means of the body must be deemed to be the most secure realities. Now we must say that reason and opinion are two things, since they differ both in origin and in nature. The one is produced by teaching, the other by persuasion; we can justify the one by true reasoning, the other is unreasoned; the one cannot be moved by persuasion, the other can; only God and a few men possess the one, all men possess the other. We must therefore agree that there are Forms distinct from the copies of them.'[5]

Plato here treats as the essential reason for believing in the

---

[1] 50 c 2.   [2] 50 c 4.   [3] 50 d 4–51 b 2.   [4] 51 b 6.
[5] 51 d 3–52 a 7.

existence of Forms the difference between knowledge and true opinion. In other words, he relies upon the elaborate argument of the *Theaetetus*[1] in which he claims to establish just this difference. The point is the same, too, on which in the *Parmenides*,[2] after pointing out the difficulties that beset the formulation of the ideal theory, Parmenides agrees with Socrates—that apart from Ideas knowledge would be impossible.

Timaeus repeats that in addition to Ideas and phenomena we must recognize a third kind of thing, 'the seat of becoming', to which he at last[3] gives the name of space, and which he describes as 'apprehended without the senses by a sort of bastard reasoning, and hardly an object of belief'.[4] This seems to be the first occurrence in Greek literature of the word χώρα in the sense of space in general, as distinct from the space occupied by any particular thing, and the first place in Plato in which spatiality or extension is pointed to as being the one inseparable accompaniment of all objects of sensation. And it is worth noting that Plato treats it not only as an inseparable accompaniment, but as something necessary to their being. 'An image, since not even the principle on which it depends is its own, but it is an ever-moving appearance of something else' (viz. of a Form) 'must come into being in something else' (viz. in space), 'clinging to existence, as best it can, on pain of not existing at all'.[5] Two further points may be noted. (1) Plato has apparently no conception answering to Aristotle's idea of matter. True, the moulding of gold into different shapes is used as a simile to throw light on the nature of space; but it is a simile which fails at a vital point. Gold is that out of which the shaped objects are made; space is not that out of which 'the things that pass into and out of it' are made, it is simply that in which they appear. And (2) these things are not thought of as substances, but as sensible qualities occupying portions of space. The expression 'passing in and out' is not to be taken literally. The things that are described as doing this do not come into space from anywhere else, nor pass into another sphere when they cease to appear in space. Their only being is in space; they are

---

[1] 187 a 1–201 c 7.   [2] 135 b 5–c 3.   [3] 52 a 8.
[4] 52 b 2.   [5] 52 c 2–5.

copies of the Forms, produced in space as a reflection of a body is produced in a mirror.

All this is a deeply interesting development of Plato's view of the sensible world, about which he has hitherto, except in one passage of the *Theaetetus*,[1] expressed no special theory at all; and so, too, is the passage which follows, the construction of the four elements out of combinations of triangular planes, and the provision, so curiously prophetic of modern physics, which it makes for transmutation of elements by rearrangement of the triangles that constitute them.[2] But in this no change in his attitude towards the Forms is involved.

The question remains, how far the contents of the *Timaeus* are meant to be a literal expression of Plato's belief. What Plato himself says on the point is to be seen in 29 b 1–d 3.

Again, these things being so, our world must necessarily be a likeness of something. Now in every matter it is of great moment to start at the right point in accordance with the nature of the subject. Concerning a likeness, then, and its model we must make this distinction: accounts are of the same order as the things which they set forth— accounts of that which is abiding and stable and discoverable by the aid of reason will themselves be abiding and unchangeable (so far as it is possible and it lies in the nature of an account to be incontrovertible and irrefutable, there must be no falling short of that); while accounts of what is made in the image of that other, but is only a likeness, will themselves be but likely, standing to accounts of the former kind in a proportion: as reality is to becoming, so is truth to belief. If, then, Socrates, in many respects concerning many things—the gods and the generation of the universe—we prove unable to render accounts at all points entirely consistent with themselves and exact, you must not be surprised. If we can furnish accounts no less likely than any other, we must be content, remembering that I who speak and you my judges are only human, and consequently it is fitting that we should, in these matters, accept the likely story and look for nothing further.

Plato's view may be put as follows: The physical world is only a likeness of the world of intelligible reality, the world of Forms.

---

[1] 155 d 5–157 c 3; cf. pp. 102–3 *supra*.

[2] The extent to which Plato anticipated modern theories of the structure of the elements is justly appreciated by P. Friedländer in *University of California Publications*, xvi (1949), 225–48.

An account of the world of Forms is to be attained by the use of pure intellect, whether this takes the higher form of dialectic or the lower form of mathematics. For such a study as that of the κοινωνία γενῶν in the *Sophistes*, and in general for his metaphysics, Plato would claim that it is true. That for which he disclaims anything more than probability is not his metaphysics but his cosmology—his account of 'the gods and the generation of the universe', where 'the gods' means the physical universe (τὸν ποτὲ ἐσόμενον θεόν, 34 a 8), the planets and stars (τῶν ἀιδίων θεῶν, 37 c 6, cf. 39 e 10, 40 b 5), and the earth (40 b 8–c 3). Even in his cosmology Plato is perfectly serious; it is not a mere play of fancy, but his attempt to get at what he thinks most likely to be the truth.

For the kernel of his account Plato would claim more than probability. And the kernel consists in the assumption that there are four things independent of one another, and all necessary for the explanation of the existence of the world as we find it. These four are the world of Forms, the Demiourgos, space, and random events in space.[1] The Forms and the Demiourgos are independent of one another. There is no foundation, anywhere in Plato, for the view that the Demiourgos is to be identified with the Form of good, or with the Forms taken as a whole. Nor does the Demiourgos make the Forms. They are present from the start as models to which he looks in making what he does make, the world as we find it.

It has sometimes been suggested that the Demiourgos is a mythical excrescence, a mere doublet of the world-soul. But Plato would have had no motive for introducing both an immanent world-soul and a transcendent divine Craftsman unless he had thought them both necessary to his account of the world as we know it. Nor is the *Timaeus* the only dialogue in which the idea of the Demiourgos appears. In the *Republic*[2] we find 'the artificer of the senses' and 'the artificer of the heavens'. In the *Sophistes*[3] we find: 'Must we not attribute the coming into being of these things out of not-being to a divine artificer and to nothing else?' In the *Politicus*[4] we find: 'The world is guided at one time by an external

[1] 30 a 3–5.   [2] 507 c 6, 530 a 6.   [3] 265 c 3–5.   [4] 270 a 3–5.

power which is divine, and receives fresh life and immortality from the renewing hand of its artificer', who is later described as its 'artificer and father',[1] as in the Timaeus[2] God is called 'the artificer and father of works'.

Thus the *Timaeus* is deistic rather than pantheistic in its theology. At the same time, the Demiourgos is not viewed as omnipotent, nor as creating the world out of nothing. He does not create the world out of nothing; on the contrary, he 'took over all that is visible—not at rest, but in discordant and un-ordered motion—and brought it from disorder into order' (30 a 3–5). Three things already existed independently of him—the un-changing Forms, the disordered world of becoming, and space, in which becoming takes place (51 e 6–52 b 5). Nor is he omni-potent in his reduction of the world to order. He cannot alter the relations between the Forms, which are determined solely by the nature of the Forms. Nor, while he aims at 'the best', can he be completely successful in this attempt; he is limited by the 'erring cause', necessity (47 e 3–48 a 7). This does not mean that in the world of becoming, considered apart from the activity of the Demiourgos, events follow necessarily from causes (on this question Plato says nothing), but that this world of disorder exer-cises a compulsive, limiting influence on the divine craftsman's work. 'Reason overruled Necessity by persuading her to guide the greatest part of the things that become towards what is best' (48 a 2–3)—but only the greatest part; on some points Reason is defeated by her. That is Plato's way of accounting for the evil and disorder that remains in the world.

These, then, according to the *Timaeus*, are the primeval realities—the world of Forms, space, random events in space, and the Demiourgos, who made the world to be as it is by moulding the random events into an image, as like as he could make it, of the eternal Forms. This general account Plato holds to be true, and the details that follow are as like the truth as he can make them.

The question may be asked, what are the Forms whose exist-ence is asserted in the *Timaeus*? The first passage that has to be considered in this connexion is 30 c 2–31 a 1.

[1] 273 b 1.   [2] 41 a 7.

What was the living creature in whose likeness the Demiourgos framed the world? We must not suppose that it was any creature that ranks only as a species; for no copy of that which is incomplete can ever be good. Let us rather say that the world is like, above all things, to that Living Creature of which all other living creatures, severally and in their families, are parts. For that embraces and contains within itself all the intelligible living creatures, just as this world contains ourselves and all other creatures that have been formed as things visible. For the god, wishing to make this world most nearly like that intelligible thing which is best and in every way complete, fashioned it as a single visible living creature, containing within itself all living things whose nature is of the same order.

Plato here treats the whole physical universe as a living creature, and says that it was formed by the Demiourgos in the likeness of the Idea of living creature. The Idea of living creature is the generic Idea of living creature in general, including as species all the various kinds of living creature.

What, then, are these kinds? The Demiourgos 'thought that this world must possess all the different Forms that intelligence discerns contained in the Living Creature that truly is. And there are four: one, the heavenly race of gods; second, winged things whose path is in the air; third, all that dwells in the water; and fourth, all that goes on foot on the dry land.'[1] Plato proceeds to identify the heavenly race of gods; they are the 'unwandering' stars, the planets, and the earth (40 b 4–c 3). He does not say whether each of these bodies was made in the likeness of a separate Idea, and it is perhaps to be supposed that he thought of the fixed stars as copies of one single Idea, that of fixed star, the planets as copies of the Idea of planet, and the earth as a copy of the Idea of earth. There must also be an Idea of bird, an Idea of Fish, and an Idea of land animal; and there will also be Ideas of the various species of bird, fish, and land animal.

But this is not all. After the passage in which Plato speaks of fire, air, earth, and water, and their transformation into one another, he goes on to say (51 b 7–c 4): 'Is there such a thing as "Fire just in itself" or any of the other things which we are always describing in such terms, as things that "are just in themselves"?

[1] 39 e 7–40 a 2.

Or are the things we see or otherwise perceive by the bodily senses the only things that have such reality, and has nothing else, over and above these, any sort of being at all?', and answers that there must be Ideas—an Idea of fire, an Idea of air, an Idea of water, an Idea of earth.

Thus there is an all-embracing Idea of living creature, subordinate Ideas of each genus and of each species of living creature, and an Idea of each of the four elements. Jackson argued that when Plato wrote the *Timaeus* he had ceased to believe in other Ideas, the metaphysical, mathematical, moral, and aesthetic Ideas which had occupied his mind in earlier dialogues. For this view there is no foundation. Jackson overlooked the very emphatic reference in 35 a 1–b 3 to the Ideas of existence, sameness, and difference, the 'greatest Kinds' of the *Sophistes*. And if moral and aesthetic Ideas are not mentioned, that is simply because the *Timaeus* is concerned not, like most of the dialogues, with human life, but with cosmology.[1]

At a certain point in the *Philebus*, Plato returns to the problem which Parmenides had put to Socrates[2]—how a Form can retain its unity and at the same time be present in many particulars. He first sets aside, as being popular, childish, and easy, two forms of the problem of how one thing can be many and many things one[3]—the question how it is that many, and opposite, qualities can be united in a single substance,[4] and the question how one thing can have many parts.[5] The real problem for the philosopher, he maintains, does not concern the things that become and perish, but units[6] like man, the ox, the beautiful, the good, i.e. Forms.

The reference to the Forms as units or monads is not paralleled elsewhere in Plato. It is called for by the particular context; what Plato does is to distinguish genuine units, completely indivisible Forms, from the kind of unity which a body may be said to be,

---

[1] I have not discussed Taylor's thesis that the *Timaeus* expresses not Plato's views, but those of a typical Pythagorean of the fifth century. This thesis, though worked out with great learning and ingenuity, has found favour with very few scholars. Ancient tradition unanimously treats the *Timaeus* as one of the most important expressions of Plato's own views towards the end of his life.

[2] *Parm.* 131 a 4–e 7.   [3] 14 c 8–10.   [4] 14 c 11–d 3.

[5] 14 d 8–e 4.   [6] ἑνάδες, μονάδες, 15 a 6, b 1.

in spite of its being divisible. The questions for the philosopher are these: '(1) whether one must maintain the existence of such completely indivisible units, and (2) how, if each is one and the same for ever, and admits of neither becoming nor perishing, it can be most surely one, and yet then be said to be either dispersed and pluralized among an infinity of things that come into being, or present as a whole in them apart from itself.'[1]

Plato does not deal with the first problem—presumably because he thinks that in suggesting an answer to the second he will have removed the main objection to asserting the existence of Forms. In dealing with the second problem, he first alludes[2] to the habit, common in the young, of going from one extreme to the other. 'As soon as a young man gets wind of a problem, he is as much delighted as if he had discovered an intellectual gold-mine; he is beside himself with delight, and loves to try every move in the game; first, he rolls the stuff to one side and jumbles it into one, then he undoes it again and takes it to pieces, to the confusion first and foremost of himself, next of his neighbour at the moment.' The right course is to proceed by degrees—first to recognize one genus, then to recognize two or three, or some other definite number of species, and then a limited number of subspecies, until one sees that the original one thing is not only 'many things, indeed an indefinite number of things',[3] but also how many species and subspecies it embraces. Plato proceeds[4] to illustrate the method by reference to the species (*a*) of letters of the alphabet and (*b*) of musical notes. What he gives is, of course, good advice. It amounts to a reiteration of the insistence on the method of division already sketched in the *Phaedrus* and exemplified in the *Sophistes* and the *Politicus*. But to break up into stages the transition from the unity of the generic Form to the infinity

---

[1] The sentence in 15 b 1–8 is difficult. It is sometimes treated as posing three questions, but there are really only two. In b 4 I read a comma after ταύτην, and I take b 2–8 to state only one question. ὅμως in b 4, which has been much suspected, is (I think) genuine, and is to be explained (in accordance with one of Badham's suggestions) by the usage stated in L. and S. s.v. ὅμως II, by which the word may be attached to the *first* of two contrasted clauses. Cf. *Lysis* 213 a 2, ὅμως καὶ μισοῦντα ἐν ἐκείνῳ τῷ χρόνῳ πάντων μάλιστά ἐστι τοῖς γονεῦσι φίλτατα, *Phaedo* 91 c 8 φοβεῖται μὴ ἡ ψυχὴ ὅμως καὶ θειότερον καὶ κάλλιον ὂν τοῦ σώματος προαπολλύηται.

[2] 15 d 4–16 a 3.   [3] 16 d 6.   [4] 17 a 8–18 d 2.

of the particular instances would in fact do nothing to alleviate
the problem of the 'one in many', if the problem were a real one.
Plato would have done better, it would seem, if he had maintained that the problem is an unreal one, that the relation of
Form or universal to particular is a perfectly intelligible, though
unique, one, and that there is no mystery about the presence of a
universal in many particulars, any more than there is about its
presence in one.

In 23 c 1–27 c 1 Plato introduces an analysis of 'the present
contents of the universe' whose bearing on the theory of Ideas has
been much discussed. He divides these contents into four classes.
He takes over from Pythagoreanism its fundamental antithesis
between the unlimited (ἄπειρον) and limit (πέρας),[1] and adds to
these what is produced by the mixture of them, and the cause of
the mixture. By 'the unlimited' we are not to understand a single
completely indefinite element, nor by 'limit' a single limiting or
defining element. 'The unlimited' is the general name for a whole
family of 'unlimiteds',[2] and 'limit' the name for a whole family of
'limits' or of 'things having the character of limits'.[3] Instances of
'the unlimited' are the hotter and colder, the violent and the
gentle, the drier and wetter, the more and fewer, the faster and
slower, the greater and smaller, the high and low in sound,
pleasure and pain.[4] Instances of limit are the ratios one to one
and two to one, and limit generally is identified with 'whatever
is a number in relation to a number or a measure in relation to a
measure'.[5] Instances of the mixture are health, music, the seasons,
beauty, strength, and many excellences of the soul, the mixed
life.[6] The cause of the mixture is identified with wisdom and
reason.[7]

It has been much debated in which of these classes, if any, the
Ideas are to be placed. We may begin by setting aside one line of
argument that has sometimes been used in support of this or that
interpretation, viz. that the doctrine of the four kinds must be
meant to throw light on the problem stated earlier in the dialogue[8]

---

[1] *Met.* 986ᵃ23.   [2] 25 a 1; cf. 23 e 4, 24 a 2–3.   [3] 25 d 3.
[4] 24 a 7, c 1, 25 c 8–10, 26 a 2, 27 c 5–9.   [5] 25 a 6–b 1.
[6] 25 e 8, 26 a 4, b 1, 5–7, 27 d 1–10.   [7] 30 a 9–e 3.   [8] 15 b 1–8.

—how an Idea can retain its unity if it is either present only partially in each of the particulars falling under it, or present whole in each of them. In fact, it must be pointed out, the doctrine of the four kinds is not put forward as a solution of this problem or as an aid to its solution; it is put forward as a preliminary to answering quite a different question, the question whether pleasure or wisdom is the better,[1] and it is to this that Plato returns after describing the four kinds.[2] Grote hits the nail on the head, as he so often does, when he says that the problem of the unity of the Idea is lost sight of in the maze of the succeeding argument; it is in fact never returned to.

No interpreter has ventured to place the Ideas in the unlimited, but each of the other three γένη has found its advocates. (1) The least plausible view is that of Zeller,[3] who identifies the Ideas with the 'cause of the mixture'. Such a view is quite incompatible with Plato's identification of the cause of the mixture with mind. The Ideas are for Plato always objects of thought, not thoughts or thinkers; we may recall that in the *Parmenides*[4] the suggestion that the Ideas are thoughts is rejected out of hand both by Parmenides and by Socrates, and that it is only by a misunderstanding that Plato has been supposed to ascribe, in the *Sophistes*,[5] life and thought to Ideas.

(2) The most ingenious interpretation is that of Henry Jackson, who places the Forms in the 'mixed class'.[6] He argues that Plato speaks of two different 'mixings'. To take the case of the hotter and colder, the effect of introducing the particular ποσόν called τὸ μέτριον is to produce an agreeable temperature that is neither too cold nor too hot, while the effect of introducing any other ποσόν is simply to produce *some* definite temperature. The one union produces a Form, in the sense of an ideal type; the other produces an actual state of temperature which is a closer or less close approximation to the type. There is no doubt that Plato's thought at some time turned to an attempt to 'generate' Idea-numbers, by a union of 'the one' with 'the great and small'; that is clear from the statements of Aristotle in *Metaphysics* A, M, and

---

[1] 22 c 7–23 b 10.   [2] 27 c 3.   [3] *Gesch. d. gr. Phil.* ii. 1⁴. 691.
[4] 132 b 3–c 11.   [5] 248 e 6–249 b 1.   [6] *J. of Philol.* x (1882), 277–84.

N. But the only concrete evidence in the *Philebus* itself that could be cited in favour of Jackson's theory is the single phrase in 24 c 6–d 1 μὴ ἀφανίσαντε τὸ ποσόν, ἀλλ᾽ ἐάσαντε αὐτό τε καὶ τὸ μέτριον . . . ἐγγενέσθαι, where Jackson urges that τὸ μέτριον is clearly distinguished from τὸ ποσόν and must mean the right degree, as distinct from some definite degree or other. But we may note that in what follows[1] only τὸ ποσόν reappears, so that clearly no great importance is to be attached to καὶ τὸ μέτριον. The whole phrase only means 'allowing both definite quantity and in particular the moderate or right quantity to come into being'. In any case, the single phrase τὸ ποσόν τε καὶ τὸ μέτριον is not nearly a sufficient basis for the imposing fabric of theory which Jackson rests upon it. One may add that there are hints all through the passage that what Plato has in his mind throughout is the genesis not of Ideas at all but only of individual things and states or activities of things. Even the introductory phrase, πάντα τὰ νῦν ὄντα ἐν τῷ παντὶ διχῇ διαλάβωμεν,[2] suggests that it is the present contents alone, not the eternal contents, of the universe that Plato is to analyse into the unlimited and limit. Cf. 24 e 7 ὁπόσ᾽ ἂν ἡμῖν φαίνηται μᾶλλόν τε καὶ ἧττον γιγνόμενα, 25 e 7 ἐν νόσοις, 26 a 6 ἐν χειμῶσιν καὶ πνίγεσιν, 27 a 11–12 οὐκοῦν τὰ μὲν γιγνόμενα καὶ ἐξ ὧν γίγνεται πάντα τὰ τρία παρέσχετο ἡμῖν γένη; That the Ideas are not included in the mixed class follows from the fact that they are called τὰ ὄντα ἀεί as opposed to τὰ γιγνόμενα, and τὰ ἀεὶ κατὰ τὰ αὐτὰ ὡσαύτως ἀμεικτότατα ἔχοντα.[3] Further, we have the fact that the process of being 'mixed' is described as 'birth into being', and its product as 'being that is compounded and *generated*'.[4] Finally, to speak of reason as the artificer[5] of the *Ideas* would be a way of speaking to which there is no parallel in Plato except the casual, and probably not seriously meant, allusion in the *Republic* to God as the maker of the Idea of bed.

It is a far cry from the doctrine of the four kinds in the *Philebus* to the generation of numbers from the One and the great and small, of which Aristotle speaks. The generation spoken of in the *Philebus* is a generation in time; the other is a purely conceptual generation, or more properly an analysis of eternal entities into their eternal components. In the *Philebus* the formal element is any one of a number of possible points along a scale, or of possible ratios between opposite qualifications; in the later theory it is a single entity, the One. In the *Philebus* the combination of the formal with the material element is effected by reason, by the divine reason at work in the physical universe, establishing such things as the seasons,[1] and by human reason in the living of a life in which both reason itself and pleasure find their due place; in the later theory there is no suggestion of an efficient cause at all. Yet there is a definite connexion between the two theories. Both are evidences of a renewed interest in Pythagoreanism. Limit and the unlimited had been fundamental opposites presupposed by the Pythagoreans;[2] they reappear in the *Philebus*, and they reappear again as the One and the great and small in Plato's later theory;[3] the very phrase 'the great and small' is taken over from the 'greater and smaller' of the *Philebus*.[4] Having in the *Philebus* recognized these two principles as involved in the world of particular things, Plato seems to have been led to think of corresponding principles as being involved in the being of the Idea-numbers.

(3) The most commonly accepted theory refers the Forms to the class of 'limit', and that is where, if anywhere, we should initially expect to find them, since Plato undoubtedly thinks of them as fixed standards, in contrast to the multiplicity and change in the sensible world. Yet on second thoughts we must hesitate. There are certain Forms which we can well suppose Plato to have thought of as being or depending on a ratio between elements. The Forms of mathematical figures such as rectangle, square, circle can easily be so reduced. The Pythagoreans treated justice as being or depending on a ratio, and Plato may have thought that all the virtues could be similarly regarded. But can we suppose him to be suggesting that all Forms can be so treated? It is difficult to believe that he could have done this without giving some explanation and defence of the suggestion. And if we look

---

[1] 26 a 6–b 3; cf. 28 d 3–30 d 8.   [2] *Met.* 986^{a}15–26.
[3] 987^{b}20–7.   [4] 25 c 9–10.

more closely at the doctrine of the four kinds the difficulty grows. The typical member of the class of 'the unlimited' is a pair of opposite qualities which represent a single scale—hot and cold the scale of temperature, high and low that of pitch, fast and slow that of velocity; and the typical member of the class of 'limit' is a definite point on that scale. By applying different limits to the unlimited of temperature you get different degrees of temperature, but there is no suggestion that the difference between, say, temperature and pitch is caused by the union of different limits with the same unlimited. Each unlimited is not totally unlimited; it is indefinite as regards its degree, but definite as regards its generic nature. The specific element in the nature of the middle C on the piano will belong to the class of the limit, the generic nature which it shares with other notes will fall on the side of the unlimited. Not all universals or natures, therefore, will fall on the side of limit, as it is here conceived.

It is impossible, then, to assign the Ideas as a whole to any one of the four classes; further, it is not in the least in Plato's mind in this passage to throw light on the nature of the Ideas. The fourfold division is one of which the origin is easy to see; it is introduced with the sole object of throwing light on the relative claims of pleasure and wisdom to be regarded as the good life; and that question is finally settled by assigning pleasure to the 'mixed class' and wisdom to the (admittedly superior) class of 'cause of the mixture.'[1] 'The unlimited' and 'limit' are for this purpose borrowed from Pythagoreanism, and the natural afterthoughts of the mixed class and the cause of the mixture are added simply as means to solving this question, without regard to any repercussion on the theory of Ideas.

The four classes which the *Philebus* refers to are best interpreted in the light of the *Timaeus*. The *Philebus* is concerned in the main not with metaphysics but with ethics, and we must not expect in it so clear a statement of metaphysical principles as we find in the *Timaeus*; but there are enough indications that Plato is expressing what is, at bottom, the same view. In the *Timaeus*[2] he says that before the universe as it is came into being there were three

[1] 27 e 5–31 a 10.   [2] 52 d 2–53 c 3.

things—being (the world of Ideas), space, becoming—and he describes becoming thus: 'All these kinds' (fire, air, water, earth) 'were without proportion or measure. They possessed indeed some rudiments of their own nature, but were altogether in such a condition as we should expect for anything when deity is absent from it. Such being their nature at the time when the ordering of the universe was taken in hand, the god then began by giving them a distinct configuration by means of shapes and numbers.' The original state he describes here is just such a world of random events as in the *Philebus* he calls 'the unlimited'. Next, we note that, as the element of limit in the *Philebus* is clearly identified with numerical and metrical definiteness, in the *Timaeus* it is precisely by the introduction of such definiteness that the Demiourgos turns the world of random events into the ordered world as it is. Cf., for example, *Tim.* 31 b 4–32 c 4, and in particular 32 c 1, 'the body of the universe was brought into being, coming into concord by means of proportion'; and again, the construction of the four elements by means of elementary triangles.[1] Finally, we may note that in both dialogues the world made by the addition of limit to the unlimited is described as a living creature composed of soul and body,[2] and the cause of the mixture is in the *Philebus* called τὸ πάντα ταῦτα δημιουργοῦν, 'that which fashions all these things', and in the *Timaeus* ὁ δημιουργός, 'the fashioner',[3] and is in both dialogues thought of as a reasonable being.[4]

Summing up the meaning and purpose of the passage, we may say that: (1) the fourfold division is introduced in order to decide the question whether reason or pleasure is to be assigned to the second place among goods, the first place having been already assigned to the life which contains both.[5] (2) To settle this problem Plato introduces an analysis of all phenomenal existence (γεγενημένη οὐσία) into (a) types of phenomenon having a certain qualitative definiteness but no quantitative definiteness (temperature, pitch, &c.) and (b) quantitative definiteness, and asserts

[1] 53 c 4–55 c 6.   [2] *Phil.* 30 a 3–7; *Tim.* 30 b 4–31 a 1.
[3] *Phil.* 27 b 1; *Tim. passim.*
[4] *Phil.* 28 c 3, 7, d 8, 31 a 7; *Tim.* 29 d 7–30 c 1.   [5] 20 e 1–22 e 3.

that it is by reason that (*b*) is introduced into (*a*). There is no reference to the Ideas, but they are presumably presupposed to be (as they are definitely said in the *Timaeus* to be) that by reference to which the divine reason introduces limit into the unlimited. (3) The cause of the mixture being clearly better than the quantitatively indeterminate, and reason being the former and pleasure one instance of the latter, the element of rational thought in our life is inferred to be superior to that of pleasure.

VIII

THE *LAWS* AND THE *SEVENTH LETTER*

THE *Laws* sticks very closely to the subjects of political theory
and law, and adds nothing to our knowledge of the theory
of Ideas; though in one passage,[1] as if to remind us that it
is still there in the background of Plato's thought, there is a brief
allusion to it. But to the expression of his metaphysical theory in
general the *Laws* makes an important contribution, which will be
considered later.[2]

Much more important, in its bearing on the theory of Ideas,
is the Seventh Letter, which, if genuine, was written in 353 or
352 B.C. The question of the authenticity of the Platonic letters
has been carefully studied by many scholars, and there are several
letters about which there is no general agreement. But the only
one which has a bearing on the theory of Ideas is the seventh,
which almost all scholars now regard as genuine. It is true that
the passage in question, the philosophical interlude which appears
in 342 a 7–344 d 2, has been thought by some scholars to be a
spurious addition to the letter; but there is weighty opinion[3]
which holds it to be highly relevant to its context and almost
necessary to it. Plato's object in this passage is to castigate the
attempt of Dionysius of Syracuse to write about the most important philosophical questions;[4] and his method is to show the
dangers of such writing when attempted without proper qualifications and proper precautions. For everything that exists, he says,
there are three things by way of which knowledge of it is to be
approached—a name, a definition, an image. Fourthly there is
knowledge about it, and fifthly there is the object itself, that
which is knowable and truly real—in other words, the Idea. He
illustrates his point by the example of the circle. There is first the

---

[1] 965 b 7–966 a 9.   [2] pp. 237, 238–9.
[3] Cf. e.g. Taylor, in *Mind*, xxi (1912), 347–53; R. Hackforth, *A.P.E.*, 99–102;
Wilamowitz, *Platon*, ii. 293; G. Pasquali, *Le Lettere di Platone*, 77–114.
[4] 341 a 8–b 3.

word 'circle'; secondly, a definition of it in a formula consisting of nouns and verbs; thirdly, a figure which we draw and rub out, or turn on a lathe and destroy—none of which things happens to the circle itself; fourthly, knowledge, understanding, and true opinion, forming one whole residing not in sounds, as the name or the definition does, nor in shapes of bodies, as the image does, but in souls, and therefore different both from the nature of the circle-itself and from the name, the definition, and the image. Understanding is nearer to the objective reality than any of the other things we have named. Further, since owing to the weakness of language the name and the definition are just as likely to indicate the mere properties of the object (τὸ ποῖόν τι) as to indicate its essence (τὸ ὄν),[1] no sensible man will venture to commit his thoughts to the weakness of language; least of all will he commit them to the irremovable weakness of *written* language. . The circle drawn or turned on a lathe is full of the opposite of the real circle, since at every point such a circle will coincide with the tangent to it; while the true circle has nothing of its contrary in it. The name never belongs to the true object, since round things might just as well have been called straight, and vice versa. The definition belongs no more securely to the real object, since it consists of nouns and verbs whose meaning is just as conventional as that of the name itself. Above all, name, definition, figure, and mental apprehension alike tend to offer a mere property instead of the essence of the object, and so produce perplexity and obscurity. It is only on a well-endowed nature, one with an affinity for the object, one which has in addition passed up and down from one to another of the four preliminaries, 'rubbing one against another',[2] testing one by another by means of question and answer, that there finally flashes forth knowledge of the object.

Of the five entities named here, three are named in a passage of the *Laws*, written presumably about the same time:[3] 'There are three points to be noted about anything . . . for one, the reality of the thing; for another, the definition of this reality; for another, its name.' The subject under discussion there is the soul, and in

---

trying to discover its real nature we do not use a sensible diagram; but in trying to discover the nature of such a thing as the circle we do, as Plato ɩɩas already said in the *Republic*, use a diagram, and that is why the 'image' appears in the Letter as one of the preliminaries. The presence of 'knowledge' as a preliminary is somewhat puzzling, since knowledge of the essence of some object is just what we are aiming at. But Plato says 'knowledge, understanding, and true opinion', and these expressions are meant to indicate such *partial* knowledge, mingled with opinion, as we start with in our search for the essence.

The passage indicates, more clearly perhaps than any other in Plato, his sense of the difficulties which attend the search for knowledge of the Ideas. But besides indicating this it gives, in the phrase 'rubbing them against one another', a most striking hint of how he thought the difficulties might in time be overcome—by comparing name, conventional definition, image, and our own preliminary ideas about the nature of the object, and noting what agreements and what disagreements there may be between any two of these, until a more accurate, and finally, if we are lucky, a precise definition is reached.

Two other things about this passage are noteworthy. One is that here, where Plato has every reason for mentioning the mathematical circle as something different both from circularity and from sensible diagrams of the circle, there is no mention of it; this suggests strongly that, late as this letter is, Plato's definite recognition of the 'intermediates' must have been later still. The other is that, so far from supporting the belief in a 'later theory of Ideas' in which Plato recognized Ideas only of the four elements and of animal and vegetable types, this passage contains the most catholic list of types of Idea to be found anywhere in Plato; he refers (though without using the word ἰδέα or εἶδος) to Ideas of straightness and curvature, of colour, of good, beautiful, and just, of every body manufactured or natural, of the physical elements, of every animal, of every character of soul, of all actions and passivities.[1]

[1] 342 d 3-8.

IX

PLATO'S 'UNWRITTEN DOCTRINES'

PROF. CHERNISS has recently contended that Plato gave no oral instruction to the members of the Academy, that Aristotle derived all his knowledge of Plato's views from the dialogues which we still possess, and that everything he says about Plato which cannot be verified from the dialogues is due to misunderstanding or misrepresentation of what Plato wrote. 'Whatever the reason may have been,' he writes,[1] 'the fact itself is certain, and its significance for the so-called "school" is momentous: Plato did not expound any physics or natural philosophy beyond that which he wrote in the *Timaeus*, and he did not give his students or associates any further exegesis of the doctrines which he set down in his dialogues.' We may first consider what the intrinsic probability of this view is.

There is a famous passage in the *Phaedrus*[2] in which Plato points out the superiority of the spoken to the written word. The passage is too long to be quoted here, but Jowett's summary may be quoted:

Writing is far inferior to recollection. Writing is like painting: it is silent ever, and, unlike speech, cannot be adapted to individuals. But there is another kind of writing graven on the tablets of the mind. What man of sense would plant seeds in an artificial garden, to bring forth fruit or flowers in eight days, and not in deeper and more fitting soil? As a pastime he may plant his fair thoughts in the garden, but his serious aim will be to implant them in his own and other noble natures.

This thought is echoed in a famous passage of the Seventh Letter which will be quoted in a later context.[3] The words are strange, coming from one who wrote so much and so well on the most difficult subjects. Yet they are natural in the mouth of Plato, who owed his inspiration to Socrates; for Socrates, so far as we know, never wrote a line, and preferred the method of spoken question and answer, in which explanations and modifications may be

[1] *R.E.A.* 72.   [2] 275 c 5–277 a 4.   [3] pp. 157–9.

introduced as the need for them arises. Even Plato's choice of the dialogue as against the treatise form reflects in another way the same preference. Is it likely, then, that Plato declined all conversation with the members of his school, in which he might have elucidated what he had written, and have expounded ideas which he had not yet committed, or was never to commit, to paper? It is really unthinkable.

There is a further point that is worth considering. The *Laws* is the longest of Plato's works, and must have occupied most of his time for the last years of his life. It is for the most part occupied with subjects far removed from metaphysics, but it is not likely that he had ceased to think about metaphysical questions. It is therefore highly probable that, rather than try to write in these years a second great work, he would then, if ever, have used at least the method of conversation, and perhaps that of lecturing, for the communication of his latest thoughts on metaphysics.

The strongest point in Prof. Cherniss's argument is one which he has effectively made—that what Aristotle says about Plato often betrays misunderstandings which a few well-chosen questions to Plato would have removed. Aristotle was not the pure blunderer that Prof. Cherniss makes him out to have been, but it must be admitted that he was too ready to adopt interpretations of Plato either because they fitted in with his own preconceptions, or because they gave him an opportunity of criticism. His long criticism in Books M and N of the *Metaphysics*, in particular, contains far too many instances of both those faults, and Prof. Cherniss has exposed many of them with great skill. But I do not think for a moment that he has established his case that all that Aristotle says about Plato that cannot be verified from the dialogues is pure misunderstanding or misrepresentation.

Having considered whether it is *likely* that Plato would have maintained the proud isolation from the members of his school—σεμνὸν καὶ ἅγιον, ἀκίνητον ἑστῶτα—that Prof. Cherniss attributes to him, we may next consider what positive evidence, if any, there is that he did not do so. There are at least nine passages in which Aristotle might be thought to be referring to sources, other than the dialogues, of his knowledge of Plato's views. The first two may be considered together. (1) In *De Gen. et Corr.* 330ᵇ13 Aristotle says 'Those who postulate two elements from the start—as Parmenides postulated fire and earth—make the intermediates . . . blends of these. . . . The same course is followed by those who advocated three, as Plato does in the divisions (ἐν ταῖς διαιρέσεσιν); for he makes that which is intermediate a blend.' And (2) in *De Part. An.* 642ᵇ10 he says 'Again, it is not permissible to break up a natural group, birds for instance, by putting its members under different bifurcations, as is done in the written divisions (αἱ γεγραμμέναι διαιρέσεις), where some birds are ranked with animals of the water, and others placed in a different class.'

In his note on passage (1) Joachim points out that the *Timaeus*[1] recognizes not one but two intermediates between fire and earth, and argues that Plato is most unlikely to have given a different account (written or unwritten) elsewhere. He holds therefore that the reference is to something quite different—to the fact that in the *Timaeus*[2] Plato makes the world-soul a blend of forms of existence, sameness, and difference, each of which forms is itself a blend of opposites. But the whole passage in Aristotle is concerned with physical elements, and it is unlikely that Aristotle would have introduced into it a reference to Plato's analysis of the world-soul. Taylor,[3] therefore, prefers to think that the allusion may be to the passage of the *Timaeus* in which Plato treats fire and earth as the primary elements, and air and water not indeed as a mixture of these but as intermediates between them; or, more likely, to the analysis, in the *Philebus*,[4] of the contents of the universe into the unlimited, limit, and the mixture of the two. To the first of these suggestions it may be objected that Plato in the *Timaeus* works so distinctly with four elements, not three, that Aristotle could hardly have cited him as believing in three only; and to the second, that a logical analysis such as we find in the *Philebus* is hardly likely to have been brought by Aristotle into a discussion of the number of the physical elements. To all three suggestions it may further be objected that the mode of reference ἐν ταῖς διαιρέσεσιν is hardly likely as a way of referring to a

---

[1] 32 a 7–b 8.   [2] 35 a 1–8.
[3] *Comm. on Plato's Timaeus*, 8 n.   [4] 23 c 4–d 1.

dialogue; Aristotle is never chary of mentioning Plato's dialogues by name when he is referring to them.

Ogle,[1] Christ,[2] and Blass[3] *may* be right in taking passage (2) to be a reference to the illustrations of the method of division in the *Sophistes* and the *Politicus*. In *Soph.* 220 b 1 the genus of swimming animals is divided into the winged and the submarine, and in *Pol.* 264 e 3–6 the herds that feed on land are divided into those that fly and those that walk—so that the natural class of birds is in fact broken up as Aristotle says it was. But the extreme difficulty of finding anything in the dialogues which can be referred to in passage (1), and the peculiarity of the mode of reference in both passages, make it probable that the reference in them is not to any dialogue but to a collection of 'Divisions' current in the Academy, which we know to have devoted itself zealously to the problem of classification. If we could be sure that the Thirteenth Letter is genuine, we should find in the words τῶν τε Πυθαγορείων πέμπω σοι καὶ τῶν διαιρέσεων[4] a reference by Plato himself to such a collection. Further, it seems fairly clear that the references in (1) and (2) must be to the *same* Divisions, and since one passage describes them definitely as Plato's and the other describes them as 'written', it follows that they were devised by Plato and written down in the Academy, though not necessarily by Plato.[5] Those Divisions probably formed the nucleus of the extant collection known as the *Divisiones Aristoteleae*.

(3) In *Met.* 1019[a]1 Aristotle says 'Some things are called prior and posterior in virtue of their nature and essence, viz. those that can exist without others and not vice versa; a distinction (διαιρέσει) which Plato used', or, according to another reading, 'was accustomed to use'. This passage has sometimes[6] been supposed to refer to such passages as *Tim.* 34 b 10–35 a 1, *Laws* 892 c 2–7, 894 c 10–e 2, 896 b 10–c 3; but none of these quite meets the case. Further, the tense is past, not present, and that

---

[1] *Arist. on the Parts of Animals*, 148.
[2] *Plat. Stud.* in *Abh. d. Philos.-Philol. Cl. Bayer. Akad.* xvii (1884), 484–9.
[3] *Apophoreton*, 54.   [4] 360 b 7.
[5] This conclusion is reached by Zeller (ii. 1[4]. 437 n. 3), by Wilamowitz (*Platon*, ii. 278–9), and by Mutschmann in his ed. of the Aristotelian *Divisiones*, xvii–xviii.
[6] e.g. by Apelt, in *Beitr. zur Gesch. d. Phil.* 226–9.

points to oral rather than to written teaching. Trendelenburg[1] supposed the reference to be to the priority and posteriority which, according to Aristotle, Plato asserted to exist among the ideal numbers, and this conjecture may well be right.

(4) In *De An.* 404^{b}16–18 Aristotle refers explicitly to Plato's analysis of the soul in the *Timaeus*; and he goes on to mention certain other doctrines which were set forth ἐν τοῖς περὶ φιλοσοφίας λεγομένοις. Opinion is much divided on the question whether the reference is to lectures by Plato or to Aristotle's dialogue Περὶ φιλοσοφίας. Prof. Cherniss takes the latter view, and argues[2] that the whole passage refers not to Plato but to Xenocrates.

The question whether ἐν τοῖς περὶ φιλοσοφίας λεγομένοις means 'in Plato's lectures on philosophy' or 'in my dialogue on philosophy' is difficult to answer. But there is not, in Aristotle or elsewhere, any other reference to oral teaching of Plato's called τὰ περὶ φιλοσοφίας, while Aristotle does refer in one other passage[3] to his own dialogue of that name. Probably, therefore, here also he is referring to the dialogue. But, as we shall show later,[4] he is referring to his account, in that dialogue, of views expressed by Plato orally.

(5) In *Met.* 992^{a}20–2 Aristotle says: 'Plato even used to object to points as being a geometrical dogma. He used to give the name of "principle of the line"—and this he often used to posit—to the indivisible lines.'

(6) In *Met.* 1070^{a}18 Aristotle says: 'And so Plato was not so far wrong when he said that there are as many Forms as there are kinds of natural object.'

(7) In *Met.* 1083^{a}32 Aristotle says: 'If 1 is the starting-point, the truth about the numbers must rather be what Plato used to say, and there must be a first 2 and 3, and the numbers must not be comparable with each other.'

(8) In *Eth. Nic.* 1095^{a}32 Aristotle says: 'Plato was right in raising this question and asking, as he used to do, "Are we on the way from or on the way to the first principles?".'

In these four passages the use of the imperfect or the aorist tense

---

[1] *De Ideis*, 81.   [2] *A.C.P.A.* 565–80.
[3] *Phys.* 194^{a}36.   [4] pp. 209–12.

points to oral teaching; and none of the references can be verified in the dialogues.

(9) Finally, there is the passage *Phys.* 209^{b}11–17: 'This is why Plato in the *Timaeus* says that matter and space are the same; for the "participant" and space are identical. It is true, indeed, that the account he gives there of the participant is different from what he says in his so-called "unwritten doctrines". Nevertheless, he did identify place and space. I mention Plato because, while all hold place to be something, he alone tried to say what it is.' In 209^{b}33–210^{a}2 Aristotle adds 'Plato, of course, if we may digress, ought to tell us why the Forms and the numbers are not in place, if "what participates" is place—whether what participates is the great and the small or the matter, as he has written in the *Timaeus*.' Putting the two passages together, we see that Aristotle ascribes to Plato's unwritten teaching an identification of the 'participant' with the 'great and small'. The reference in 209^{b}14 is the only perfectly explicit reference in Aristotle to Plato's unwritten teaching, but it is in itself enough to refute the contention that all that Aristotle says about Plato is derived from the dialogues; for this purpose one reference to the unwritten teaching is as good as a hundred would have been. Indeed, we may go farther and conclude that what Aristotle tells us in the *Metaphysics* about the great and small is derived not from the dialogues but from the unwritten teaching. But at the same time these passages convey a warning not to accept Aristotle as an infallible guide to what Plato said; for Plato's 'space' was not the same either as his 'great and small' or as Aristotle's 'matter'.

Other ancient authorities have much to say about these unwritten doctrines. The oldest reference outside Aristotle is in Aristoxenus,[1] a slightly younger contemporary of Aristotle. He quotes Aristotle as having said of most of the audience that attended Plato's lectures (ἀκρόασιν) on the Good that 'they came, every one of them, in the conviction that they would get from the lectures some one or other of the things that the world calls good; riches or health, or strength—in fine, some extraordinary

[1] *Harm. El.* ii. 30–1.

gift of fortune. But when they found that Plato's reasonings were of mathematics—numbers, geometry, and astronomy—and, to crown all, to the effect that there is one Good,[1] methinks their disenchantment was complete. The result was that some of them sneered at the thing, while others vilified it.'

Of many references in the Greek commentators on Aristotle to Plato's lectures on the Good, the most important is that in Simplicius *in Phys.* 453.25–455.14. Simplicius there says that Plato expounded the doctrine of the One and the indefinite dyad in his discourses on the Good. These were, he adds, attended by Aristotle, Heracleides, Hestiaeus, and other members of the school, who wrote them down in the enigmatic form in which they were delivered; but Porphyry interpreted them, in his commentary on the *Philebus*. Simplicius proceeds to quote from Porphyry, and also from Alexander of Aphrodisias. Alexander himself tells us[2] that Plato's teaching about the One and the indefinite dyad (or plurality) was recorded in Aristotle's treatise *On the Good*—which was based on his notes of Plato's lectures.

Simplicius[3] identifies the unwritten doctrines which Aristotle refers to in *Phys.* 209[b]14 with the lectures on the Good. There is no necessity to limit the unwritten teachings of Plato which Aristotle knew to one particular course of lectures; but his knowledge about the theory of Idea-numbers seems to have been mainly derived from that source.

I have spoken of a 'course of lectures', not of a single lecture, and this must now be justified. Simplicius uses the words ἀκρόασις and συνουσία in this connexion,[4] but he also uses the plural λόγοι,[5] and the plural συνουσίαι,[6] which is also used by Philoponus[7] and by Asclepius.[8] ἀκρόασις may mean a single lecture, but it may also mean a course of lectures; the whole of Aristotle's *Physics* is in the manuscripts called Φυσικὴ ἀκρόασις. The evidence, then, points to a course rather than to a single lecture, and that is also what the general probabilities point to.

---

[1] This seems the most probable translation of καὶ τὸ πέρας ὅτι ἀγαθὸν ἔστιν ἔν.
[2] *In Met.* 56.33–5, 85.17, 250.17–20, 262.18–26.
[3] *In Phys.* 545.23.   [4] Ibid. 151.10, 454.18.
[5] Ibid. 453.28, 503.12.   [6] Ibid. 542.10, 12, 545.24.
[7] *In. Phys.* 515.30, 521.10, 14.   [8] *In Met.* 77.4.

Thus we have evidence good in quality, though not very great in bulk, that Aristotle had access both to unwritten teachings of Plato and to a collection of 'divisions' not to be found in the dialogues, but either written down by Plato, or more probably compiled from his unwritten teaching; and that one part of this teaching, the lectures on the Good, was occupied precisely with those later developments of the ideal theory with which Aristotle acquaints us in Books A, M, and N of the *Metaphysics*.

We may now turn to consider what Aristotle says about these later developments of Plato's theory, and ask whether what he says could well be based entirely, as Prof. Cherniss maintains, on the dialogues. One fact strikes our attention immediately. Aristotle refers very freely to Plato's dialogues by name; anyone who looks at Bonitz's Index to Aristotle, s.v. Plato, will find some fifty explicit examples. But Aristotle never cites any dialogue as evidence of any of the later developments which we shall presently be studying. That in itself suggests very strongly that it is from another source, the 'unwritten teachings', that he derives his knowledge of these developments.

The impression we thus derive is greatly strengthened when we look at what he says about them. Take one of the most remarkable of them, the derivation of the ideal numbers from the One and the great and small. According to Prof. Cherniss, what Aristotle says about this depends in part on the *Philebus* and in part on hints scattered through the *Sophistes* and the *Timaeus*. All that Aristotle says about the great and small has to be traced to the phrases 'greater and smaller' and 'more and less' in the *Philebus*.[1] But there two things are noticeable. One is that these phrases are, in the *Philebus*, no more prominent than 'hotter and colder', 'more and less violent', 'drier and wetter', 'faster and slower'. The other is that the analysis there offered is an analysis not of numbers, but of things and events in the phenomenal world. It is reasonable to suppose that the line of thought which Plato in the *Philebus* applies to the phenomenal world was later extended by him to the ideal numbers; but it is unreasonable to suppose that Aristotle has no more basis than the *Philebus* for what

[1] 25 c 9.

he says of the 'great and small' as the material principle of number.

As the basis of what Aristotle says about the One as the formal principle, Prof. Cherniss puts forward the following facts: that in the dialogues 'every idea is an immutable and indivisible unit; in the *Philebus* they are designated "henads", "monads", and "units"; in the *Timaeus* the ideas are distinguished from their phenomenal manifestations by being called each "indivisible", which term Xenocrates employed to read into this passage his own derivation of numbers from the One; and in the *Sophist*, even where the intercommunion of ideas is explained, Plato insists that each idea is a unit, different from every other and from all others together. What he says in this last dialogue shows that, as the being of each idea comes to it from the idea of Being and the difference of each from the single idea of Difference, so the unity of each idea must come to it from the idea of One.[1] No other source than this need be hunted for Aristotle's statement that the One is the formal cause or essence of the Ideas.'[2]

It is, of course, true that Plato often emphasizes the unity and indivisibility of every Idea. But it is a long way from this to what Aristotle says, not of the nature of each Idea, but of the successive derivation of the number-series. It is highly probable that there is a good deal of misinterpretation in what Aristotle says; but it is difficult to suppose that he had nothing more to misinterpret than Prof. Cherniss gives him. Where in the dialogues, to take one instance out of many, shall we find any basis whatever for Aristotle's statement that Plato carried the derivation of the numbers only as far as the number 10?[3] Knowing as we do that there were 'unwritten teachings' and that Aristotle knew them, it is only reasonable to suppose that it was in them that he found the basis of what he says of Plato's later views.

It is certain, then, that Plato did give some oral instruction on philosophy, and therefore we need not hesitate to accept what Aristotle says about Plato merely because we find no support for it

---

[1] Though it may be noted that the Idea of One is not mentioned at all in the *Sophistes*.

[2] *R.E.A.* 51.   [3] *Phys.* 206ᵇ32.

in the dialogues. But the greatest care is needed if we are (*a*) to discover when it is of Plato, and not of some other member of the Academy, that he is speaking, and (*b*) to allow for possible misinterpretations of Plato by Aristotle; and Prof. Cherniss has done notable work in exploring these difficulties.

Much of what Aristotle says about the theory of Ideas in *Metaphysics* A refers to Plato by name; but even there we must be careful in our study of the passages in which he says 'we' (i.e. we members of the Academy) 'do so-and-so'; for that does not necessarily mean that the master did likewise. When we turn to Books M and N the difficulties are much greater. They arise not only from the queerness of the doctrines discussed, but also from the fact that Aristotle hardly ever tells us whom he is speaking about; Plato is mentioned only once,[1] Speusippus and Xenocrates never, yet there is no doubt that these three are the subjects of the whole discussion. Not only does Aristotle not say whom he is speaking about, but he diverges disconcertingly from the discussion of one view to that of another. The greatest care is therefore needed in sorting out the passages which refer to Plato from those in which one of his followers is referred to. To this task we must now turn.

There are six passages[2] in which Aristotle distinguishes three views held within the Academy—that which distinguished the 'intermediates' or mathematical entities from the Ideas, that which recognized only the former, and that which identified the two; and there are other passages[3] which mention two of these views. In *Met.* $987^{b}14$–18 Aristotle expressly attributes the first of the three views to Plato; how are the others to be assigned?

From two passages in other Books in which Speusippus is mentioned by name,[4] we learn of two features of his system: (1) that he recognized more classes of entities than the three (Ideas, mathematical objects, sensible objects) recognized by Plato, and treated them in detachment from one another, recognizing separate principles for each; but that, like Plato, he started with

---

[1] $1083^{a}32$. The *Phaedo* is mentioned in $1080^{a}2$.
[2] $1069^{a}33$–6, $1076^{a}19$–22, $1080^{b}24$–30, $1083^{a}17$–$^{b}8$, $1086^{a}2$–13, $1090^{b}13$–$1091^{a}5$. This last passage needs special consideration, which will be found on pp. 208–9.
[3] $1080^{b}11$–16, $1086^{a}29$–32, $1090^{a}4$–28.   [4] $1028^{b}21$–4, $1072^{b}30$–$1073^{a}3$.

the One as his first principle; (2) that he regarded values as emerging late in the evolution of the universe, and thought of the first principles and their earliest products, numbers, as not possessing goodness.

Now the theory referred to in the first of these passages is clearly the same which in $1075^b37–1076^a4$ and in $1090^b13–29$ is described as making nature 'a chain of disconnected incidents, like a bad tragedy'; and in these two passages the thinkers in question are described as 'making mathematical number the first' or as 'asserting the existence only of the objects of mathematics'. Thus Speusippus is clearly identified as the thinker who recognized the existence of mathematical objects but denied that of Ideas. We are left, therefore, with Xenocrates as the thinker who identified the two.

By following up this clue it is possible to identify many passages of the *Metaphysics* as referring to Speusippus or to Xenocrates, and to learn a good deal about their respective views.[1] To Speusippus we may refer, in some cases with certainty and in others with high probability, the following passages: $1028^b21–4$, 1069^a36, $1072^b30–1073^a3$, $75^a36–7$, $^b37–1076^a4$, $1076^a21–2$, $1080^b14–16$, 25–8, $1083^a20–31$, $1085^a32–^b9$, $^b27–31$, $1086^a2–5$, 29–30, $1087^b6–9$, 16–17, 27, 30–3, $1090^a7–15$, 25–8, $^b13–20$, $1091^a33–^b1$, $^b22–5$, $32–1092^a3$, $1092^a11–17$, $35–^b1$. To Xenocrates we may assign $1028^b24–7$, 1069^a35, $1076^a20–1$, $1080^b22–3$, 28–30, $1083^b1–8$, $1086^a5–11$, $1090^b20–32$. To Plato we may assign $987^a29–988^a17$, 988^a26, $990^a29–32$, $991^b3–9$, $995^b16–18$, $996^a4–7$, $997^b1–3$, $998^b9–11$, $1001^a9–12$, $1002^b12–32$, $1010^b11–14$, $1019^a1–4$, $1025^a6–13$, 1026^b14, $1028^b19–21$, $1053^b9–13$, $1057^b8–9$, $1059^b3–12$, $1060^b6–12$, 1064^b29, 1069^a34, $1071^b31–3$, $37–1072^a2$, $1073^a20–2$, $1076^a19–20$, 1077^a11, $1080^a2–8$, $^b11–14$, 24–5, $1081^a24–5$, $1083^a31–6$, $1084^a12–17$, 1085^b7, 9–10, $1086^a11–13$, $31–^b5$, $1087^b13–16$, 1089^a19, $1090^a4–7$, $^b20–7$, $32–1091^a5$, $1091^b35–1092^a3$. This dissection shows that Books M and N are as much occupied with Plato's followers as with Plato himself; the reason why they pay much more attention to Speusippus than to Xenocrates is that

---

[1] I have indicated the lines on which such an identification proceeds, in my edition of the *Metaphysics*, i. lxxi–lxxvi.

Aristotle considered the view of Xenocrates, who confused ideal with mathematical numbers, to be much the worst of the three.[1] While the dissection has a good deal of value, it remains true that there are many other passages in which the reference is doubtful or more general, so that many problems remain on our hands.

[1] 1083^{b}1–8.

X

ARISTOTLE'S ACCOUNT OF PLATO'S EARLIER DOCTRINE

ARISTOTLE'S main account of the theory of Ideas is found in two passages of the *Metaphysics*, A. 987ª29–ᵇ14 and M. 1078ᵇ9–32, which read as follows:

1. After the systems we have named came the philosophy of Plato, which in most respects followed these thinkers,[1] but had peculiarities that distinguished it from the philosophy of the Italians.[1] For in his youth he first became familiar with Cratylus and with the Heraclitean doctrines that all sensible things are ever in a state of flux and there is no knowledge about them, and these views he retained in later years. Socrates, however, was occupying himself with ethical matters, neglecting the world of nature as a whole but seeking the universal in ethical matters; he was the first to concentrate attention on definitions. Plato accepted his teaching, and held that the problem applied not to sensible things but to entities of another kind—for this reason, that a general definition could not be a definition of any sensible thing, since such things were always changing. He, then, called things of this other sort Ideas, and sensible things, he said, were all named after these, and in virtue of a relation to these; for it was in virtue of participation that the many have the same name as the Forms.[2] Only the name 'participation' was new; for the Pythagoreans say that things exist by imitation of numbers, and Plato says they exist by participation, changing the name. But what the participation or imitation of the Forms might be, they left an open question.

2. Now, regarding the Ideas, we must first examine the ideal theory itself, not connecting it in any way with the nature of numbers,[3] but

---

[1] i.e. the Pythagoreans.

[2] I now think the true reading in 987ᵇ9 is κατὰ μέθεξιν γὰρ εἶναι τὰ πολλὰ ὁμώνυμα τοῖς εἴδεσιν. It is probable that an early copyist, not recognizing the significance of τὰ πολλά (the many, as opposed to the one), and taking it to mean 'the majority', introduced τῶν συνωνύμων as a gloss, and that the gloss got incorporated in the text of the manuscripts, and drove out ὁμώνυμα in that of Aᵇ, Alexander, and Asclepius. ὁμώνυμος, not συνώνυμος, is Aristotle's usual way of expressing the relation of the particulars to the Ideas in Plato's system (990ᵇ6, 991ª6), and it is also Plato's way (*Phaedo* 78 e 2, *Parm.* 133 d 3, *Tim.* 52 a 5). The interpretation of τὰ πολλὰ τῶν συνωνύμων as meaning 'the many consisting of the συνώνυμα' seems to me most unlikely.

[3] i.e. without discussing Plato's later theory of Idea-numbers.

taking it as it was originally understood by those who first maintained the existence of the Ideas. The supporters of the theory of Forms were led to it by the fact that on the question about the reality of things they accepted the Heraclitean sayings which describe all sensible things as ever passing away, so that if knowledge and thought are to have an object there must be some other and permanent entities, distinct from those that are sensible; for there could be no knowledge of things which were in a state of flux. But Socrates was occupying himself with the moral virtues, and in connexion with them became the first to seek for general definitions. . . . It was natural that Socrates should be seeking the essence, for he was seeking to get reasoned conclusions, and the essence of the thing reasoned about is the starting-point of reasoning about it. . . . Two things may be fairly ascribed to Socrates—inductive arguments and general definition, both of which are connected with the starting-point of knowledge. But Socrates did not make the universals or the definitions exist apart; these thinkers, however, gave them separate existence, and this was the kind of thing they called Ideas.

This account is repeated in brief in M. 1086^a37-^b5:

They [the believers in the Ideas] thought that the particulars in the sensible world were in a state of flux and none of them was stable, but that the universal was apart from these and something different. Socrates gave the impulse to this theory . . . by reason of his definitions, but he did not separate universals from individuals; and he was right in not separating them.

We must consider separately the three ingredients which Aristotle describes as having entered into Plato's theory. (1) We know very little about Cratylus; all that has come down to us about him from antiquity is contained in one page of Diels.[1] It may be inferred with fair certainty from *Crat.* 429 e 5 that he was an Athenian, and 440 d 5 says definitely that he was considerably younger than Socrates. It is presumably in consequence of the latter fact that Diogenes Laertius says[2] it was only after Socrates' death that Plato associated with Cratylus. Aristotle definitely describes Plato as having associated with him before he came under the influence of Socrates, and Aristotle is much more likely to have known the facts than Diogenes.

[1] *F.V.*⁵ ii. 69–70.   [2] iii. 6 (8).

With regard to the teaching of Cratylus we have, in addition
to what Aristotle says here, his statement elsewhere[1] that Cratylus
'in the end did not think it right to say anything but used only
to move his finger, and to criticize Heraclitus for saying that it is
impossible to step twice into the same river; for *he* thought one
could not do it even once'. In the dialogue that bears his name,
he appears as a convinced Heraclitean.[2]

There is no difficulty in accepting Aristotle's statement that
Plato associated first with Cratylus; for Plato was already a man
of twenty-eight to thirty when Socrates died, and plenty of time
had elapsed for him to have had a brief association with Cratylus,
followed by a longer and more important one with Socrates.
Even without Aristotle's testimony we should know that Plato
had been influenced by Heracliteanism. There is a striking passage in the *Symposium*[3] in which he speaks of the transitoriness of
all things human—not only of hair, flesh, bones, blood, and the
whole body, but of habits, traits of character, opinions, desires,
pleasures, pains, fears, knowledge. In a passage of the *Phaedo*[4] the
same thought is repeated, and there the transitoriness of such
things is contrasted with the eternalness of the Forms, equality
itself, beauty itself.

In these passages the transitoriness of sensible things is stated as
a matter of common observation. In the *Theaetetus*[5] Plato takes a
step forward. He introduces a theory which, he says, has been
held by Protagoras and by other distinguished men. There is,
however, no trace of it in what we know about Protagoras or
about anyone else before Plato himself; and those scholars[6] are
probably right who hold it to be a theory developed by Plato on
the basis of Heraclitean and Protagorean teaching. Whether or
not he was the author of the theory, it is clear that he held it,
since it is on the assumption of its truth that he proceeds to criticize the capacity of perception to yield knowledge,[7] and since he
states it again in the *Timaeus*.[8] The theory is that all physical

---

[1] 1010[a]12.   [2] *Crat.* 440 d 7–e 2.   [3] 207 d 2–208 b 6.
[4] 78 c 10–79 a 11.   [5] 155 d 5–157 c 2.
[6] e.g. Jackson, *J. of Philol.* xiii (1885), 255–6; Burnet, *Gk. Phil.* i. 242; Cornford,
P.T.K. 49.
[7] 181 b 8–183 c 7.   [8] 45 b 2–d 3, 67 c 4–68 b 5.

so-called things are not things, but slow motions, that our sense-
organs also are slow motions, and that perception is the result of
the meeting of these motions.

Plato was, then, as Aristotle says, convinced of the truth of
Heraclitus' doctrine that the world of sense is in constant flux,
and that what is in constant flux cannot be known. But he was
equally convinced that knowledge exists, and therefore that there
must be non-sensible entities which are the objects of knowledge.
Thus the theory of Ideas was built on the foundation of
Heracliteanism.

(2) It is no longer necessary to argue against the view of Burnet
and Taylor that the theory of Ideas as we find it in the dialogues
down to and including the *Phaedo* and the *Republic* was the work
of Socrates and not of Plato; the judgement of scholars generally
has pronounced against this view.[1] It is clearly incompatible with
what Aristotle says in the passages we have quoted, and it is inconceivable that Aristotle, who was for nineteen years, during
Plato's lifetime, a member of the Academy, should not have
known Plato's own view, and that of the school, about the contribution Socrates had made to the formation of the theory.

It is necessary, however, to consider two passages which were
much emphasized by Burnet and Taylor as evidence for their
view. One of these is a passage in the Second Letter:[2] 'When a
thing has once been committed to writing, it is impossible to
prevent it from gaining publicity. It is for this reason that I myself
have never written anything on these subjects. There is not, and
there never will be, a written treatise (σύγγραμμα) of Plato's.
Those that are called his are really the teaching of Socrates
restored to youth and beauty.' The other is a passage in the
Seventh Letter:[3]

There neither is nor ever will be a treatise (σύγγραμμα) of mine on the
subject. For it does not admit of exposition like other branches of
knowledge; but after much converse about the matter and a life lived

---

[1] For discussions of this view cf. for example G. C. Field, *P.C.* 202–38; Lodge,
Robin, Shorey, and Heidel in *Proceedings of the Sixth International Congress of Philosophy*, 559–88; also my edition of the *Metaphysics*, i. xxxiii–xlv, and my address to
the Classical Association in 1932.

[2] 314 c 1–4.   [3] 341 c 4–342 a 1.

together, suddenly a light, as it were, is kindled in one soul by a flame that leaps to it from another, and thereafter sustains itself. Yet this much I know—that if the things were written or put into words, it would be done best by me, and that, if they were written badly, I should be the person most pained. Again, if they had appeared to me to admit adequately of writing and exposition, what task in life could I have performed nobler than this, to write what is of great service to mankind and to bring the nature of things into the light for all to see? But I do not think it a good thing for men that there should be a disquisition, as it is called, on this topic—except for some few, who are able with a little teaching to find it out for themselves. As for the rest, it would fill some of them quite illogically with a mistaken feeling of contempt, and others with lofty and vainglorious expectations, as though they had learnt something high and mighty.

The Second Letter is open to grave suspicion. Most scholars have come to the conclusion that it is spurious, and a study of the arguments put forward, for instance, by Prof. Hackforth,[1] Prof. Field,[2] and Prof. Pasquali[3] would convince most readers that the rejection is right. If that is so, the passage is pretty obviously an imitation of the passage in the Seventh Letter; and certain features in the context suggest that the writer has misunderstood the 'philosophical digression' in that letter. Even if the Second Letter be genuine, what Plato says would not drive us, in the face of the general tradition of antiquity,[4] to treat the dialogues of Plato as mere essays in biography; Plato's saying that all he had done was to 'present Socrates restored to youth and beauty' could still be taken as only a graceful acknowledgement of all he owed to his great teacher.

What Plato says in the Seventh Letter is that he has written no σύγγραμμα περὶ αὐτῶν, 'no treatise on these subjects'. What is a σύγγραμμα, and what are 'these subjects'? The sequel, the 'philosophical digression' which we have considered elsewhere,[5] makes it clear that the subjects are the Ideas and the method of getting to know them. While the word σύγγραμμα is often used of any writing, it has a special tendency to mean a prose treatise.[6] Now

---

[1] *A.P.E.* 42–51.   [2] *P.C.* 200–1.   [3] *Le Lettere di Platone*, 173–95.
[4] For which see Prof. Field, *P.C.* 214–38.
[5] pp. 139–41; cf. esp. 342 e 2–343 a 4.
[6] Cf. *Laws*, 810 b 6, Isoc. 2. 7 (7. 42), Galen 16. 532.

none of Plato's dialogues is a σύγγραμμα in this sense; Aristotle classed the 'Socratic dialogues', of which Plato's are the chief, with the mimes of Sophron and Xenarchus, and regarded both the dialogues and the mimes as poetic in character in spite of their being in prose.[1] Though the Ideas appear in dialogue after dialogue, there is no dialogue which could be called a treatise on the Ideas. Thus these two passages do nothing to establish the view that Socrates was the author of the theory of Ideas.

The part Aristotle assigns to Socrates in the history of philosophy is a comparatively modest one. In his review of previous philosophers he passes[2] direct from the Pythagoreans to Plato, and introduces Socrates incidentally as one of the influences that affected Plato's development. This treatment of him is justified, because it is the history of metaphysical thinking that Aristotle is writing, and Socrates was not a metaphysician.

It is to Socrates' search for definitions that Aristotle ascribes his influence on Plato's metaphysics, and we need not doubt that the search for definitions was one of Socrates' main interests; to this extent Plato's early dialogues may be accepted as historically accurate. Even the practically minded Xenophon bears witness to this interest when he says:[3]—'Socrates would hold discourse, from time to time, on what concerned mankind, considering what was pious, what impious; what was noble, what ignoble; what was just, what unjust; what was sanity, what insanity; what was fortitude, what cowardice; what a state was, and what the character of a statesman; what was the nature of government over men, and the qualities of one skilled in governing them.' Xenophon in fact, in his long account of Socrates' conversation, gives very few examples of such discussion;[4] but that is because his practical mind did not share this interest.

Aristotle, it will be noted, apportions very precisely the credit due respectively to Cratylus and to Socrates for the origination in Plato's mind of the theory of Ideas. Plato, he says, accepted Socrates' teaching about the importance of definitions; but it was the Heraclitean teaching about the changingness of all sensible

---

[1] *Poet.* 1447^{b}9–20.　　　[2] 987^{a}29.　　　[3] *Mem.* i. 1. 16.
[4] Cf. i. 2. 41, 44; iii. 9. 1–13; iv. 6. 1–12.

things that led Plato to the conclusion that there must be other, unchanging things to serve as the objects of definition. The theory of Ideas sprang from this contact of flint with steel. Aristotle's estimate of Socrates' contribution to the formation of the theory was not made casually. 'Two things', he says elsewhere,[1] as though the question had been much discussed, 'may be *fairly ascribed* to Socrates—inductive arguments and general definition, both of which are connected with the starting-point of science; but he did not treat the universals or the definitions as existing apart; they [the believers in Ideas], however, gave them separate existence, and this was the kind of thing to which they gave the name Ideas.' We can hardly doubt that this estimate—echoed by his statement that Socrates 'gave the impulse to the theory'[2]—is a correct estimate of the facts.

(3) Aristotle comes to the Pythagoreans rather late in his account of the pre-Socratics—after Empedocles, Leucippus, and Democritus—and describes them as having been 'contemporaneous with and earlier than these'.[3] Thus it is not very early thinkers that he has in mind. He hardly ever mentions Pythagoras, and never in connexion with the theory of Ideas; he is rather thinking of philosophers who flourished between, say, 470 and 400, and it is likely that he had chiefly in mind Philolaus, who was probably born about the middle of the fifth century.[4] In describing the views of the Pythagoreans he sometimes credits them with saying that things are numbers,[5] sometimes with saying

---

[1] 1078^{b}27–32.   [2] 1086^{b}3.   [3] 985^{b}23.
[4] Philolaus is one of the two important Pythagoreans (other than Pythagoras himself) named by Plato, who had heard from Cebes and Simmias of their association with Philolaus when Philolaus visited Thebes (*Phaedo* 61 d 6–e 9); Plato had no doubt learned from them something about Philolaus' views. There is a certain amount of later tradition connecting Plato with Philolaus; D.L. 3. 6 (8) says that when Plato was twenty-eight, after visiting Megara and Cyrene he went to Italy to see Philolaus, and D.L. 8. 84–5 says that (much later) Plato wrote to Dion asking him to buy Pythagorean books from Philolaus, and himself bought or otherwise procured the one book Philolaus had written. But the one leading Pythagorean with whom, as we can learn from the Seventh Letter (338 c 5–339 d 6, 350 a 5–b 5), Plato was really intimate was Archytas, who was pretty much of his own age. Here, too, later tradition adds something which may or may not be true— that after Socrates' death Plato visited in succession Egypt, Italy, and Sicily, and in Italy 'was much with' Archytas (Cic. *de Rep.* 1. 10. 16).
[5] 987^{b}27–8.

that things imitate numbers;[1] and it may be that the two descriptions reflect different elements in early Pythagorean theory.[2] We can hardly suppose a relatively late thinker like Philolaus to have meant seriously that all things are numbers and nothing more, but we can easily suppose him to have said 'all things are number', meaning that all things have a numerical character, and that that is the most important thing about them. That is the view expressed in the fragments attributed to him,[3] and even if (as is probable) these are not genuine, they may very well record his view. This view probably arose originally from the discovery that the chief concordant intervals—the octave, the fifth, and the fourth—correspond to the ratios of length $1 : 2$, $2 : 3$, $3 : 4$ between two vibrating strings—a discovery that may well go back to Pythagoras himself. From this immensely important discovery the Pythagoreans were led to suspect that a definite numerical structure underlies every qualitative distinction. Some of their dicta were sound, more were fanciful, but the principle was sound enough—that qualitative distinctions rest upon quantitative facts.

Aristotle does not describe the theory of Ideas as springing from Pythagorean views; he says that it 'followed' them,[4] and 'followed' very probably means 'resembled' rather than 'originated from'.[5] He does not represent Plato as having, in the early form of his ideal theory, had numbers in his mind at all. He points out, indeed, the affinity between the part played by numbers in the Pythagorean theory and the part played by Ideas in the Platonic,[6] but he does not suggest that the one theory was derived from the other, and in describing Plato's doctrine as in most respects following the Pythagorean, he probably has chiefly in mind the late Platonic theory of Idea-numbers.[7] The earlier Platonic view he describes as due to two sources *other* than Pythagoreanism—

---

[1] Ibid. 11.   [2] Cf. J. E. Raven, *Pythagoreans and Eleatics*, 62–3.

[3] e.g. fr. 4 καὶ πάντα γα μὰν τὰ γιγνωσκόμενα ἀριθμὸν ἔχοντι· οὐ γὰρ οἷόν τε οὐδὲν οὔτε νοηθῆμεν οὔτε γνωσθῆμεν ἄνευ τούτου.

[4] 987ᵃ30.   [5] Cf. Bywater's note on *Poet.* 1449ᵇ10 ἠκολούθησεν.

[6] 987ᵇ7–14.

[7] 987ᵇ18–988ᵃ1. The view expressed above is confirmed by the fact that in *Met.* M. 4, where Aristotle is concerned only with Plato's ideal theory, not with his theory of Idea-numbers, the Pythagoreans are introduced only in a parenthesis (1078ᵇ21–3).

the positive conclusion that Plato drew from the negative teaching of Cratylus, and the impulse he received from Socrates' search for definitions.

Aristotle does not say when or how Plato came under Pythagorean influence; he certainly does not suggest that it was through Socrates, and his language suggests rather the opposite. The most natural supposition is that Plato's first knowledge of Pythagoreanism came from Simmias and Cebes, the Pythagoreans from Thebes who form part of the Socratic circle depicted in the *Phaedo*, and that he learned much more about the system during his visit to south Italy about 388, eleven years after Socrates' death. But it is noteworthy that even as late as the *Phaedo*, which was probably written some years after that visit, there is nothing to suggest that the theory of Ideas there put forward owes anything to Pythagoreanism; it is only Plato's views about the destiny of the soul that seem to do so. It is not till we come to the *Timaeus* and the *Philebus* that we find the theory of Ideas beginning to be influenced by the Pythagorean theory that 'all things are numbers', and it is only in the still later theory of Idea-numbers that this influence reaches its height. Whether this was the result of further contacts with Pythagoreans during Plato's second and third journeys to Sicily,[1] or of further meditation on what he had learned long before about Pythagorean views, it is impossible to say.

Of the greatness of the Pythagorean influence on Plato during this later period there can be no doubt. Not only do we find the 'limit' and the 'unlimited' of the *Philebus* already present among the first principles recognized by some of the Pythagoreans; we find unity and plurality (Plato's One and his 'indefinite dyad') in that list;[2] and we find goodness associated with limit and unity, and badness with the unlimited and plurality, as they were by Plato.[3]

---

[1] About 367 and 361.

[2] 986ª22–6. Mr. Raven points out (*Pythagoreans and Eleatics*, 184–5) that, while limit, the unlimited, and the mixture of them are introduced in the *Philebus* as something obvious, the cause of the mixture is introduced with great hesitation; he suggests, with much probability, that this last is a new feature which Plato is adding to the Pythagorean theory.   [3] 988ª14–15.

Aristotle says that Plato's main divergences from the Pythagorean doctrine were due to his σκέψις ἐν τοῖς λόγοις. The phrase is pretty clearly a reminiscence of *Phaedo* 100 a 1–3, where ἐν λόγοις σκοπούμενον τὰ ὄντα is Socrates' description of his own method. As we have seen,[1] λόγοι there probably means 'statements' rather than 'definitions', but in view of what Aristotle has said earlier of Plato's debt to Socrates' study of definitions, *he* probably uses λόγοι in the latter sense. The best commentary on Aristotle's meaning is to be found in two other passages dealing with the Platonists—*Met.* 1069ª27, where he says that they treat genera as substances διὰ τὸ λογικῶς ζητεῖν, and contrasts them with the old thinkers, who treated particular things as substances; and 1084ᵇ23–32, where he says that they accepted an erroneous theory of units because they at the same time considered them from the point of view of mathematics and therefore treated them as the constituents of numbers, and from the point of view of general definitions, and therefore dwelt on the unity that is predicable of any number. The Pythagoreans were doing what the other pre-Socratics did, trying to find the ultimate constituents of things, and they (so Aristotle holds, at least) thought of numbers as being constituents of things very much as other thinkers had thought of water or air as being their constituents, i.e. as being the very stuff of which they are made. Plato, on the other hand, following in the footsteps of Socrates, was interested in the universal character of a set of things, and this led to two divergences between his doctrine and that of the Pythagoreans. He did not view the One and the numbers as the stuff of which things are made, but as their formal principle, and therefore placed them 'apart from sensibles'; and he did not confine himself to the Pythagorean language about 'numbers', but spoke of 'Ideas' and thought of them as essentially the objects of definition.

In Aristotle's account of the influences that went to mould Plato's metaphysics one misses any reference to the Eleatics. We might feel tempted to include them among the 'Italians' whose views those of Plato are said to resemble; but the parallels which Aristotle proceeds to draw are only between Plato and the

[1] pp. 27–8.

Pythagoreans, and it is of these that he elsewhere[1] uses the word 'Italians'.

This apparent gap in Aristotle's account would be filled if we could accept Diogenes Laertius' statement[2] that Plato studied not only under Cratylus but under Hermogenes, who 'held the views of Parmenides'. But there is no other evidence that supports this; it is probably a mere inference from Hermogenes' appearance in the *Cratylus* as Cratylus' opponent. Hermogenes was a member (apparently an inconspicuous member) of the Socratic circle,[3] and we have no good ground for supposing either that he was an Eleatic or that Plato learned from him.

Parmenides is the chief speaker in the dialogue that bears his name, and in the *Sophistes* and the *Politicus* the chief speaker is an Eleatic stranger. But it must be admitted that they do not speak as mouthpieces of specifically Eleatic views, nor do we find Plato in these dialogues leaning to such views. In the *Parmenides*, the criticisms of Plato's early theory are not made from a specially Eleatic point of view; and in the *Sophistes* Plato for the first time clearly draws the conclusion that reality must include something that changes as well as something that does not—a most un-Eleatic view. Plato, when he speaks of Parmenides, always speaks of him with the respect he deserves as the founder of rationalism, but beyond the acceptance of rationalism Plato does not seem to have been specially influenced by the Eleatic philosophy; he nowhere shows any tendency towards thorough-going monism.

---

[1] *Meteor.* 342^{b}30; *Met.* 987^{a}10, 988^{a}26.
[2] iii. 6 (8).   [3] *Phaedo* 59 b 7.

XI

THE POPULATION OF
THE WORLD OF IDEAS

WE may next take account of a passage of great interest[1] in which Aristotle criticizes the theory of Ideas, with reference to various arguments current in the Academy. The passage runs as follows; for convenience of reference I divide it into sections.

Of the ways in which we [i.e. we Platonists; for in Book A Aristotle writes as a member, though a recalcitrant member, of the Academy] prove that the Forms exist, none is convincing; for [A] from some no inference necessarily follows, and [B] from some there arise Forms of things of which we think there are no Forms. For [1] according to the arguments from the existence of the sciences there will be Forms of all things of which there are sciences; [2] according to the 'one over many' argument there will be Forms even of negations; [3] according to the argument that there is an object for thought even when the thing has perished, there will be Forms of perishable things; for we have an image of them. Further [C], of the more precise arguments, [1] some establish Ideas of relative terms, and [2] others introduce the 'third man'.

The fullest and best discussions of this passage are to be found in Robin's *Théorie Platonicienne*,[2] in Prof. Cherniss's *Aristotle's Criticism of Plato and the Academy*,[3] and in Wilpert's *Zwei aristotelische Frühschriften über die Ideenlehre*.[4] Our discussion of it will be limited in two ways. (1) We shall not be concerned with the merits of Aristotle's arguments. These form an interesting topic; but our object is to trace the history of Plato's views rather than to assess their value; and in any case our judgement of their value is likely to be determined by other considerations than those which Aristotle brings forward. And (2) we shall not be concerned with the views of Plato's followers; for our subject is not the Academy, but Plato. What we shall try to discover is what evidence there is

---

[1] 990^b8–17.
[3] pp. 226–318.
[2] pp. 173–98.
[4] pp. 15–118.

that Plato at any time recognized Ideas of any of the types here named by Aristotle, and what evidence there is that he ever ceased to recognize such Ideas. The latter question was vigorously raised by Henry Jackson, who argued that there was a 'later theory of Ideas' held by Plato in which only Ideas of animal types and of the four elements were recognized.

We need not concern ourselves with the precise nature of the arguments for Ideas which Aristotle refers to. From Alexander's commentary we may learn that there were various forms of the argument from the sciences (Aristotle's use of the plural is itself enough evidence for this); and Alexander in fact sets out three forms.[1] But the setting out of a list of arguments is not in Plato's manner, and we may feel pretty sure that the formulation was the work of the school (though no doubt based on hints in the dialogues, and probably also in Plato's oral teaching); and for this reason they will not be gone into in detail.

We will start with the arguments from the sciences—(B) (1). What were the objects of science to which the (or some) Platonists denied the rank of Forms? A little lower down[2] Aristotle says 'According to the assumption on which our belief in the Ideas rests, there will be Forms not only of substances but also of many other things (for the concept is single not only in the case of sub-stances but also in the other cases, and *there are sciences* not only of substance but also of other things, and a host of other such difficulties confronts them). But, according to the logic of the case and the opinions held about the Forms, if Forms can be shared in there must be Ideas of substances only.' Here Aristotle tells us what the 'other things' are which the Platonists do not believe to have Ideas corresponding to them though the argu-ment from the sciences should lead to a belief in such Ideas; they are all things that are not substances. We need not concern our-selves with Aristotle's argument; for it is certain that, whoever the members of the Academy were who believed only in Ideas of substances, Plato was never among them. In the earlier

---

[1] 79. 5–15. Alexander's knowledge of them was derived from Aristotle's early work Περὶ Ἰδεῶν (Al. 79. 4).

[2] 990^b22–9.

dialogues things like goodness and beauty are the most typical examples of Ideas. In the *Parmenides* they are among the Ideas of whose existence he was most sure. In the *Sophistes* 'the greatest Forms' are existence, sameness and difference, rest and motion. In the Idea-number theory, which belongs to the latest period of his life, the primary Ideas are oneness, twoness, and the like. Everywhere except in the *Timaeus* Ideas of substances play a very subordinate part.

Most scholars seem to have overlooked the explanation which Aristotle himself gives in $990^b 22-9$ of his statement ibid. $11-13$ that the Platonic arguments from the sciences lead to Ideas of things of which nevertheless the Platonists think there are no Ideas. Relying on Alexander's interpretation,[1] they think the things referred to are not 'things other than substances', but *works of art*. Since Alexander bases himself on Aristotle's *De Ideis*, we may take it that, according to Aristotle, works of art were a second class of things Ideas of which were not admitted by the Platonists, though according to the arguments from the sciences they should have been admitted. To this question we shall return later.[2]

We turn now to (B) (2): 'According to the "one over many" argument there will be Forms even of negations; and yet we say there are not.' We have to ask (*a*) whether the theory of Ideas really implies that there are negative Ideas, and (*b*) whether Plato ever denied that there are such Ideas.

There are three kinds of term which might in a very general way be called negative terms, and we must ask these questions about all of them. (*a*) There are first the terms, beloved by some logicians but never used in ordinary life, which are purely negative in their meaning—terms like 'not-good', 'not-beautiful', 'not-tall'. Plato touches on such terms in the *Sophistes*, but his attitude towards them is not altogether clear. In 257 e 2-4 he says 'the existence of the not-beautiful consists of its being marked off from a single definite kind of existing things'—*from* a kind, not *as* one. But in 257 e 9 he says 'According to this argument is the beautiful any more and the not-beautiful any less a reality?', and the answer that is expected and is forthcoming is 'No'. And in

[1] 79.22–80.6. [2] pp. 171–5.

258 b 9 he says, 'Should we now make bold to say that "that which is not" is undoubtedly a thing that has a nature of its own—just as the tall was tall and the beautiful was beautiful, so too with the not-tall and the not-beautiful—and in that sense "that which is not", also, on the same principle, both was and is what-is-not, a single Form to be numbered among the many realities?' The doctrine is that not-being (which is identified with difference) is a genuine Form, indeed one of the greatest Forms. Of this Form Plato says,[1] 'We have shown that the nature of the different has existence and is parcelled out over the whole field of existing things with reference to one another'; and he might be supposed to mean that purely negative terms like 'not-beautiful', 'not-good' stand for specific Ideas embraced under the generic Idea of not-being or difference. But he never says this, and his meaning is as likely to be that the Idea of difference is parcelled out among all the *individual things* that are not beautiful or are not good. He expresses himself more definitely in the *Politicus*,[2] where he says that 'barbarian' (if it only means not-Greek) and 'not-ten-thousand', though they stand for parts of the genera man and number, do not stand for species of them, i.e. that there is *no* Idea of not-Greek or of not-ten-thousand.

(β) Secondly, there are terms negative in form but in fact having a positive as well as a negative meaning. Plato occasionally refers to Ideas answering to such terms, e.g. to the Idea of impiety and to the Idea of injustice,[3] and there is no evidence that he ever ceased to believe in the existence of such Ideas. Nor was there any reason why he should; for such words clearly stand not only for the absence of a quality—since not everything that is not just is unjust—but also for the presence of another positive quality.

(γ) Thirdly, there are terms not negative even in form, but definitely suggesting the absence of some desirable quality—terms such as 'sickness', 'evil', or 'ugly'. These, too, have a positive as well as a negative significance. Ideas answering to such terms are referred to in mature as well as in early dialogues,[4] and

---

[1] 258 d 7.   [2] 262 c 8–263 e 1.
[3] *Euthyph.* 5 d 2–5; *Rep.* 476 a 4–7 (cf. 402 b 9–c 8); *Tht.* 176 e 3–177 a 2.
[4] *Phaedo* 105 c 4; *Rep.* 476 a 4; *Tht.* 186 a 8.

there was no reason why Plato should cease to recognize them. It *might* be possible for a theory of Ideas to dispense with an Idea of evil and with Ideas of its species, and to explain all evil in the sensible world as due to the fact that the relation of the phenomenal to the ideal is never one of perfect instantiation but always one of imitation which falls short of its pattern. But there is nothing to show that Plato ever took this line.

Socrates' hesitation, in the *Parmenides*,[1] to recognize Ideas of mud, hair, and dirt was presumably due to the suggestion of unpleasantness or else of triviality which such words suggested. But Parmenides' advice to Socrates, which represents Plato's better thoughts, was that he should discard such doubts and follow his general principle.[2] The same line of thought is to be found in the *Sophistes*,[3] where he divides the purification of living bodies into that effected by medicine and that effected by bathing, and adds that 'the dialectical art never considers whether the benefit to be derived from the purge is greater or less than that to be derived from the sponge, and has no more interest in the one than in the other'.

Of these various types of 'negative term', it seems to have been about the first that Aristotle says that the argument of the 'one over many' involved Ideas corresponding to them, which nevertheless the Academy did not recognize; for Alexander's examples[4] are 'not-man', 'not-musical', 'not-horse', 'not-wood', 'not-white'. If Plato had ever resolved negation into assertion, had analysed '*A* is not *B*' into '*A* is not-*B*', then—on the general principle that where one thing is asserted of many, a single Idea is being asserted—he would have had to recognize purely negative Ideas. But there is no evidence that he ever so analysed negation. On the other hand there is no evidence that he ever ceased to recognize Ideas answering to general terms which, though negative in form, imply a positive meaning. There is thus no evidence of a change of view on his part.

(B) (3) Aristotle goes on to say that 'according to the argument that there is an object for thought even when the thing has

---

[1] 130 c 5–d 9.
[2] 130 e 1–4.
[3] 226 e 8–227 c 6; cf. *Pol.* 266 d 4–9.
[4] *In Met.* 80.18–81.13.

perished, there will be Forms of perishable things; for we have an image of these'. The form of the argument described as τὸ νοεῖν τι φθαρέντος must have been somewhat as follows: 'Supposing we find, by study of a particular sensible equilateral triangle, that it must be equiangular; we retain this knowledge even after the particular triangle has been broken up; therefore the object of our knowledge must be another entity, which still exists, and such entities, which exist independently of their particular embodiments in individual things, are just what we call Ideas.' Aristotle argues that by parity of reasoning, since we can remember a perishable individual thing even after it has ceased to exist, there ought on Platonic principles to be an idea of such an individual. Plato's answer would no doubt have been that to argue thus is to ignore the difference between knowledge of universal truths and memory. In the former we are aware of an eternal connexion between entities themselves eternal, and therefore different from any perishable individual. In the latter we are aware (if for argument's sake it be admitted that memory is a kind of awareness) of an individual thing in which certain universals were connected, but we have no awareness that these are eternally connected, and therefore there is no reason to suppose that there is a complex universal consisting of them as so connected, i.e. an Idea of the perishable thing.

Here again we have no ground for supposing that there was any change in Plato's view; for it is certain that at no time would he have said that there is a separate Idea answering to each perishable individual thing.

(C) Aristotle goes on to say[1] 'Of the more precise arguments [1] some recognize (ποιοῦσιν) Forms of relative terms, of which we say there is no independent class, and [2] others mention (λέγουσιν) the "third man".' This sentence does not continue the illustration of Aristotle's statement[2] that the Platonic arguments for the existence of Ideas involve the recognition of Ideas which the Platonists do not in fact recognize. For in [1] he does not say 'some of the arguments set up Ideas of relative terms, of which we do not recognize Ideas'; he says 'which we do not

---

[1] 990ᵇ15.   [2] Ibid. 10-11.

recognize as a separately existing class'; he does not deny that the Platonists recognize Ideas of relative terms, but gives a reason why they should not have done so.[1] And in [2] λέγουσιν must mean 'mention', not 'involve as a consequence',[2] and must refer to the infinite regress argument used in the *Parmenides*; and that was an argument not to prove the existence of Ideas, but to show a difficulty which belief in them involved. In fact the sentence we are considering starts the more general line of thought which is continued in the next and following sentences, in which arguments used by the Platonists not to prove the existence of Ideas, but about Ideas (περὶ τῶν εἰδῶν)[3] are shown to have consequences unwelcome to the school.

Ideas answering to relative terms were recognized in the ideal theory as early as the time of writing of the *Phaedo*, where indeed the Ideas of equality and inequality are taken as primary examples of Ideas.[4] Such Ideas recur with equal prominence in the *Republic*,[5] and in the *Parmenides*, where they are recognized as a distinct class of Ideas.[6] Forms of sameness and difference (two of the 'greatest kinds') occur in the *Sophistes*[7] and in the *Timaeus*.[8] Plato, at least, seems never to have denied the existence of purely relative Ideas.

So far, then, we have found no evidence that Plato at the end of his life denied the rank of Ideas to anything to which he had earlier conceded that rank. There are, however, two other passages of which we must take account. In *Met.* 991[b]6 Aristotle says 'we [i.e. we Platonists] do not recognize Forms of such things as house or ring', and in 1070[a]18 he approves Plato by name for saying (on the assumption that Forms exist) that 'there are Forms as numerous [i.e. presumably only as numerous] as the things [i.e. the kinds of thing] that exist by nature'.

Plato expressly assumes the existence of Forms of artefacta not

---

[1] As Alexander points out (83.33), Aristotle is expressing the same thought which he expresses in the *Ethics* (1096[a]21-2) by saying that that which is relative 'is like an offshoot and accident of being'.

[2] This is not the usual view, but I have the support of Jackson (*J. of Philol.* x (1882), 255, n. 2), and of Wilpert (*Z.a.F.I.* 77-8).

[3] 990[b]18.

[4] 74 a 2-77 a 5.

[5] 479 b 3-7.

[6] 133 c 8.

[7] 254 e 2-256 e 3.

[8] 35 a 1-8.

only in the *Cratylus* and in the *Republic*, where Forms of shuttle, auger, bed, and table are mentioned by name,[1] but also in the *Timaeus* and in the *Laws* (in both of which, as in the *Cratylus* and the *Republic*, the good craftsman is said to work with his eye on the Form of that which he is making),[2] and in the Seventh Letter.[3] Artefacta do not occur among the kinds of thing, the existence of Forms of which is discussed in the 'first part' of the *Parmenides*, but we cannot infer from this that when he wrote that dialogue Plato denied or doubted the existence of such Forms. There is nothing improbable in the story Diogenes Laertius tells,[4] that when Diogenes the Cynic said to Plato 'I see a table and a cup, but certainly not tableness and cupness', Plato replied 'Naturally, for you have eyes, by which a cup or a table is perceived, but not reason, by which tableness and cupness are seen.'

On the other hand, Aristotle's statement derives some support, or seems to do so, from the remark made by Proclus,[5] that 'Xenocrates placed on record this definition of the Idea as one satisfactory to the Founder—"a pattern-like cause of the things that from time to time are constituted according to nature—a separable and divine cause".' (αἰτία παραδειγματικὴ τῶν κατὰ φύσιν ἀεὶ συνεστώτων . . . χωριστὴ καὶ θεία αἰτία.) And we can hardly set against the statements of Aristotle we have quoted his more general statements[6] that the Platonists recognized Ideas 'of all things that are spoken of universally', and that Plato himself said that the many individual things have the same names as the Forms by virtue of participation in them.

Here, then, we *seem* to have definite evidence of a divergence from the doctrine of the *Republic*, that there is an Idea answering to every common name; how is this to be explained? The question has been well discussed by Robin.[7] He considers various hypotheses. (*a*) It may be said that when Plato speaks of Forms of artefacta he is speaking loosely and half-humorously.[8] In reply it must be pointed out that Forms of artefacta are required by the

---

[1] *Crat.* 389 b 1–d 3; *Rep.* 596 b 3–597 a 3.

[2] *Tim.* 28 a 6–b 1; *Laws* 965 b 7–c 8.   [3] 342 d 3–e 2.

[4] 6.2.53.   [5] *In Parm.* 691 Stallbaum.

[6] 1078ᵇ32–4, 987ᵇ8–10.   [7] *T.p.I.N.* 174 n.

[8] So Proclus *in Tim.* 29 c, i. 344.5–14 (Diehl); Bonitz, *Arist. Met.* 2.118–9.

general doctrine that wherever there is a common name there is a Form, and that the Forms of bed and table play an essential part in Plato's argument against art in the tenth Book of the *Republic*.[1] (*b*) It may be said that Aristotle has misinterpreted Plato in saying that he recognized only Forms of natural objects.[2] But Aristotle's interpretation is supported by the definition of 'Idea' which Xenocrates described as commending itself to the Founder. (*c*) It may be said that Plato changed his opinion.[3] This view cannot be definitely rejected; but we can at least say that there is no evidence, in Plato or in what we read about him elsewhere, of such a change. (*d*) It may be suggested that it was only Plato's followers that changed the theory. Beckmann supposed[4] that the name of Plato was substituted for 'the believers in Ideas' in the one place (*Met.* 1070^{a}18) where he is definitely named in this connexion in the text of Aristotle. There is some evidence for this,[5] but the weight of the evidence is against it. (*e*) Robin suggests that Plato rejected Forms of the products of the *imitative* arts, the copies which merely reproduce the outward form of their originals, but did not reject Forms of the products of the useful arts, which have a form dictated by their end as truly as natural objects have one; and that Aristotle misinterpreted him as having denied Forms of the latter also. This suggestion agrees with the doctrine of the *Republic*,[6] where the actual bed stands at one remove from the Form just as a natural object does, the painted bed at two removes. There is no Form of the painted bed; the pattern to which the painter looks is not a Form but the actual bed. In the *Republic*,[7] too, the whole class of manufactured things (i.e. the products of the useful arts) is put in the same section of the Line as living things, the second section; and in the *Sophistes*[8] the products of imitative art are said to be to the products of useful art as dream-images, shadows, and

---

[1] 596 a 5–602 b 11.   [2] So Zeller, *Plat. Stud.* 262.
[3] So Zeller, *Ph. d. Gr.* ii. 1^4. 703 f., 947; Heinze, *Xenokr.* 53 f.; Jackson, *passim*.
[4] *Num Plato artefactorum ideas statuerit*, 29–35.
[5] Alexander as reported by Averroes had οἱ τὰ εἴδη τιθέμενοι ἔφασαν, but all the manuscripts of Aristotle have Πλάτων (or ὁ Πλάτων) ἔφη. Themistius' paraphrase, which agrees with Averroes, is so free as hardly to count.
[6] 596 b 6–10, 597 b 2–598 d 6.
[7] 510 a 5–6.   [8] 265 c 1–266 d 7.

reflections are to living things, and would therefore belong to the first and lowest division of the Line (though not mentioned in the Line passage).

The question whether Plato ever denied the existence of artefacta has been fully and well discussed by Prof. Cherniss,[1] who comes to the same conclusion as Robin, and supports it by much additional evidence. Of the passages bearing on the question, the only one in which Aristotle mentions Plato by name is that in which he says 'Plato recognizes Forms just as many as the things that exist by nature'; his other reference may equally well refer to some Platonist who had gone farther than his master by denying the existence of Forms of any artefacta, not merely of Forms of products of the *imitative* arts. The question is, what Plato meant by the word φύσει, 'by nature'; is this opposed to 'by art' or to 'contrary to nature'? Aristotle takes it in the former sense; but, as we have seen, Plato habitually puts the products of the useful arts on the same level as living things, on the ground that they answer the real needs of human nature. In discussing the principles on which classification should be based, Plato more than once insists that not any and every subdivision of a class which ingenuity can devise answers to a subdivision ordained by nature. In the *Phaedrus*[2] he insists that we ought 'to divide a genus into species at the joints established by nature, and not try to break up any part, like a bad cook'. In the *Politicus* he insists that while every species is a part of a genus, not every part is a species,[3] and lays down the rule 'let every part have at the same time a Form',[4] i.e. be not an arbitrary subdivision but one that answers to a real articulation in the nature of things. It is highly probable that it was to this principle, and not to any distinction between natural and manufactured products, that Plato was referring when he said 'there are Forms as many as the things that exist by nature'.[5] As positive evidence that he was not putting the products of art in general (i.e. those of the useful as well as those of the imitative arts) on a lower level of reality than those of nature, we have the words in his latest work,[6] 'The legislator should defend the claim

[1] *A.C.P.A.* 235-60.
[2] 265 e 1-3.
[3] 263 a 2-b 11.
[4] 262 b 1.
[5] *Met.* 1070ª18.
[6] *Laws*, 890 d 1-8.

of law itself *and of art* to be natural, or no less real than nature, since they are products of mind in accordance with sound reasoning.'

If this very probable conjecture is right, there is no real evidence that Plato ever denied the existence of Ideas answering to the objects of the useful arts. But early Platonists evidently did so; for Aristotle says distinctly[1] that they did not recognize Ideas of house and ring.

We come to the conclusion, then, that there is no real evidence that there was a later theory of Ideas in which Plato denied the existence of Ideas which he had earlier recognized. It may be added that, as we have already seen,[2] the fullest list of types of Idea to be found anywhere in Plato is in one of his latest writings, the Seventh Letter.

[1] 991^{b}6.   [2] p. 141.

XII

THE IDEAL NUMBERS

ARISTOTLE'S general account of Plato's later Metaphysics runs as follows:[1]

Further, besides sensible things and Forms he says there are the objects of mathematics, which occupy an intermediate position, differing from sensible things in being eternal and unchangeable, from Forms in that there are many alike, while the Form is in each case unique.

Since the Forms were the causes of all other things, he thought their elements were the elements of all things. As matter, the great and the small were first principles; as essential reality, the One; for from the great and the small, by participation in the One, came the numbers.[2] But while he agreed with the Pythagoreans in saying that the One is substance and not a predicate of something else, and that the numbers are the causes of the reality of other things, the positing of a dyad and the construction of the indeterminate out of a great and small, instead of treating it as one, is peculiar to him; and so is his view that the numbers exist apart from sensible things; *they* say that the things themselves are numbers, and do not place the objects of mathematics between the numbers and sensible things. His divergence from the Pythagoreans in making the One and the numbers separate from things, and his introduction of the Forms, were due to his inquiries in the region of definitions (for the earlier thinkers had no tincture of dialectic), and his making the other entity besides the One a dyad was due to the fact that the numbers, except the prime numbers, could be aptly produced out of the dyad as out of some plastic material.[3] Yet

[1] 987b14–988a15.

[2] In 987b22 τοὺς ἀριθμούς can hardly be either the predicate or in apposition to τὰ εἴδη. It is not certain which of the two phrases should be omitted. τοὺς ἀριθμούς is rather surprising, because Aristotle has said nothing about Plato's identification of the Ideas with numbers; but that Plato did identify them is for Aristotle so much a matter of common knowledge that he does not notice his omission to state it here.

[3] ἐκμαγεῖον. The word is not used elsewhere by Aristotle. Alexander (57.6) takes it as meaning a hollow mould, and some modern scholars have followed him. In Plato it means sometimes a plastic material, sometimes a copy taken in such a material, sometimes a pattern or archetype. Aristotle clearly treats the great and small as the quasi-material element, the One as the formal element, in the formation of the numbers, so that ἐκμαγεῖον must mean a plastic material, as it does in *Tht.* 191 c 9, 196 a 3, and probably in *Tim.* 50 c 2, where Plato uses it to illustrate his view about space.

what actually happens is the opposite of this; the theory is not a reasonable one. For they make a plurality of things out of the matter, and the Form generates only once, but what we observe is that only one table is made from one matter, while the man who applies the form, though he is one, makes many tables. And the relation of the male to the female is similar; the latter is impregnated by one copulation, but the male impregnates many females. Yet these are analogues of those first principles.

Plato, then, declared himself thus on the points in question; it is evident from what has been said that he has used only two causes, the essential and the material (for the Forms are the essential cause of all other things, and the One is the essential cause of the Forms); and it is evident what the underlying matter is, of which the Forms are predicated in the case of sensible things, and the One in the case of Forms, viz. that this is a dyad, the great and the small. Further, he has assigned the cause of good and that of evil to the elements, one to each of the two.

With the first statement made here—that Plato treated mathematical objects (i.e. numbers and spatial figures) as intermediate between Forms and sensible things—we have dealt in our examination of the *Republic*,[1] and it is only necessary to repeat that it is a doctrine which in the dialogues Plato seems from time to time to be on the verge of stating but never quite states. One would be disposed to think that it was probably the earliest development of his metaphysical theory beyond the point reached in the dialogues; but doubt is cast on this by its absence in the metaphysical section of the Seventh Letter.[2]

The other features mentioned by Aristotle may be summarized as follows: (1) Plato says the elements of the Forms are elements of all things.

(2) Plato says 'the great and the small' are the material element, the One the essential or formal element, in the Forms, the numbers (identified by Aristotle with the Forms) being produced by the participation of the great and the small in the One.

(3) While the treatment of the One as a substance, not an attribute, and the treatment of the numbers as formal causes of sensible things, resemble the Pythagorean views, the treatment of

[1] pp. 58–65.　　　　　　　　　　　[2] Cf. p. 141.

the indeterminate as a duality composed of the great and small is new.

(4) This analysis of the indeterminate is due to the fact that the numbers (except the prime numbers) can be aptly generated from a dyad as from a plastic material.

(5) The Forms are made the formal cause of sensible things, and the One the formal cause of the Forms; the material cause both of the Forms and of sensible things is the dyad of the great and small.

(6) The formal cause is the cause of the good, the material cause the cause of the evil, in the world.

The problems we have to consider are the following: (A) What are the numbers Aristotle is speaking of? (B) What are the principles they are derived from? (C) How are they generated? (D) What is their status relatively to the world of Ideas?

(A) The general answer to this question is not in doubt. The numbers, the generation of which by Plato is being considered, are Forms, distinguished by Plato both from sensible things and from the numbers which are according to him the objects of arithmetic. They are universals, characteristics, things such as we refer to by words ending in -ness or -ity.

The existence of Ideas such as oneness, twoness, and so on, is implied in the doctrine that there is an Idea answering to every common name,[1] and is explicitly maintained in the *Phaedo*,[2] where Plato says that every two is such by sharing in the Idea of twoness, and every one is such by sharing in the Idea of oneness. In the *Hippias Major*[3] Socrates points out the difference between most Ideas, which characterize each and all of a number of individual things, and Ideas of number, which characterize a group but not its individual members. These ideal numbers were distinguished both from the sensible numbers (i.e. numerable groups) recognized by 'the many' and from the abstract numbers of 'the philosophers' (i.e. of the mathematicians).[4]

For the Greeks number connotes plurality, so that 1 is not a number[5] but the first principle of number,[6] that *from* which

---

[1] *Rep.* 596 a 6–8.   [2] 101 b 9–c 9.   [3] 300 d 5–302 b 3.
[4] *Phil.* 56 d 4–57 a 2.   [5] *Met.* 1088ᵃ6.   [6] *Met.* 1016ᵇ18, &c.

number starts; Plato accordingly assumes its existence, does not set out to derive it.

The series of numbers has no limit in the upward direction; but there is good evidence to show that Plato assigned, as the Pythagoreans had done before him, a prerogative position to the numbers from 2 to 10. We should know from the *Metaphysics* only that some members of the Academy did so,[1] but in *Phys.* 206[b]32 Aristotle says that Plato 'makes number extend to the number 10'. We must, however, not take this too literally; Plato cannot have supposed that a group of eleven members is not characterized by eleven-ness, as much as a group of ten by ten-ness. But he saw that he must stop his 'generation' of numbers somewhere, and he naturally stopped at the limit suggested by the Greek system of numeration, which is purely decimal. He may have thought that his procedure was further justified by the fact that within the series 2 to 10 there are already examples of the three types of number into which the Greeks divided numbers—2 and its powers, odd numbers, and products of an odd number multiplied by 2 or a power of 2;[2] thus he may have thought that if he could generate the numbers up to 10 he could generate all the numbers.

There is a further consideration which may well have led Plato to end his 'generation' of the numbers with the number 10. 1 was undoubtedly, for him, the formal principle of the ideal numbers; and according to one passage in which (as will be argued later[3]) he is referred to,[4] we read that 2 was the formal principle of the line, 3 that of the plane, 4 that of the solid. And in another passage in which it is at least probable that he is referred to,[5] not only is that stated, but also that 1 was the formal principle of reason, 2 that of science, 3 that of opinion, 4 that of sensation. He could account therefore both for the formal structure of the sensible world and for that of the mind without going beyond the sacred τετρακτύς of the Pythagoreans, $1+2+3+4 = 10$.

For the Greeks of Plato's time the term 'number' applied only

[1] 1073[a]20, 1084[a]12–[b]2.   [2] 1084[a]3–7, Philolaus (?) fr. 5.   [3] pp. 208–9.
[4] 1090[b]20–4.   [5] *De An.* 404[b]18–27; cf. pp. 214–5.

to natural numbers. They had no zero and no negative numbers, and they did not apply the name 'number' to fractions or to irrationals.[1] Thus it was the integers from 2 to 10 that Plato set himself to derive.

Aristotle ascribes to Plato, by name, the view that the numbers are οὐ συμβλητοί,[2] and he attacks this view by asking whether, then, the units in each number are also ἀσύμβλητοι or not, and by pointing out objections to either alternative.[3] The meaning of συμβλητός in Aristotle is 'comparable'; and in his view two things are comparable if and only if they are multiples of a single unit. His own view[4] is that the number 2 contains two units and the number 3 three units, so that the two numbers are obviously comparable.

This criticism is a complete mistake. When Plato described the numbers as incomparable (which we must take it from Aristotle that he did), by the number 2 he meant twoness and by the number 3 threeness; and it is no fancy, but the simple truth, that twoness is not a part of threeness. A group with three members has as part of itself a group with two members, but Plato is not speaking of groups but of universals, and what he says of universals is plainly true. The view, then, that numbers are incomparable has nothing to do with the special views which Plato later developed about the generation of the number series, or with the reduction of all Ideas to numbers; it is a necessary consequence of the recognition of twoness, threeness, &c., as Forms, to be distinguished from the groups which are simply exemplifications of these Forms. It is found as early as the *Phaedo*:[5]

Would you not be afraid to say that ten exceeded eight by, and by reason of, two, rather than by, and by reason of, manyness; or that two cubits exceed one cubit by a half, rather than by greatness? For there is the same liability to error in all these cases.—Very true.— Again, would you not be cautious of affirming that the addition of one to one, or the division of one, is the cause of two? You would loudly asseverate that you know of no way in which anything comes into

---

[1] The evidence for these limitations is well stated in Van der Wielen, *I.P.* 13–17.
[2] 1083^{a}34.
[3] 1080^{b}37–1083^{a}17.
[4] 1080^{a}30–3, 1081^{b}12–17.
[5] 101 b 4–c 7.

existence except by participation in its own proper essence, and that in the case of numbers you know of no cause of two except participation in duality—this is the only way to make two, and the participation in one is the way to make one.

It may be noted, though Aristotle does not mention the point, that something exactly corresponding to this is true of geometrical Ideas. These also are, in the same sense, incomparable. A particular square may be larger than a particular triangle, but squareness is not larger than triangularity; it is an indivisible unit, as every Idea is described in the *Philebus*[1] as being.

In *Met.* 1080ª17 Aristotle says that one view which may be held about the number series is that it has within it a distinction of before and after, and he elucidates this by the phrase 'each number being different in kind'; and in 1080ᵇ11 he says that some of the Platonists (and other passages make it clear that Plato himself is included) distinguished ideal from mathematical number as being that which has this characteristic. Plato recognized, in fact, that, while a particular group with two members differs, as such, from a group with three members only in size and not in nature, the ideal numbers are a series of different natures which display a growing degree of complexity as we pass from twoness to threeness, and so on. This recognition is quite independent of the generation of the numbers from the One and the great and small. It is a recognition of the plain fact that 2 is definable as the successor of 1, and 3 as the successor of 2, in the series of natural numbers.

Now in the *Nicomachean Ethics*[2] Aristotle says of 'those who introduced the doctrine of the Ideas' (which must of course include Plato himself) that 'they did not recognize Ideas of things in which there is a distinction of before and after; for which reason they did not set up an Idea of the numbers'. This has often been interpreted as meaning that they did not recognize Ideas of the separate numbers; but that would run counter to all that we learn from the *Metaphysics* about Plato's distinction of the ideal from the mathematical numbers. What Aristotle says is that the Platonists did not recognize *an* Idea of *the numbers*, an Idea,

[1] 15 a 1–b 2.   [2] 1096ª17.

that is to say, of number in general. This is a surprising statement.
Aristotle himself held something very similar to the principle
that over things which have a serial order there is no common
universal; he expresses this thought, with modifications which
need not concern us, in four passages—in *Met.* 999ᵃ6–10, in
E.E. 1218ᵃ1–10, in *De An.* 414ᵇ20–33, and in *Pol.* 1275ᵃ34–ᵇ5.
In the first of these passages he might be supposed to be speaking
merely dialectically (for the whole of Book B of the *Metaphysics* is
dialectical), and in the second to be speaking as one not yet con-
verted from Platonism; but the last two seem to express his
mature view. The underlying notion in them seems to be that a
truly generic nature must be one that is expressed equally, though
differently, in a diversity of species, and that this is true neither
of the nature of soul nor of that of constitution. Similarly, we may
suppose, some Platonists (we do not know whether Plato was
among them) held that number or plurality was not a genuine Idea,
because the successive numbers exhibit plurality only unequally.[1]

(B) We now turn to the first principles from which Plato derived the ideal numbers—the One and the great and small. The
entities to be 'generated' from the two principles are neither
'sensible numbers' (groups of two, three, &c., things) nor
'mathematical numbers' (the entities which mathematicians
speak of when they say 2 and 3 makes 5, without regard to any
particular groups of two or three things), but ideal numbers (i.e.
twoness, threeness, &c.). Plato made no attempt to 'generate'
oneness, but he believed, of course, in the existence of oneness, no
less than in that of twoness and threeness; it follows that the One
which he presupposed as a generating principle was simply oneness, the Idea of One.

As regards the 'great and small', Taylor made the ingenious
suggestion[2] that the phrase points to a method, known to the
Greeks *possibly* as early as the time of Plato,[3] of arriving at

[1] On the subjects dealt with in the last four pages, and on many other aspects of
Platonic doctrine, a flood of light was thrown by Cook Wilson's article *On the
Platonist Doctrine of the ἀσύμβλητοι ἀριθμοί*, in *Class Rev.* xviii (1904), 247–60.

[2] In *Mind* xxxv (1926), 419–40 and xxxvi (1927), 12–33, reprinted in *P.S.* 91–150.

[3] Though the earliest mention of it is in Theo Smyrnaeus (*fl. c.* A.D. 115–40)
(ed. Hiller, pp. 42.10–45.8).

approximations to the value of √2 by approaching its value alternately from the side of the too little and from that of the too great. They set out a column of 'side-roots' and a corresponding column of 'diagonal-roots'. The first number in each column was 1. Each subsequent side-number was formed by adding to the previous side-number the corresponding diagonal-number; each subsequent diagonal number was formed by adding to the previous diagonal-number *twice* the corresponding side-number. Thus we have

Side-numbers	Diagonal-numbers
1	1
2	3
5	7
12	17
29	41
70	99
⋮	⋮

It can easily be verified that $\frac{1}{1}, \frac{3}{2}, \frac{7}{5}, \frac{17}{12}, \frac{41}{29}, \frac{99}{70}$ are successively closer approximations to the value of √2, alternately less and greater than it. Taylor thought that Plato knew this method,[1] and that it suggested to him the use of the phrase 'the great and small' for the material principle in the generation of the integers. Taylor failed, however, to show that the side and diagonal numbers have anything to do with the great and small. There is no real connexion between the evaluation of surds and the derivation of integers, except one which is fatal to Taylor's interpretation, viz. that the evaluation of surds *presupposes* the existence of the integers; none of the ancients who wrote about the great and small suggest any connexion, nor do those who describe the method of evaluating surds use the phrase 'the great and small'; and when Taylor comes to the actual generation of the integers, it is only with regard to the generation of the odd numbers that he makes use of the joint approach from below and from above. His explanation of the 'great and small', therefore, cannot be accepted;[2] but on the merits and demerits of Plato's actual

---

[1] He certainly knew that $\frac{7}{5}$ is an approximation to the value of √2 (*Rep.* 546 c 4–5), and Heath (*Hist. of Gk. Math.* i. 93) thinks the method was Pythagorean.

[2] I have discussed it at length in Ross and Fobes, *Theophrastus' Metaphysica*, 50–4.

derivation of the integers, and of Aristotle's criticism of it, he says much that is true and important.

Aristotle sometimes speaks of 'the great and small', but oftener of 'the great and the small'. The difference is important; the second phrase suggests two principles, the first a principle having two characteristics. Though he sometimes presses the second alternative,[1] there can be no doubt that the first represents Plato's meaning. The best clue Aristotle gives to this is given in *Phys.* 206^{b}27, where he says: 'Plato made the indeterminates dual, because they are supposed to exceed all limits and to proceed *ad infinitum* in the direction both of increase and of reduction.' A similar account is given by a Platonist of the first generation, Hermodorus, quoted in Simplicius' commentary on the *Physics*.[2] But we must look also to Plato himself. We have found in the *Philebus*[3] the distinction between the unlimited and limit, and we have found the unlimited described by the phrases 'the more and less' and 'the greater and smaller'.[4] We have found him saying of 'everything now in the world'[5] that it both has a character of its own (e.g. that of being temperature[6]) which may exist in any degree, and a definite degree of that character. There was no reference there to numbers. But we must suppose that he came similarly to distinguish bare plurality from definite degrees of plurality; and 'the great and small' is simply another name for what one of his followers[7] called, perhaps more happily, πλῆθος, bare plurality. We can see now the justification for Aristotle's statement[8] that Plato thought the elements of the numbers were also the elements of all other things. In his study of the numbers Plato found them to presuppose the same two elements—limit (which he now calls the One) and the unlimited (now called the great and small)—into which he had in the *Philebus* analysed sensible phenomena.

There has been much discussion of the rather unimportant question whether Plato used the phrase 'the indefinite dyad' as a name for the material principle in the generation of the num-

---

[1] 1083^{b}23-8, 1087^{b}12-16; *Phys.* 203^{a}15, 206^{b}27-8.

[2] 247.30-248.18.   [3] 23 c 4-26 c 2.

[4] 24 a 9, c 5, 25 c 9.   [5] 23 c 4.

[6] 24 a 7.   [7] Probably Speusippus.   [8] *Met.* 987^{b}18-20.

bers. Aristotle nowhere explicitly ascribes the phrase to him, as he does the phrase 'the great and small'.[1] But he uses the complex phrase 'those who make the dyad an indefinite composed of great and small',[2] which at least suggests that Plato used both phrases; and other passages point in the same direction.[3] Theophrastus, Hermodorus, Alexander, Simplicius, Syrianus, and Asclepius use the phrase freely in describing Plato's doctrine. 'The indefinite dyad' is simply a name for the unlimited as being capable of being indefinitely great and indefinitely small.[4]

The fullest account of the line of thought from which the One and the indefinite dyad emerged as the supreme principles from which numbers, Ideas, points, lines, planes, tridimensional figures, and bodies were successively derived is given by Sextus Empiricus.[5] All things (τὰ ὄντα) were divided into three groups: (1) absolutes, like man, horse, plant, earth, water, air, fire; (2) contraries, such as good and bad, just and unjust, advantageous and disadvantageous, holy and unholy, pious and impious, in movement and at rest, health and disease, pain and painlessness, life and death; (3) relatives, like right and left, up and down, double and half, greater and smaller, more and less, sharp and flat (in pitch). The second group was distinguished from the third by two characteristics: (a) the genesis of one of two contraries is the destruction of the other, while the destruction of one of two relatives is the destruction of the other; (b) there is always a mean between relatives, but never a mean between contraries. The One, i.e. oneness, was treated as the generic nature of everything in the first group; i.e. being the single thing that it was was the common character of every self-subsisting thing. The equal and the unequal were the genera under which all contraries fell, e.g. rest fell under the equal because it does not admit of differences of degree, movement fell under the unequal because it admits of such differences. Relatives fell under the genus of excess and defect. But while the equal and the unequal together formed the genus under which contraries fell, the equal itself fell under the

---

[1] In 987[b]20, 26, 988[a]13, 26.   [2] In 1088[a]15.
[3] 987[b]25-7, 33, 988[a]13, 1083[b]23-36, 1090[b]32-1091[a]5.
[4] Cf. Robin, *T.p.I.N.* 641-54 and my note on *Met.* 1081[a]14.
[5] *Adv. Math.* x. 258-83.

genus of the One (because the equality of the One with itself is the primary case of equality), and the unequal fell under the heading of excess and defect. Finally, excess and defect fell under the indefinite dyad, because excess and defect involve two things of which one exceeds the other. Thus the One and the indefinite dyad emerged (ἀνέκυψαν)[1] as the supreme principles of all things. The scheme is accurately represented by Wilpert[2] as follows:

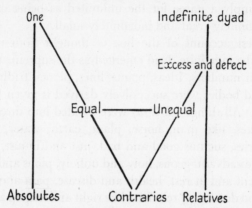

Sextus' account is vague as to the authorship of this scheme. At the beginning of the passage he speaks of Plato, but later of Pythagoras, the Pythagoreans, and 'the children of the Pythagoreans'. And in two respects the scheme he presents is unplatonic. He speaks of the indefinite dyad as itself derived from the One by the addition of the One to itself,[3] whereas Aristotle's account makes it abundantly clear that the indefinite dyad was an independent principle. And he speaks of the One as derived from the 'first unit',[1] whereas Aristotle's account makes it clear that for Plato there was no such distinction—the One was a first principle, and there was no suggestion of a derived One. But there are two pieces of evidence which show that the scheme Sextus sets out is in the main Platonic. His account appears in an abbreviated form in a passage[4] in which Simplicius quotes the account of Plato's doctrine given by a Platonist of the first generation, Hermodorus; and a part of it appears in Alexander's

---

[1] *Adv. Math.* x. 276.
[2] *Z.a.F.I.* 191.
[3] *Adv. Math.* x. 261.
[4] *In Phys.* 247.30–248.18.

account[1] of the One and the great and small, which he claims
to derive from Aristotle's *De Bono*,[2] i.e. from Aristotle's account
of Plato's lectures on the Good. That the theory is not Pythagorean is confirmed by the fact that Aristotle distinctly says[3] that
the substitution of the great and small for the indefinite was one
of the points which distinguished Plato's view from the Pythagorean.[4] It seems clear that in the main Sextus is describing Plato's
line of thought; his reference to the Pythagoreans is only one
example of a very general tendency in late Greek writers to find
Pythagoreanism everywhere.[5]

(C) We must now examine the method of the generation of the
numbers. There is a passage in Plato which offers a 'generation'
of the numbers. In the 'second hypothesis' of the *Parmenides*, in
which he reasons to the *positive* conclusions that may be deduced
from the assumption that there is a One, he argues as follows:[6]
If there is a One, its being is different from its unity, so that we already
have two things. And the difference of its being from its unity is different
from either its unity or its being, so that we already have three things.
And three is odd, two even. And if there are two and three, there must
be twice and thrice. And if there are two and twice, and three and
thrice, there must be twice two and thrice three. And if there are three
which occur twice and two which occur thrice, there must be twice
three and thrice two. Thus there will be even multiples of even sets,
odd multiples of odd sets, odd multiples of even sets, and even multiples
of odd sets. That being so, there must be no number left which must
not necessarily be. Therefore if a One is, there must be number.

This proof is rather perfunctory, since it makes no provision for
prime numbers other than 2 and 3. If we are right in our view
of the 'second part' of the *Parmenides*, the argument is an exercise
in dialectic rather than exposition of doctrine; and in any case

---

[1] *In Met.* 56.13-18.   [2] Ibid. 33-5.   [3] 987b25-7.

[4] There are interesting points of contact between Sextus' account and the
Categories, which considers the questions, which of the categories admit of degree
(3b33-4a9, 6a19-25, b20-6, 10b26-11a14), and whether the existence of one of
two correlatives involves the existence of the other (7b15-8a12). The distinction
between relatives and contraries, and the question which contraries admit of a
mean, reappear in the later part of the *Categories* (the Post-predicaments), in
11b32-12a25. This confirms the view that the line of thought recounted by Sextus
is Academic, not Pythagorean. The point is well argued by C. J. de Vogel in
Mnemosyne, ii (1949), 205-16.

[5] For which cf. G. C. Field, *P.C.* 175-6.   [6] 143 a 4-144 a 5.

the 'generation' of numbers here offered bears no resemblance to that about which Aristotle informs us. It makes no use of principles answering to the One and the great and small, but produces the numbers by the ordinary processes of addition and multiplication.

Aristotle tries to show[1] that the generation ascribed to the Idea-numbers was a generation in time, but this interpretation may be firmly set aside, and is probably mere dialectic on his part. What Plato offered was a logical deduction of numbers, stated in temporal terms 'in order to assist contemplation of their nature.'[2] In other words, he was distinguishing two elements in the being of every ideal number—pointing out that twoness, for instance—a group's being a group of two—involved its being (a) a plurality and (b) a definite plurality. The implication of these two elements in its being he described metaphorically as its generation from the great and small, which made it a plurality, and the One, which made it the particular plurality it was.

Aristotle says[3] that Plato's reason for making the second of the generative principles a dyad was that the numbers ἔξω τῶν πρώτων could be aptly generated out of a dyad as out of a plastic material. This statement is difficult to interpret; the difficulty is that of understanding what is meant by οἱ πρῶτοι ἀριθμοί. Aristotle often uses the phrase to designate Plato's ideal, as opposed to mathematical, numbers, but plainly that cannot be the meaning here, where it is precisely the generation of the ideal numbers that is in question. Taylor suggested[4] that 'except the first numbers' means 'except 1 and 2', and Becker[5] holds that, with or without the insertion of καί before ἔξω, the words mean 'beyond the first numbers' (1 and 2); but these interpretations are open to the objection that for the Greeks 1 was not a number but the 'first principle of number',[6] and Taylor's interpretation is open to the further objection that, so far from being something that could not be aptly generated from the first principles, the

---

[1] 1091ª23–9. [2] 1091ª28–9. [3] 987ᵇ33–988ª1.
[4] In *Mind*, xxxvi (1927), 22–3 (=*P.S.* 135–6).
[5] O. Becker, in *Quellen u. Studien zur Geschichte der Mathematik, Astronomie u. Physik*, Abt. B, i. 4 (1931), 483 n.
[6] Cf. 1088ª6–8.

number 2 offers the first and most obvious example of such derivation.[1]

Toeplitz[2] thinks that the products of the One and the great and small were not numbers but ratios, and that the meaning is that the ratios, except those that were between numbers prime *relatively to one another*, could be aptly generated from ratios between numbers that *were* prime relatively to one another, e.g. the ratios 2 : 4, 3 : 6, 4 : 8 from the ratio 1 : 2. But both Plato and Aristotle have the perfectly good word λόγος for ratio, and there is no reason to suppose that they could have used ἀριθμός in that sense.[3]

The meaning 'ideal' being excluded, the only other natural interpretation of πρῶτοι here is 'prime'; it is the standing word for 'prime' in Greek arithmetic. But prime numbers are not the only ones that cannot, in Aristotle's view, be aptly derived from the One and the great and small; since for him the great and small is essentially a duplicator, only 2 and its powers can be aptly derived from it.[4] The numbers that cannot be aptly so derived fall into three groups: (a) prime odd numbers, (b) non-prime odd numbers, (c) multiples of an odd and an even number. It has been proposed to emend the passage by reading περιττῶν 'odd', or to interpret πρώτων as meaning 'odd', so as to cover cases (a) and (b) alike. The omission of any reference to (c) would not in itself be fatal to these suggestions; Aristotle's meaning might be that if once the odd numbers could be generated, the generation of their even multiples would offer no new difficulty. But there is no external evidence for the emendation, and no parallel in Greek literature for the interpretation. We are driven, then, to suppose that Aristotle means 'except the primes'.

In that case Aristotle overlooks cases (b) and (c). Even this omission is not very serious; his meaning may be that if Plato could have derived the prime numbers, as well as 2 and its powers, from his principles, the composite numbers would have offered

[1] 1081ᵃ23–5, 1083ᵇ23–5, 1091ᵃ9–12.
[2] O. Toeplitz, in *Quellen u. Studien*, &c. Abt. B, i. 1 (1929), 22.
[3] Plato has also for it the phrase πρὸς ἀριθμὸν ἀριθμὸς ἢ μέτρον πρὸς μέτρον (*Phil.* 25 a 8), which is inconsistent with the use of ἀριθμός alone in the same sense.
[4] 1091ᵃ9–12.

no difficulty; 6 could be generated from 3, and 10 from 5, as 2 would already have been generated from 1, and 9 from 3 as 3 would have been already generated from 1.

It might be objected to this interpretation of πρώτων that 2, which Aristotle repeatedly describes as the first number generated by Plato, is itself a prime number. But Van der Wielen[1] is probably right in suggesting that Plato followed a Pythagorean classification in which prime numbers were a subdivision of odd numbers and 2 was not a prime number.[2]

The generation of the number 2 is described by Aristotle as follows:

1081ᵃ23, 'The units in the ideal 2 are generated at the same time, whether, as the first holder of the theory held, from unequals (coming into being when these were equalized) or in some other way.'

1083ᵇ23, 'Does each unit come from the great and small when these are equalized, or one from the small, the other from the great?'

Ibid. 30, 'If each of the two units' (in the ideal 2) 'proceeds from both the great and the small, equalized. . . .'

Ibid. 35, 'The function of the indefinite dyad was to double.'

1091ᵃ10, 'The great and the small cannot in any way generate number other than that got from 1 by doubling.'

Ibid. 24, 'Some thinkers present even number as produced first from unequals—the great and small—when these are equalized.'

The passage from 2 to 4 is thus described:

1081ᵇ21, 'They say 4 came from the ideal 2 and the indefinite 2; it was two 2's other than the ideal 2.'

1082ᵃ13, 'The indefinite 2, as they say, received[3] the definite' (i.e. ideal) '2 and made two 2's; for its nature was to double what it received.'

Ibid. 33, 'The units in the ideal 2 generate the four in 4.'

The passage from 4 to 8 is thus described:

1082ᵃ28, 'Let the 2's in 4 have no order of priority; yet these are prior to those in 8, and as 2 generated them, they generated the 4's in the ideal 8.'

---

[1] *I.P.* 131.

[2] Nicomachus, *Introductio Arithmetica*, 1. ii. 2.

[3] 'Received', not took; for the rôle of the great and small was passive, akin to that of the female in copulation, or that of a plastic material (988ᵃ2–7).

Aristotle has much less to say about the generation of numbers other than 2 and its powers. What he says is as follows:

1083ᵇ28, 'How is it with the units in the 3 itself? One of them is an odd unit. But perhaps it is for this reason that they give the 1 itself the middle place in odd numbers.'

1084ᵃ36, 'This is why they identify the odd with 1; for if oddness depended on the number 3, how would 5 be odd?'[1]

1091ᵃ23, 'These thinkers say there is no generation of the odd numbers.'

Robin offers two alternative accounts. In his first, provisional, account[2] he supposes two processes to have been at work—duplication and the addition of 1. But in his further consideration of the matter[3] he substitutes for the second of these processes one of splitting a difference; he supposes that in certain cases an upward movement from a smaller number met a downward movement from a larger number, and both movements were arrested halfway and an intermediate number was produced. While Taylor thinks the use of the term 'great and small' is in some way connected with the method of evaluation of roots by alternative approach from below and from above, he sees that this has no *close* connexion with the generation of integers, and in his account of the latter he follows Robin, but adds one new point. In some of the passages we have quoted,[4] Aristotle describes the numbers as produced by equalization of the great and the small; and Taylor explains this by reference to a passage in the *Ethics*[5] where Aristotle, considering a case in which one party has wronged another, so that the one has more and the other less than he should, describes the judge as 'equalizing' by putting both parties into a position intermediate between that of the gainer and that of the loser. Here, then, equalizing means splitting the difference, and Taylor holds that it is by a similar process that 3, 5, 7, and 9 are produced from 2 and 4, from 4 and 6, from 6 and 8, and from 8 and 10 respectively. This suggestion is, however,

---

[1] The meaning of this is very obscure.

[2] *T.p.I.N.* 280–2.   [3] pp. 442–50.

[4] 1081ᵃ25, 1083ᵇ24, 31, 1091ᵃ25; in 1081ᵃ24 the phrase is assigned explicitly to Plato.

[5] 1132ᵃ6–10, 24–30.

put out of court by the fact that it is only in connexion with 2 and its powers, which are produced not by splitting a difference but by doubling, that Aristotle uses the word 'equalize'.

Taylor suggests some minor variations of Robin's second suggestion, but in the end expresses a preference for that suggestion itself.[1]

These interpretations are open to certain objections. (1) It is unlikely that Plato, who insisted that the ideal numbers had a fixed order,[2] would have produced them in any other than their natural order, and in particular that he would have brought in the sacred number 10 in any position other than the final one. Aristotle has much to say in criticism of the Platonic theory, but he nowhere complains that it produced the numbers in an unnatural order, and in two passages he seems to imply the opposite. In 1081^a17–29 he argues as follows: 'If the units are incomparable each with each, the number-series so produced (i) cannot be mathematical number, since this consists of comparable units, and (ii) cannot be ideal number, since the number 2 will not be the first product of the One and the indefinite dyad, and be followed by the successive numbers as it is said—2, 3, 4—because the first of the two units in 2 will be prior to 2.' If (as the argument seems to imply) 'as it is said' means 'as the Platonists say', the passage indicates that the numbers were generated in their natural order (though not every number was necessarily generated *from* the immediately previous one). The same conclusion is suggested by 1080^a33–5, 'ideal number is counted thus— after 1, a distinct 2 which does not include the first 1, and a 3 which does not include the 2, and the rest of the number-series similarly'.

It is so improbable that Plato would have generated the numbers in any other than the natural order that one is tempted to suggest a variant on Robin's first interpretation, in which by the alternate use of multiplication and addition the numbers can be generated in their natural order. Robin's two suggestions and this third suggestion may be set out as follows:

---

[1] *Mind*, xxxvi (1927), 19–20 (= *P.S.* 131–2).
[2] 1080^b12.

A	B	C
$1 \times$ ind. $2 = 2$ ⎫	$1 \times$ ind. $2 = 2$ ⎫	$1 \times$ ind. $2 = 2$ a
$2 \times$ ind. $2 = 4$ ⎬ a	$2 \times$ ind. $2 = 4$ ⎬ a	$2+1 = 3$ b
$4 \times$ ind. $2 = 8$ ⎭	$4 \times$ ind. $2 = 8$ ⎭	$2 \times$ ind. $2 = 4$ a
$2+1 = 3$ ⎫	$\dfrac{2+4}{2} = 3$ c	$4+1 = 5$ b
$4+1 = 5$ ⎬ b		$3 \times$ ind. $2 = 6$ a
$8+1 = 9$ ⎭	$3 \times$ ind. $2 = 6$ a	$6+1 = 7$ b
$3 \times 2 = 6$ ⎫	$\dfrac{4+6}{2} = 5$ ⎫	$4 \times$ ind. $2 = 8$ a
$5 \times 2 = 10$ ⎭ a		$8+1 = 9$ b
$6+1 = 7$ b	$\dfrac{6+8}{2} = 7$ ⎬ c	$5 \times$ ind. $2 = 10$ a
	$5 \times$ ind. $2 = 10$ a	
	$\dfrac{8+10}{2} = 9$ c	

('ind. 2' = the indefinite dyad, a stands for multiplication, b for addition, c for splitting a difference. In none of these schemes is any number used in the generation of another unless it has first itself been generated.)

If addition was used at all, it is probable that it was used as in C rather than as in A. But (2) each of these three schemes is open to the objection that it uses two different methods for the generation of different numbers; we should have expected Plato to use a single method. At this point we may consider (i) A and C together, and (ii) B.

(i) Did Plato use addition at all, in his generation of the numbers? Aristotle's testimony on this point is difficult to interpret. In 1081^{b}12–20 he says, 'Whether the units are undifferentiated or different each from each, number must be counted by addition, e.g. 2 by adding to 1 another 1, 3 by adding another 1 to the 2, and 4 similarly. This being so, numbers cannot be generated as the Platonists generate them, from the 2 and the 1; for 2 becomes part of 3, and 3 of 4, and the same happens in the case of the succeeding numbers.' This suggests that in the Platonic scheme 3 was *not* produced by adding 1 to 2, and in fact that addition was not used at all. On the other hand in 1083^{b}28–30 Aristotle says, 'How is it with the units in the ideal 3? One of them is an odd unit. But perhaps it is for this reason that they give 1 itself the middle place in odd numbers.' This suggests that the odd numbers *were* produced by adding 1 to the previous even numbers.

We may feel sure, however, that Plato did not produce the odd numbers by adding 1 to even numbers; for to do so would be to treat the One as part of the 'material' of the odd numbers, whereas it is clear that he treated it as a formal principle pure and simple. We must reject schemes A and C alike, and suppose that in the last-quoted passage Aristotle is speaking not of Plato but of some dissentient member of his school.

(ii) There is nothing in the accounts given by Aristotle or by the ancient commentators which definitely supports scheme B. The nearest approach to such support is to be found in the passage of the *Physics*[1] which says 'Plato made the indeterminates two in number, because they are supposed to exceed all limits and to proceed *ad infinitum* in the direction *both of increase and of diminution*'; but that cannot be said to give very definite support to scheme B. More probably it is only a way of saying that by 'the great and small' Plato meant indefinite plurality, ranging from 2 to infinity. Scheme B cannot be rejected outright, but neither can it be said to be definitely established.

A new line of interpretation was opened up by Stenzel in his book *Zahl und Gestalt*. He starts[2] from a typical example of the method of division preached and practised in the *Sophistes* and *Politicus*:

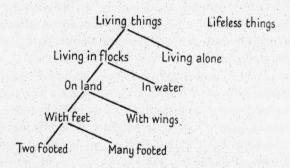

where the class of lifeless things could, of course, be dichotomized as Plato dichotomizes that of living things. Then[3] on the analogy

---

[1] 206[b]27.   [2] p. 11.   [3] p. 31.

of this diagram he offers the following diagram as representing Plato's generation of the numbers:

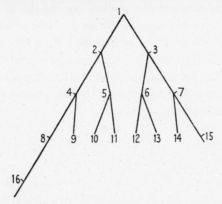

Stenzel's account is so vague that it is impossible to see exactly what his theory is. His whole treatment of the problem is open to fatal objections. (*a*) It is based on the assumption that Plato's derivation of the numbers is to be explained by reference to the method of διαίρεσις expounded and illustrated in the *Sophistes* and the *Politicus*. But there is no real analogy between the two diagrams he uses to illustrate his theory. The numbers 2 and 3 are not species of the genus 1, as living things and lifeless things are species of the genus 'things that come into being'. (*b*) In all that Aristotle says about the matter—and it must be remembered that Aristotle is our only original authority for the Platonic derivation of the numbers—there is no suggestion that διαίρεσις has anything to do with it. What Aristotle says is that the One was the formal element, and the great and small the quasi-material element, in the generation of the numbers. What this suggests, as the starting-point of Plato's derivation of the numbers, is not διαίρεσις at all, but the πέρας and the ἄπειρον of the *Philebus*; Stenzel entirely ignores this clue. (*c*) He ignores the detailed hints which Aristotle gives about the derivation of particular numbers.[1]

Stenzel's view was considerably improved upon by O. Becker,[2]

[1] For a fuller criticism of Stenzel's view, cf. Van der Wielen, *I.P.* 220–4.
[2] In *Quellen u. Studien zur Geschichte der Mathematik, Astronomie u. Physik*, Abt. B, i. 4 (1931), 464–501.

who, however, followed him in supposing the derivation of the numbers to have been by dichotomy. He thinks that by the 'generation' of the number 2 Plato meant the dichotomy of a generic Idea into two specific Ideas. For the production of the powers of 2 he relies on further dichotomy. He illustrates the production of 2, 4, 8 by the following diagram,[1] where the filled-in circles stand for the units produced by dichotomy, and the empty circles for units which are produced by dichotomy and cancelled by further dichotomy:

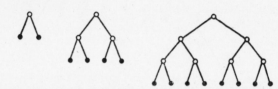

He sees that the number 3 could not be produced, as in Stenzel's hypothesis, by the same dichotomy which yields the number 2, and for the production of 3 and of other odd numbers he relies on further dichotomy of *one* of the units produced by a previous dichotomy:[2]

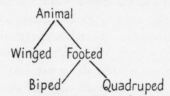

This he illustrates by the following division of the genus animal:

Animal

Winged   Footed

Biped   Quadruped

The main lines of Becker's view are laid down in the following propositions: 'Thus there lies before us a dichotomy in which not the numbers themselves but the units in the numbers are the members.'[3] 'It is these units that correspond to the Ideas.'[4] 'The halving of a monad is according to the Platonic doctrine nothing other than the division of a genus into two differentiae.'[2] 'That which in the ideal number and in the chain of Ideas is compared

[1] *Quellen u. Studien*, &c., p. 462.   [2] Ibid. 468.   [3] Ibid. 467.   [4] Ibid.

is the single units in the number and the single Ideas in the chain. To the whole ideal number corresponds the whole definition, and therewith the definiendum as a whole.'[1] His theory, then, seems to be that Plato was led to his identification of Ideas with numbers by recognizing that as the being of any Idea except a *summum genus* involves a generic element and one or more differentiae, so the being of any number involves two or more units. A *summum genus*, which cannot be analysed into a generic and a differential element, would be represented by 1; a class-Idea including a generic and one differential element (e.g. 'animal with feet') would be represented by the number 2, one with a generic and two differential elements by the number 3, and so on. That seems to be what Becker at one time says. But in the diagrams reproduced above, the number 2 answers not to an Idea with a generic and one differential element, but to a class divided into two species, the number 4 to a class divided into four subspecies, the number 8 to a class divided into eight sub-sub-species; and again the number 3 not to an Idea with a generic and two differential elements, but to a genus divided into one species and two sub-species of another species. Thus Becker seems not to have made up his mind whether a number answers to the totality of the elements in a single Idea or to the totality of classes into which a genus is divided.

The fundamental part of his theory is, however, that 'to the Ideas in the dichotomic scheme (the chain of Forms) answer the units of the ideal numbers, not these numbers themselves'.[2] In other words, an ideal number is not a single Idea, but a group o Ideas, each of which answers to one of the units involved in the ideal number (or rather, presupposed by it, since it is clear that in Plato's view an ideal number did not *contain* units); an ideal number is a 'number of Ideas' in the sense of a group of Ideas. In support of this thesis Becker quotes a number of passages[3] in which ἀριθμός in the singular occurs in conjunction with the plural of εἶδος or of ἰδέα. But an examination of these passages shows that in them ἀριθμός is used not of a particular ideal number

---

[1] Ibid. 473.   [2] Ibid. 467.
[3] 1080^{b}12, 1081^{a}21, 1083^{b}3, 6–7, 1090^{b}33, 37, *De Philosophia* fr. 9.

but of the whole range of ideal numbers, just as ὁ μαθηματικὸς ἀριθμός is used collectively of the mathematical numbers. This is pointed out by Van der Wielen,[1] who also shows[2] that certain other passages[3] relied on by Becker do not prove his point.

The main objections, however, to Becker's view are the same as those which apply to Stenzel's view—that it makes no attempt to explain the phrase 'the great and small' and the function of the great and small, which Aristotle describes as being (with the One) the basis of the whole theory of ideal numbers, that it ignores the many hints Aristotle gives about the method of generation of particular numbers, and that it links up the theory with the dichotomies of the *Sophistes* and the *Politicus*, and neglects its much more probable connexion with the 'limit' and the 'unlimited' of the *Philebus*. For all its great ingenuity, it seems that his theory cannot be accepted.

Another attempt at explanation of Plato's theory is that of O. Toeplitz,[4] who suggests[5] that 'Plato's mysterious Idea-numbers, the "indefinite pair" (the ἀόριστος δυάς) or, as he himself calls it, the "great and small" (the μέγα καὶ μικρόν) are the epistemological incarnation of the mathematical "ratios" (λόγοι)—that α : β is the indefinite pair, which can appear under the most different phenomenal forms, perhaps as ratio of the most different pairs of whole numbers, or of two planes, &c. Whether the precise meaning of the adjective ἀόριστος is that with the pair which represents the same λόγος one can nevertheless deal very differently, or that the two members of the pair, the great and small, themselves spring from the world of the unlimited, is a question which must for the present be postponed.'

As we have seen, Toeplitz's interpretation of the difficult passage *Met.* 987ᵇ33–988ᵃ1 is that 'the different pairs of quantities which stand in the ratio 1 : 2, e.g. 2 : 4, 3 : 6, 4 : 8 . . . are the different copies of a single mould which binds them all into one concept, one ἕν, the λόγος or the "number" (in the new sense) 1 : 2'.[6]

---

[1] p. 235.   [2] pp. 235–6.
[3] *Phil.* 18 c 3–6; *Met.* 987ᵇ20–2, 1080ᵃ30–5, 1081ᵃ32–5, 1082ᵃ33–6, ᵇ23–6.
[4] *Quellen u. Studien zur Geschichte der Mathematik, Astronomie u. Physik*, Abt. B, i. 1 (1929), 3–33.   [5] Ibid. 10.   [6] Ibid. 22.

Thus apparently the indefinite dyad is ratio in general, 'the One' is a generic name for all possible ratios stated in their lowest terms, e.g. 1 : 2, 1 : 3, and the ideal numbers are ratios produced by the operation of the One on the indefinite dyad, i.e. 2 : 4, 3 : 6, &c., produced by the ratio 1 : 2; 2 : 6, 3 : 9, &c., produced by the ratio 1 : 3, and so on. Much in this is far from clear. The initial identification of 'the mysterious Idea-numbers' with the indefinite dyad is already a sign of confusion, since Aristotle's testimony distinguishes the two most clearly. Another sign of confusion is the description of the ratios stated in their lowest terms as the mould of which the Idea-numbers are copies.[1] This implies that Toeplitz takes Aristotle's ἐκμαγεῖον, which clearly in the context[2] means 'plastic material', to be a mould impressed on such a material. In general, there is great difficulty in discovering exactly what Toeplitz takes 'the One' and 'the great and small' to stand for. And, in addition, there is no evidence to show that in the time of Plato ἀριθμός could have been used to mean 'ratio', for which Plato has his own expressions, λόγος and πρὸς ἀριθμὸν ἀριθμός.[3]

One thing of value, however, that remains in Toeplitz's account is his reminder that the notion of ratio, to which Plato himself refers in the *Philebus*[4] in describing the nature of πέρας, may have played *some* important part in his theory of the Idea-numbers. To this possibility we shall return presently.[5]

Van der Wielen's account[6] of the generation of the Idea-numbers is based on a passage in Simplicius' commentary on the *Physics*,[7] in which, after referring to Plato's use, in his lectures on the Good, of the One and the great and small as elements in the constitution both of sensible things and of intelligible things (i.e. of the Idea-numbers), he goes on to say that Porphyry interpreted the doctrine as follows in his commentary on the *Philebus*:

Plato himself classes the more and the less, and the 'exceedingly' and the 'slightly' (τὸ σφόδρα καὶ τὸ ἠρέμα) as belonging to the class of the unlimited. For wherever these are present, advancing in respect of intensification and relaxation, that which shares in them does not come

[1] p. 22.   [2] 988ᵃ1.
[3] The former, *passim*; the latter in *Phil.* 25 a 8.
[4] 25 a 6–b 3, d 11–e 2.   [5] pp. 200–2.
[6] *I.P.* 118–37.   [7] 453.25–454.7.

to a stand and to a limit, but goes on to the indefiniteness of infinity. So, too, it is with the greater and the less, and with the great and the small, which Plato uses as their equivalents. Let us take some limited magnitude, e.g. a cubit, and let it be bisected; if we left the one half-cubit undivided, but divided the other and added it little by little to the undivided part, the cubit would have two parts, one diminishing and the other increasing, without limit. For in dividing the cubit we should never come to an indivisible part, since the cubit is a continuum and a continuum is divided into perpetually divisible parts. Such an unceasing process of cutting reveals a certain infinity enclosed within the cubit, or, rather, more than one, the one advancing towards the great and the other towards the small.

There is a passage[1] in which Aristotle envisages a similar division of a line as yielding an 'infinite by addition' and an 'infinite by division', and concludes by saying, 'It is for this reason that Plato also made the infinites two in number, because it is supposed to be possible to exceed all limits and to proceed *ad infinitum* in the direction both of increase and of reduction.'

On the basis of the Porphyry passage Van der Wielen suggests that Plato used a divided line, as he had done long before, to illustrate a philosophical doctrine. The line may be represented thus:

Aristotle describes the genesis of the ideal numbers as due to the One as the formal element and to the great and small as the material element. This Van der Wielen interprets as meaning that if $\Gamma\varDelta$ (which is capable of being divided at any point $\varPi_n$) be divided at its middle point $\varPi_1$, the form One, i.e. the ratio $1:1$, which is the ratio of $\Gamma\varPi_1$ to $\varPi_1\varDelta$, transforms the indeterminate ratio of $\Gamma\varDelta$ to $\varPi_n\varDelta$ into the determinate ratio $(2:1)$ of $\Gamma\varDelta$ to $\varPi_1\varDelta$, and thus generates the number 2. If $\varPi_1\varDelta$ be divided at its mid-point $\varPi_2$, the ratio $1:1$ of $\varPi_1\varPi_2$ to $\varPi_2\varDelta$ transforms the indeterminate ratio of $\Gamma\varDelta$ to $\varPi_n\varDelta$ into the determinate ratio $(4:1)$ of $\Gamma\varDelta$ to $\varPi_2\varDelta$, and thus produces the number 4; and a

[1] *Phys.* 206[b]3-29.

similar process will yield the ratio 8 : 1, and thus produce the number 8.

Van der Wielen's theory of the generation of the ideal numbers is in some ways the best of those that have been advanced. It is based on a very careful study of all the evidence in Aristotle and elsewhere. It makes full use of the important clue given by Plato when he identifies the 'limit' and the 'unlimited' of the *Philebus*, which are clearly the ancestors of the One and the great and small, with definite ratio and the absence of definite ratio.[1] But there remains a great gap in this account; it makes Plato generate only 2 and its powers.

In fact, however, by an exactly similar method Plato might have generated each number from its predecessor:

$$\Gamma \qquad\qquad\qquad\qquad \Pi^1 \quad\; \Pi^2 \qquad\qquad\qquad \Delta$$

If $\Gamma\Delta$ is divided at its mid-point Π^1, the ratio 1 : 1 of $\Gamma\Pi^1$ to $\Pi^1\Delta$ makes the ratio of $\Gamma\Delta$ to $\Pi^1\Delta$ to be 2 : 1 and thus generates the number 2. If $\Gamma\Delta$ be then divided at Π^2 so that the ratio of $\Gamma\Pi^2$ to $\Pi^2\Delta$ is 2 : 1, that makes the ratio of $\Gamma\Delta$ to $\Pi^2\Delta$ to be 3 : 1 and thus creates the number 3. And so *ad infinitum*.

Van der Wielen recognizes[2] the possibility of this method of generation of the numbers other than 2 and its powers, but sets it aside on the ground that it is inconsistent with the statement in *Met.* A. 6 that the One is the formal principle in the generation of *all* the numbers. But there is no inconsistency; the One is indeed the active principle in the generation of all the numbers, but that does not imply that it intervenes afresh at each stage; its function is to initiate the process, as the ratio 1 : 1 in fact does. Such a situation is just what Aristotle's criticism in A. 6[3] implies:

The theory is not a reasonable one. For they make many things out of the matter, and the form generates *only once*, but what we observe is that only one table is made from one matter, while the man who applies the form, though he is one, makes many tables. And the relation of the male to the female is similar; for the latter is impregnated by one copulation, but the male impregnates many females; yet these are analogues of those first principles.

[1] 24 e 7-25 b 3.   [2] *I.P.* 132-3.   [3] 988ª1-7.

Aristotle's criticism is that a single form operating on a single matter can produce only one result, while the Platonists generate many products from one matter though the form operates only once; and that is just what happens in a chain reaction such as we may suppose Plato to have had in mind. If we can accept Van der Wielen's interpretation of the One as the ratio 1 : 1, we can follow him in saying that the One, i.e. the ratio 1 : 1 between the two parts of the line, entails the ratio 2 : 1 between the whole line and one of its halves; and then the One need not intervene again, for the 2 will similarly entail the 3, and so *ad infinitum*.

This interpretation is not to be rejected on the ground of Aristotle's statement[1] that only the composite numbers could be aptly generated from Plato's two principles, or his statement[2] that 'the great and the small cry out against the attempt to generate from them numbers other than 2 and its powers', or his statement[3] that 'they say there is no generation of the odd numbers'; for he also says clearly that Plato claimed to generate *all* the ideal numbers. The first two statements imply only that Aristotle holds Plato's attempt to have failed when applied to prime numbers, or when applied to any number except 2 and its powers, and the third statement may well refer to some of Plato's followers, not to Plato.

Yet the positive evidence for Van der Wielen's ingenious interpretation is very slight. Porphyry does not say that Plato used a divided line in connexion with the ideal numbers; nor does Porphyry himself use it to illustrate the mode of their generation, but only to illustrate the meaning of 'the great and small'. There is, too, something rather naïve in the procedure of dividing a line in two and then using the ratio between the parts to generate the number 2; one is rather reluctant to ascribe this procedure to Plato. We may well look for another interpretation. We must examine Aristotle's evidence once more.

For Aristotle, the function of the One is to equalize,[4] and that of the great and small to double. As regards the former function, the word, or at least the idea behind it, must be Plato's own. For

---

[1] 987^{b}33–988^{a}1.   [2] 1091^{a}9–12.
[3] 1091^{a}23.   [4] 1081^{a}25, 1083^{b}24, 31, 1091^{a}25.

of the various phrases which Aristotle uses for the material principle of the numbers, 'the unequal' is one of those which seem
most clearly to go back to Plato himself,[1] and if so, the function
he assigned to the One must have been that of removing the inequality. But what does this mean? In what sense was the great
and small unequal? Aristotle thought it was because the great
and small were two things, which must be unequal because the
one was great and the other small. His view comes out most
clearly in *Phys.* 203[a]15 and 206[b]27, where he says, 'Plato made
the indefinites two in number'. But it is far more probable,
particularly in view of the undoubted descent of 'the great and
small' from 'the more and less' of the *Philebus*, that Plato did not
mean by it two things, but one thing, indefinite plurality, which
was called 'the unequal' simply because it was capable of being
particularized into unequal numbers ranging from 2 to infinity;
indeed, in one passage,[2] Aristotle complains that Plato 'treats the
unequal, or the great and small, as being one'. If Plato meant
by 'the unequal' indefinite plurality, the function of the One,
described as equalization, must have been that of imparting
definiteness, of imposing definite form on indefinite plurality.

We have no such guarantee that the expression 'doubling' for
the function of the great and small goes back to Plato. May it not
be that Aristotle's use of it is due to the same misunderstanding,
that of supposing Plato's great and small to be two things, not
one indefinite thing? If this supposition be right, the function of
the great and small was not strictly that of doubling (though its
first task was that of furnishing matter for the formation of the
number 2), but simply that of furnishing unlimited plurality on
which the One, the principle of definiteness, imposed successive
specifications and thus produced the successive numbers. In one
passage[3] Aristotle actually describes the great and small as
'giving plurality'.

If Plato had thought of the function of the great and small as
being simply that of doubling, the only number that could be
produced by the impact of the One on the great and small would

---

have been the number 2. The number 4 could then be described
as produced by the impact of the number 2 on the great and
small,[1] and the number 8 by the impact of the number 4 on the
great and small.[2] On this basis the only numbers that could be
produced would be 2 and its powers.[3] For the other numbers
Plato would have had to rely on some quite different method of
production; but it is most improbable that he would have used
fundamentally different methods for the production of different
numbers. It is surely more likely that he used a single method
—that the One, the principle of limit or definiteness, imposed
successive definite degrees on the indefinite manyness and indefinite fewness of the great and small. The number 2 had the
maximum of fewness, the minimum of manyness, the number
3 the next possible degree of fewness and of manyness; and so on.

It is probable, then, that Aristotle's account was radically
warped by a misconception of what Plato meant by the great and
small. It was also warped by Aristotle's failure to recognize the
truth of Plato's conception of an ideal number as not a sum of
units but itself a unitary Idea.[4] For such misconceptions Aristotle
was not entirely to blame; for the ancient authorities agree in
describing Plato's lectures on the Good as having left his hearers
guessing at their meaning. As evidence that there is a certain
amount of misunderstanding in Aristotle's account of Plato's
'generation of the numbers', one may point to two passages in the
Physics which have already been commented on.[5] It may also be
that some of Aristotle's criticisms are directed not against what
Plato had said, but against what Speusippus or Xenocrates
guessed him to have meant, or against some new 'generation of
the numbers' devised within the Academy; for in Metaphysics M
and N Plato is only once mentioned by name,[6] and of the passages in which the generation of particular numbers is described
only one[7] clearly refers to him.

What I suggest, then, is that in Plato's generation of the ideal
numbers the One answers exactly to the 'limit' of the Philebus,
and the great and small to the 'unlimited' of the Philebus. The

---

[1] 1081b21, 1082a13, 33.   [2] 1082a28-31.   [3] 1084a5-6.   [4] Cf. pp. 180-1.
[5] p. 147 supra.   [6] 1083a32.   [7] 1081a23-5.

successive numbers were the result of successive applications of limit or definiteness to unlimited plurality. A great deal of what Aristotle says will be due to his interpretation of the great and small as two things, a great and a small. From this follows his description of it not as supplying plurality but as 'doubling'. From this also follows his statement that the combination of the two principles cannot aptly generate the odd numbers, and his more extreme statement that it can only yield the number 2 and its powers. Much of what he says may be directed not against Plato but against Xenocrates, who, as Aristotle says, confused the ideal with the mathematical numbers, and may therefore have given a more mathematical type of generation of them than Plato did. He may well have spoken of 2 and its powers as produced by successive doublings, and it may be he who made the One the middle unit in odd numbers,[1] i.e. treated them as produced by adding 1 to the previous even numbers.

(D) The question of the relation of the ideal numbers to the Ideas in general can be considered better when we have first examined Plato's view of the 'things after the numbers', and of the relation between the Ideas and soul.

[1] 1083ᵇ29.

XIII

THE 'THINGS AFTER THE NUMBERS'

THERE are three passages in which Aristotle refers to a belief, held by some part of the Platonic school, in spatial entities as a class of things 'after the numbers' or 'after the Ideas':

992^{b}13–18, 'Nor can it be explained either how the lines, planes, and solids *that come after the numbers* exist or can exist, or what significance they have; for these can neither be Forms (for they are not numbers), nor the intermediates (for these are the objects of mathematics), nor the perishable things. This is evidently a distinct *fourth class*.'

1080^{b}23–8, 'The case of lines, planes, and solids is similar. Some think that those which are the objects of mathematics are different from *those which come after the Ideas*; and of those who express themselves otherwise some speak of the objects of mathematics and in a mathematical way—viz. those who do not make the Ideas numbers nor say that Ideas exist; and others speak of the objects of mathematics, but not mathematically.'

1085^{a}7–9, 'Similar difficulties occur with regard to *the classes of things posterior to number*—the line, the plane, and the solid.'

Aristotle's whole treatment of the Platonic school in Books M and N of the *Metaphysics* is based on a distinction between those who recognized the existence of Ideas, as distinct from the objects of mathematics, those who denied the existence of Ideas, and those who identified them with the objects of mathematics. We have already shown[1] (and this is, I believe, common ground for all students of the subject) that it was Plato who recognized the existence of all three entities, Speusippus who denied the existence of Ideas, and Xenocrates who identified them with the objects of mathematics. Thus neither Speusippus nor Xenocrates had three other classes, from which he could distinguish as a fourth class the things after the Ideas or after the numbers. This being so, each of the first two passages quoted above makes it plain that it was Plato who believed in the things 'after the numbers' or 'after the Ideas'.

[1] pp. 151–2.

Aristotle's usual account of Plato's doctrine is that he distinguished three types of entity—the Ideas, the objects of mathematics, and sensible things. The recognition of a fourth class, next after the Ideas in hierarchical order, must clearly have been a later development in Plato's thought. There are two passages of the *Metaphysics* which throw light on its origin.[1] In 1036ª26–ᵇ17 Aristotle points out that when a form is found in conjunction with a variety of materials, as the circular form may be found either in bronze, in stone, or in wood, it is easy to see that the material is no part of its essence; but that when a form is always combined with the same material, or set of materials, as that of man is with flesh and bones, it becomes doubtful whether the definition should contain a reference to the material. This difficulty, he adds, is felt by some people about the circle itself. It is debated whether spatial extension belongs any more to the essence of a line than bronze or stone does to.that of a statue, and some of the Platonists call duality the line itself, while others call it the Form of (i.e. only the formal element in) the line, because the line cannot be identified with what is only its formal element. And in 1043ª29–36 Aristotle alludes to the question whether the essence of the line is twoness embodied in length or simply twoness.

Up to a certain time, then, Plato was satisfied to distinguish simply between Ideas, mathematical objects, and sensible things;[2] but when he had identified the Ideas, or rather the highest, most abstract, Ideas, with numbers, he had to recognize a lower class of Ideas, each of which included in its very essence a reference to spatial extension as well as to number, so that the Idea of line, for instance, was 'twoness in length'. These Ideas were to the objects of geometry and to sensible spatial objects as the Idea-numbers were to the objects of arithmetic and to sensible numbered groups; they differed from mathematical objects by being unique, and from sensible objects both by being unique and by being eternal and unchangeable.

We have now to consider whether Plato assigned generative principles to these ideal 'magnitudes'; and we shall consider first

[1] The significance of these is very well brought out by Van der Wielen, in *I.P.* 144–7.   [2] 987ᵇ14–18, 1028ᵇ18–21.

the question of material principles. In the third of the passages in which these magnitudes are referred to,[1] and in two others,[2] Aristotle speaks of Platonists who treated the long and short as the material principle of the ideal line, the broad and narrow as that of the plane, the deep and shallow as that of the solid. In none of the passages is this doctrine expressly ascribed to Plato, but, as we have seen, it was Plato who believed in this 'fourth class'; further, in each passage it is pointed out that these material principles are forms of the great and small; and since the treatment of the great and small as the material principle of Idea-numbers is expressly ascribed to Plato, it is at least natural to suppose that it was he who held the corresponding view about lines, planes, and solids, and that as by the great and small he meant indefinite plurality, by the long and short he meant indefinite extension in one dimension, by the broad and narrow indefinite extension in a second dimension, and by the deep and shallow indefinite extension in a third dimension.

The conclusion that Plato was among those who held this view is confirmed by two other passages. In 1085[a]31–4 it is distinguished from another view which was pretty certainly that of Speusippus,[3] and in 1090[b]37–1091[a]1, a passage which certainly refers to Plato,[4] we are told that he generated spatial magnitudes from a great and small other than that from which he generated the Idea-numbers; this clearly refers to the long and short, the broad and narrow, the deep and shallow.

Apart from the two passages already considered[5] in which the number 2 is referred to as the formal cause of the line, the most explicit reference in the *Metaphysics* to *formal* causes assigned to the spatial entities by the Platonists is found in 1090[b]20–4, where Aristotle says: 'The believers in the Ideas derive spatial magnitudes from matter and number—lines from the number 2, planes doubtless from 3, solids from 4—or they use other numbers, which makes no difference.' This occurs in a passage[6] which is some-

---

[1] 1085[a]7–12.   [2] 992[a]10–13, 1089[b]11–14.

[3] Since in it the material principle of number is referred to as πλῆθος, which was probably his name for it.

[4] Οἱ πρῶτοι δύο τοὺς ἀριθμοὺς ποιήσαντες, 1090[b]32.

[5] 1036[b]12–17, 1043[a]29–36.   [6] 1090[b]20–32.

times taken[1] to refer solely to Xenocrates, but a closer examination shows this not to be the case. It begins with the words 'As for the believers in the Ideas, this difficulty passes them by'. Then, after the reference to the formative principles of the spatial entities, Aristotle continues:

But will these spatial magnitudes be Ideas, or what is their manner of existence, and what do they contribute to things? These contribute nothing, as the objects of mathematics contribute nothing. But not even is any theorem[2] true of them ⟨except for someone who chooses to tamper with the objects of mathematics and invent doctrines of his own. But it is not hard to assume any random hypotheses and spin out a long string of conclusions; these thinkers, then, in clinging *in this way* to the objects of mathematics as well as the Ideas, are in error⟩. Those who first posited two kinds of number, that of the Forms and that which is mathematical, neither have said nor can say how mathematical number is to exist and from what it is to be derived.

Here the phrase 'the believers in Ideas' includes both Plato and Xenocrates and marks them off from Speusippus, who has been dealt with in ᵇ13–20, and the assignment of the numbers 2, 3, 4 to the line, the plane, and the solid is ascribed to both. But the phrase, 'These contribute nothing, as the objects of mathematics contribute nothing', shows that Aristotle has *primarily* in mind a thinker who distinguished Ideas from the objects of mathematics, i.e. not Xenocrates but Plato. It is only in the passage I have enclosed in brackets that Xenocrates is exclusively referred to; and immediately after it Aristotle returns to Plato.

With this passage must be considered one from the *De Anima*:[3]

In the same way Plato in the *Timaeus* fashions the soul out of his elements; for like, he holds, is known by like, and things are formed out of the principles or elements.[4] (l. 18) Similarly also, ἐν τοῖς περὶ φιλοσοφίας λεγομένοις, it was set forth that the Living-Creature-itself is compounded of the Idea itself of the One together with the primary length, breadth, and depth, everything else being similarly constituted. (l. 21) Again in yet other terms, reason was said to be the One, science the dyad (because it goes undeviatingly to one point), opinion the number of the plane, sensation the number of the solid. For the

---

[1] e.g. by me formerly.
[2] i.e. any mathematical theorem.
[3] 404ᵇ16–27.
[4] *sc.* so that soul must be so too.

numbers were identified with the Forms themselves or principles, and
are formed out of the elements. (l. 25) Now things are apprehended
either by reason or by science or by opinion or by sensation, and these
same numbers are the Forms of things.

I have left the words ἐν τοῖς περὶ φιλοσοφίας λεγομένοις un-
translated, because their meaning is disputed. Some think they
refer to lectures of Plato on philosophy, and these have sometimes been identified with the lectures on the Good. Others think
they refer to Aristotle's dialogue *On Philosophy*, in which he stated
and commented on the most important doctrines of earlier philosophers, including Plato and his school. Van der Wielen[1] takes
the words in the former sense, and holds that the whole passage
refers to Plato; Prof. Cherniss[2] takes them in the latter sense, and
holds with equal conviction that the whole passage except the
first sentence refers to Xenocrates. The question whether ἐν τοῖς
περὶ φιλοσοφίας λεγομένοις means 'in Plato's lectures on philosophy' or 'in my *De Philosophia*' is not crucial; for even if the
latter view be right (as I think it is), the reference may well
be to Aristotle's report of Plato's doctrine.[3] The whole passage
404ᵇ16–27 reads more naturally if taken as referring throughout
to Plato; and it may be noted that when in ᵇ27–30 Aristotle comes
to mention a view which is certainly that of Xenocrates, he
marks the transition by saying 'some thinkers thought' so and so.

We have found, in *Met.* 1090ᵇ20–4, a passage which ascribes to
Plato what is recognizably the same view about lines, planes, and
solids. And there is a passage in Theophrastus[4] which confirms
the view that the whole of the *De Anima* passage refers to Plato.
The passage runs as follows:

Most people go to a certain point and then stop, as those do who set
up *the One and the indefinite dyad*; for after generating numbers *and
planes and solids* they leave out almost everything else, except to the
extent of just touching on them and making this much plain, that some
things proceed from the indefinite dyad, e.g. place, the void, and the

---

[1] *I.P.* 158–68.　　　　　　　　　　　　[2] *A.C.P.A.* 565–80.
[3] This is how Philoponus (75.34–76.1) takes the passage; Simplicius expresses,
more briefly, the same view (28.7–9). Themistius takes the passage to refer to the
views of Xenocrates (11.37–12.7), but also to those of Plato (12.28).
[4] *Met.* 6ᵃ23–ᵇ9.

infinite, and others *from the numbers and the One*, e.g. *soul* and certain other things . . . but of the heavens and the remaining things in the universe they make no further mention; and similarly the school of *Speusippus* does not do so, nor does any of the other philosophers except *Xenocrates*; for he does somehow assign to everything its place in the universe, alike objects of sense, objects of reason or mathematical objects, and divine things as well.

Here Plato is clearly referred to, in distinction from Speusippus and Xenocrates, in the earlier part of the passage, and a view both about spatial magnitudes and about the soul identical with that mentioned in the *De Anima* is ascribed to him.

Finally, that Plato did assign the numbers 2, 3, 4 to the line, the plane, and the solid is confirmed by the fact that these assignments occur in the passage of Sextus Empiricus[1] which we have seen good reason to regard as a summary of Platonic doctrine.[2]

What, then, is the view so far as lines, planes, and solids are concerned? It is that the Idea of line was derived from the number 2 and indefinite length, the Idea of plane from the number 3 and indefinite breadth, the Idea of solid from the number 4 and indefinite depth. To this we can assign an intelligible meaning. For Plato the objects of mathematics, those of arithmetic and of geometry alike, formed a whole, intermediate between Ideas and sensible things. It is natural, then, that he should have attempted a 'generation' of the Ideas of the geometrical entities, corresponding to that which he gave of the Ideas of numbers.

The system was at least a symmetrical one. The ideal numbers were derived from the One and the great and small, indefinite plurality. The Idea of line was derived from the number 2 and the long and short, indefinite length. The Idea of plane was derived from the number 3 and the broad and narrow, indefinite breadth. The Idea of solid was derived from the number 4 and the deep and shallow, indefinite depth. The Idea of line was 'twoness embodied in length',[3] twoness because two points determine the simplest line, the straight line. The Idea of plane was 'threeness embodied in breadth', threeness because three points determine the simplest plane figure, the triangle. The Idea of

---

[1] *Adv. Math.* 10.278–80.　　　[2] Cf. pp. 185–7 *supra*.　　　[3] 1043ᵃ34.

solid was 'fourness in depth', fourness because four points determine the simplest solid, the tetrahedron.

What, we may now ask, is the meaning of the words in the passage from the *De Anima*: 'The Living-Creature-itself is compounded of the Idea itself of the One together with the primary
length, breadth, and depth, everything else being similarly
constituted'? The doctrine which Aristotle is reporting evidently
ran on the same lines as that of the *Timaeus*. Now in the *Timaeus*[1]
the sensible world is called 'a living creature with soul and
reason'; and therefore the 'Living-Creature-itself' can hardly be
anything but the Idea after which, according to the *Timaeus*, the
Demiourgos modelled the sensible world. In view of Aristotle's
frequent use of the word πρῶτος to distinguish ideal from mathematical numbers, the 'primary length, breadth, and depth' will
be the Ideas of length, breadth, and depth. Thus the Idea of
the sensible world is a composite Idea, having as its elements the
Idea of One and the formal or ideal elements in the line, the
plane, and the solid, i.e. the Ideas of -2, 3, and 4. That is a
picturesque way of saying that number and three-dimensional
extension are the fundamental structural features of the sensible
world—a view which the *Timaeus* expounds at length. 'Everything else being similarly constituted' I take to mean that the
same elements that are present in the Idea of the sensible world
are present in the Idea of each of its parts—of each living creature, whether it be a star, an animal, or a plant.

The remainder of the *De Anima* passage I reserve for the next
chapter.

[1] 30 b 8.

XIV

THE IDEAS AND SOUL

THAT great Platonist, Léon Robin, held the view[1] that Plato assigns to soul a special affinity with the 'intermediates', the objects of mathematics. It is unlikely that Plato would have held so strange a view, and there is no evidence that he held it. Yet there is evidence for saying that Plato held the soul to be in some sense intermediate between Ideas and sensible things, as he held the objects of mathematics also (though for quite a different reason)[2] to be. There is a passage in the *Phaedo*[3] which describes the soul as akin to the Ideas and more real than bodies: 'The soul is most like the divine, immortal, intelligible, uniform, indissoluble, and unchangeable; whereas the body is most like the human, mortal, multiform, unintelligible, dissoluble, and perpetually changing.' There is the assertion in the *Sophistes*[4] that soul has true being, no less than the Ideas. There is the saying in the *Laws*[5] that 'soul is among the primal things, elder-born than all bodies and prime source of all their changes and transformations'. Above all there is the passage in the *Timaeus*[6] in which he assigns to soul forms of existence, sameness, and difference intermediate between those proper to Ideas and those proper to bodies. With this passage we may connect Aristotle's statement[7] that 'Plato in the *Timaeus* constructs the soul out of the elements; for like, he maintains, is known by like, and things are composed of the ultimate elements'. Robin supposes[8] the elements in question to be the One and the indefinite dyad, which would at once connect the soul with the ideal numbers. But the *Timaeus* says nothing about the One and the indefinite dyad; the only elements it assigns to soul are being, sameness, and difference. That it is of these that Aristotle is thinking is shown, too, by his statement that Plato's reason for assigning the same elements to soul as to sensible things is that

---

[1] *T.p.I.N.* 479–98. [2] *Met.* 987ᵇ14–18. [3] 80 a 10–b 5.
[4] 248 e 6–249 b 4. [5] 892 a 2–7. [6] 34 c 4–35 b 1.
[7] *De An.* 404ᵇ16–18. [8] *T.p.I.N.* 310.

like can only be known by like—precisely the reason Plato gives in the *Timaeus* passage[1] for ascribing being, sameness, and difference alike to Ideas, souls, and bodies. The argument is correctly summarized by Proclus:[2] 'Since the soul consists of three parts, Existence, Sameness, and Difference, in a form intermediate between the indivisible things and the divisible, by means of these she knows both orders of things . . . for all knowing is accomplished by means of likeness between the knower and the known.'

Later, however, Plato seems to have offered another account of the analogy between the soul and the objects of its awareness. Theophrastus tells us[3] that Plato derived the soul from the numbers and the One. And Aristotle, in the *De Anima*,[4] immediately after pointing out that in the *Timaeus* Plato used the principle of 'like knows like', goes on to say:

Similarly also ἐν τοῖς περὶ φιλοσοφίας λεγομένοις it was set forth that the Animal-itself is compounded of the Idea-itself of the One together with the primary length, breadth, and depth, everything else being similarly constituted. Again, it was put in another way: Reason is the monad, science the dyad (because it goes undeviatingly to a single conclusion), opinion the number of the plane, sensation the number of the solid. The numbers are expressly identified with the Forms themselves or principles, and are formed out of the elements; now things are apprehended either by reason or by science or by opinion or by sensation, and these same numbers are the Forms of things.

That Plato treated the numbers 2, 3, 4 as the formal principles of the line, the plane, and the solid, I have tried to show elsewhere.[5] And in this passage the assignment of 1, 2, 3, 4 to the mental faculties is so interlocked with the assignment of 2, 3, 4 to the line, the plane, and the solid that we are bound to suppose Aristotle here also to be referring to Plato. Reason was correlated with the One because it is the direct apprehension of a single Idea. Science was correlated with the number 2 because it goes from a single datum to a single conclusion (so Aristotle says), and the ancient commentators on the *De Anima* are therefore probably right in saying that opinion was correlated with the number 3 because it moves indifferently from a single datum either to a true or to a false conclusion;[1] alternatively it may have been correlated with the number of the plane[2] because, as from a point on a plane lines may be drawn in any direction, so from a single datum opinion may draw any one of a number of conclusions.

The reason given by the ancient commentators for the correlation of sensation with the number 4—that the objects in the sensible world are solids, and 4 was the number assigned to the solid—is not on the same lines as their account of the other correlations, but it derives support from a passage in the *Laws*:[3] 'The condition under which coming-to-be universally takes place—what is it? Manifestly it is effected whenever its starting-point has received increment and so come to its second stage, and from this to the next, and so by three steps acquires perceptibility to percipients.' This is Plato's way of saying that neither a point (ἀρχή), nor a line (ἀρχὴ λαβοῦσα αὐξήν), nor a plane (ὁπόταν εἰς τὴν δευτέραν ἔλθῃ μετάβασιν), but only a solid (ὁπόταν εἰς τὴν πλησίον μετάβασιν ἔλθῃ) is a possible object of perception.

In his latest phase, then, Plato established a correlation between four faculties of the soul and four types of geometrical object. Between sensation and the solid he recognized a direct correlation, treating one as the proper object of the other. Between reason and the point, between science and the line, between opinion and the plane, he recognized no direct correlation, but he correlated both reason and the point with its One, science and its line with its number 2, opinion and its plane with its number 3.

[1] *Philop.* 79.28; *Simp.* 29.6; *Them.* 12.9.   [2] i.e. 3.   [3] 894 a 1–5.

XV

THE IDEAS AND THE IDEAL NUMBERS

WE are now in a better position than we have hitherto been to consider the relation, in Plato's system, between the ideal numbers and the Ideas in general. On the one hand there is an imposing array of passages[1] in which Aristotle says, or clearly implies, that for Plato all the Ideas were numbers. On the other hand there is an important passage in which Theophrastus says[2] that the numbers (i.e. the ideal numbers) were more fundamental than the Ideas (i.e. the other Ideas). 'Plato in reducing things to the ruling principles might seem to be treating of the other things' (i.e. sensible things) 'in linking them up with the Ideas, *and these with the numbers,* and in proceeding from the numbers to the ruling principles.' There is here an apparent contradiction. Aristotle identifies the ideal numbers with Ideas in general; Theophrastus places the ideal numbers above the other Ideas, intermediate between them and the first principles, i.e. the One and the 'great and small'. *Prima facie,* Aristotle's evidence has more weight than that of Theophrastus, since Theophrastus probably learned from Aristotle what he knew about Plato's 'unwritten doctrines'. But Theophrastus' statement is very definite, and it receives support from a passage in which Sextus Empiricus says:[3] 'The Ideas, which are incorporeal, are according to Plato prior to bodies, and each of the things that come into being is modelled on them; but they are not the *first* principles of existing things, since while each Idea taken separately is said to be a unity, by virtue of its inclusion of another or other Ideas it is said to be two or three or four, so that there is something higher than their nature, namely number, by participation in which "one" or "two" or "three" or yet higher numbers are predi-

---

[1] *De An.* 404ᵇ24–5; *Met.* 987ᵇ18–25, 991ᵇ9–10, 992ᵇ13–18, 1073ᵃ17–19,1080ᵇ11–12, 1081ᵃ5–17, 1082ᵇ23–4, 1083ᵃ17–20, 1086ᵃ11–13, 1090ᵃ16–17, 1091ᵇ26, *De Phil.* fr. 9.

[2] *Met.* 6ᵇ11–14.

[3] *Adv. Math.* 10. 258. Attention has been called to this passage, and to what follows it, by P. Wilpert in *Zwei aristotelische Frühschriften über die Ideenlehre.*

cated of them.' Further, one of the passages in which Aristotle himself refers to the question casts some doubt on his identification of the Ideas with numbers: 'If the Ideas are not numbers, neither can they exist at all. For from what principles will the Ideas be derived? It is *number* that comes from the One and the indefinite dyad, and the principles or elements are said to be principles and elements of *number*, and the Ideas cannot be ranked as either prior or posterior to the numbers.'[1] The last clause of this passage suggests that Aristotle's statement that Plato identified the Ideas with numbers was based on his inference from what Plato said, rather than on a plain statement by Plato.

We must consider the general probabilities. Aristotle says that according to the Pythagoreans all things were numbers.[2] But this statement, taken strictly, attributes to the Pythagoreans an impossible attitude. To form the very conception of number, a high degree of abstraction was needed; but people capable of this could not also be capable of completely identifying the concrete things of daily life, men and women, stocks and stones, with such things as twoness, threeness, and the like. Only a primitive savage could be capable of so complete a confusion, but a primitive savage could not even have formed the abstract conception of number. Now the Pythagoreans of the fifth century were not primitive savages; they were members of perhaps the cleverest race the world has known, in the heyday of its civilization. We can only conclude that if they said, 'all things are numbers', what they meant was that at the basis of all things lies a certain arithmetical structure. We know some of the instances they had in mind. They knew that the ratios $1:2$, $2:3$, $3:4$ lay at the base of the melodic intervals; they knew many of the ratios that exist between geometrical figures. Starting from such facts as these, they made the bold generalization that number lies at the base of everything, and they may well have said, to express this, 'all things are numbers', which really means no more than that 'things exist by imitation of the numbers', as Aristotle in one passage[3] expresses their view.

---

[1] 1081^{a}12–17.
[2] 987^{b}27–8, 1083^{b}17, 1090^{a}20–3. [3] 987^{b}11.

It is reasonable to suppose that Aristotle's statement that according to Plato all the Ideas were numbers is to be similarly explained.[1] We have already found that Plato recognized an arithmetical element in the being of the line, the plane, and the solid. But he did not identify these with the numbers 2, 3, 4; he treated these numbers as the formal element in the being of the line, the plane, and the solid, and space or extension as the material element; the line was twoness in length (his way of saying 'in one dimension'), the plane threeness in breadth (i.e. in two dimensions), the solid fourness in depth (i.e. in three dimensions). Is it not likely, then, that he also treated other Ideas besides those of line, plane, and solid as having a formal element which was a number, and a 'material' element 'in' which that number was embodied? Here again the Pythagoreans had shown the way. They had said that justice is a square number,[2] and that meant that justice was fourness embodied or illustrated in two persons and two possessions to be distributed or exchanged between them.[3]

It is probable, then, that Plato did not identify the Ideas with numbers, but only assigned numbers to Ideas; i.e. he regarded some Ideas as monadic, others as dyadic, and so on. If we look for specimens of his assignment of numbers to ideas, we find two passages that look promising. In *Met.* 1081ª11 Aristotle says, 'This 3 is no more man-himself than any other 3', and in 1084ª14, 'If the number 3 is man-himself.' But in 1084ª25 he says, 'If man is the number 2'; so that he is clearly making suppositions for argument's sake; and so is he when he says,[4] 'If 4-itself is the Idea of anything, as of horse or of white.'

There are two other references which may be considered together. One is in *Met.* 1084ª32–7, where we are told that members of the Academy 'generate the derivatives—e.g. the void, proportion, the odd, and the other things of this kind—within the decade. For some things—e.g. movement and rest, good and evil —they assign to the first principles, and the others to the numbers.

---

[1] I now think that in my edition of the *Metaphysics* I took Aristotle's statement too literally, and that Robin was right in accepting Theophrastus' statement as more accurate than Aristotle's (*T.p.I.N.* 450–68). Cf. C. J. de Vogel in *Studia Vollgraff*, 165–78.

[2] Arist. *M.M.* 1182ª14.   [3] *Eth. Nic.* 1131ª18–20.   [4] 1084ª23.

This is why they identify the odd with the One.' The second passage is Theophrastus, *Met.* 6ᵃ23–ᵇ3, which has been quoted on pp. 210–11 above.

Both passages in all probability refer to Plato and his orthodox followers; the first, because it refers to the limitation of the number-series to the numbers from 2 to 10, which in *Phys.* 206ᵇ32 is definitely ascribed to Plato; the second, because the persons referred to are explicitly distinguished from Speusippus and Xenocrates. The Aristotelian passage is confused; the void, proportion, and the odd seem to be connected with the numbers, while movement and rest, good and evil, are connected with the first principles (the One and the indefinite dyad), and yet the odd is identified with the One, which is not a number but a first principle. The Theophrastus passage, again, when it describes the soul as derived from the numbers and the One, is too vague to be (taken alone) of much use; we could not, either from his statement or from Aristotle's, discover with certainty with what number Plato connected any one Idea.

We have found, however, two passages which enable us to do so.[1] One is *Met.* 1090ᵇ20–4, where Aristotle says that those who believe in Ideas 'derive lengths from the number 2, planes presumably from the number 3, and solids from the number 4'. The other is *De An.* 404ᵇ18–25, where the same view is again recorded, and it is added that reason was identified with the One, science with the number 2, opinion with the number 3, sensation with the number 4. What these two passages have in common is that they show that Plato connected a particular Idea with a particular number when he thought that the Idea included a definite number of elements in its being. Linearity involved two points, planarity three, and solidity four. Reason involved one object of apprehension, science involved a premiss and a conclusion, opinion involved a premiss and two possible opposite conclusions, sensation involved a solid object, which in turn involved four points (not in one plane).

Incidentally, we may note that Plato's assignment of the number 2 both to the line and to science, of the number 3 both

[1] I have tried to show on pp. 208–12 that these passages refer to Plato.

to the plane and to opinion, of the number 4 both to the solid and to sensation, confirms the view we have reached on other grounds, that he did not, strictly speaking, identify the Ideas with numbers, but assigned numbers to Ideas, i.e. classified the Ideas as respectively monadic, dyadic, triadic, &c.

As to the general principles on which, apart from these instances, Plato connected a particular Idea with a particular number we have no definite information. But it would be safe to say that he assigned a given number to a given Idea if and only if he thought that the Idea in some way involved that number of elements; and we can perhaps be a little more definite than this. Stenzel, and the school of interpreters who follow him, interpret the ideal number theory in the light of the 'division' preached and practised in the *Sophistes* and the *Politicus*. On this basis the number 1 would be assigned to any *summum genus*, the number 2 to a species coming immediately under a *summum genus* (since it would contain two elements, a generic and a differential), and so on. But this is not the principle on which the numbers 2, 3, 4 were assigned to the line, the plane, and the solid, and the numbers 1, 2, 3, 4 to reason, science, opinion, and sensation; for a line is not a kind of point, a plane a kind of line, a solid a kind of plane, nor is science a kind of reason, opinion a kind of science, sensation a kind of opinion. Plato's assignment of numbers to these entities is much more on the lines of the Pythagorean assignment of the number 4 to justice. On this analogy we may fairly suppose that Plato would assign 1 to the Idea of being, and 2 to that of sameness and to that of difference. Assignments of other numbers to other Ideas might easily be conjectured; but the extreme paucity of actual assignments reported in Aristotle or elsewhere suggests that Plato confined himself in the main to stating his general principle, and gave few illustrations of it.

If Plato did not identify the Ideas with numbers, but only assigned numbers to Ideas, i.e. classified Ideas as monadic, dyadic, &c., the theory is by no means the wild phantasy which at first sight it seems to be; in it Plato was in fact only carrying the effort of abstraction to a farther point than it had already been carried in abstracting Ideas from sense-particulars.

XVI

THE IDEAS AND SENSIBLE THINGS

IN his summary of the latest phase of Plato's metaphysics, Aristotle says not only that Plato treated the One and the great and small as being respectively the formal and the material principle involved in the being of the Ideas, but also that he treated the *Ideas* and the great and small as the principles involved in the being of sensible things;[1] and we have now to consider the interpretation of this statement. Aristotle's language suggests that the material element in sensible things was identical with the material element in the Ideas, but it is hardly credible that Plato in his construction of sensible things simply added a second dose of the very same principle that he had already used once in the construction of the Ideas. For the most obvious fact about bodies is their spatial extension, and this they could not be supposed to derive either from the Idea-numbers or from the great and small which Plato used in constructing the Idea-numbers, which was simply indefinite plurality. In the *Timaeus* he had clearly recognized space as something which was as necessary for the existence of sensible things as the Ideas of which they were copies; and we can hardly believe that he ever went back on this doctrine.[2]

Aristotle touches on this question in his discussion of 'place' in the *Physics*; 'Plato in the *Timaeus*', he remarks,[3] 'says that matter and space are the same; for the participant (τὸ μεταληπτικόν) and space are identical. It is true, indeed, that the account he gives there of the participant is different from what he says in his so-called unwritten teaching. Nevertheless, he did identify place and space.' And later[4] he says, 'Plato ought to tell us why the Forms and the numbers are not in place, if what participates is place—whether what participates is the great and small or the matter, as he has called it in the *Timaeus*.' These allusions show clearly that Aristotle had not read his *Timaeus* very carefully; they contain two obvious errors. 'The participant' is a fair

---

[1] 988ᵃ8–14.   [2] Cf. *Laws* 894ᵃ1–5, quoted on p. 215.
[3] 209ᵇ11–16.   [4] Ibid. 33–210ᵃ2.

paraphrase of Plato's 'receptacle' (ὑποδοχή) or 'seat' (ἕδρα)[1] of becoming. But in the first place Aristotle is wrong in identifying this with the 'matter' which plays so large a part in his own philosophy. The word ὕλη occurs in the *Timaeus*,[2] but in quite a different context and with quite a different meaning; and Plato makes it clear that he conceives of space not as the matter of sensible things, but as the field in which they come into being. He lays himself open to misunderstanding when he illustrates the function of space by referring to it as a sort of plastic material (ἐκμαγεῖον),[3] and compares it to a lump of gold which can be shaped and reshaped.[4] But that is only a comparison; his account taken as a whole makes it clear that he regards space not as a material to be shaped into sensible things, but as the field in which they come to be. And secondly, what this field receives is not the Ideas (as Aristotle's objection implies) but the copies of the Ideas.[5]

Since Aristotle certainly makes these mistakes, it is easy to suppose that he made yet another. Plato may well have used, in his account of the genesis of the Idea-numbers, the phrase 'the participant' or some equivalent, but Aristotle must be mistaken in supposing that by it Plato meant the same participant which he uses in the *Timaeus*; for what he needed in the derivation of sensible things was unlimited extension, but in the derivation of the Idea-numbers indefinite plurality. Again, Plato may have used the phrase 'the great and small' in both connexions, but that phrase is applicable to indefinite extension at least as well as to indefinite plurality.

If this line of thought be correct, Aristotle's statement that 'the underlying matter of which the Forms are predicated in the case of sensible things, and the One in the case of the Forms, is a dyad, the great and small'[6] is due partly to a hasty reading of the *Timaeus*, and partly to a hasty conflation of what Plato had written in the *Timaeus* about the generation of sensible things with what he had said in his 'unwritten teachings' about the generation of the Ideas. Plato did not, as Aristotle says, use the

---

[1] 49 a 6, 52 b 1.   [2] 69 a 6.   [3] 50 c 2.
[4] 50 a 5–b 6.   [5] 50 c 5; cf. 51 e 6–52 b 2.   [6] 988ª 11–14.

same participant in his construction of the ideal numbers and in his construction of sensible things, but in the one case indefinite plurality and in the other indefinite extension. There could not be a number unless there were oneness and plurality, since each number was both a single Form and a species of the genus plurality. There could not be sensible things unless there were Ideas of which they were imperfect exemplifications and extension in which they must exist, 'on pain of not existing at all'.[1]

At this point a query naturally arises. Plato has already, it would seem, used indefinite extension (the long and short, &c.) in the generation of the ideal line, plane, and solid. Does he use the same indefinite extension in the generation of sensible things? The answer is, I think, not far to seek. The 'ideal solid' is not a solid; it is solidity; and the 'space' involved in its being is not space but spatiality; the 'ideal solid' is fourness exhibited in spatiality. Thus space itself, that which *has* spatiality, is still there, to be used in the generation of sensible things which are exemplifications of 'fourness exhibited in spatiality'.

None of our evidence suggests that the mathematical entities, which Plato treated as intermediate between the ideal numbers and magnitudes on the one hand and sensible numbered groups and sensible shapes on the other, played a part in the generation of the latter. The One and indefinite plurality were the necessary presuppositions of the ideal numbers; the ideal numbers and indefinite spatiality were the necessary presuppositions of the ideal figures; the ideal figures and space were the necessary presuppositions of sensible things; the mathematical entities disappear from view. What, then, did Plato think about them in his latest period? We do not know; but we may conjecture that he came to think of them as mathematical fictions. He certainly so thought of the point;[2] and it has been a great puzzle why he did so. It becomes more intelligible if we suppose that he not only thought a point having position but no magnitude impossible, but also thought a line having length but no breadth or depth,

---

[1] *Tim.* 52 c 5.

[2] 'Plato even used to object to points as being a geometrical dogma. He used to give the name of "principle of the line"—and this he often used to posit—to his "indivisible lines"' (992ª 20–2).

and a plane having length and breadth but no depth, impossible. The *Ideas* of position, length, breadth, and depth remained for him real and distinct; but it may be suggested that he had come to think that the supposition of the existence of points, lines, and planes as defined by the mathematicians was simply a necessary device for making possible the study of solids.

It must be remembered that in the *Timaeus*, to explain the existence of the sensible world Plato posits only three things, apart from the Demiourgos—the Ideas, 'the things that enter into and pass out of space', and space itself.[1] Further, the things that enter into and pass out of space are not the 'intermediates' which are the objects of mathematics; for they are sensible and generated[2] while the intermediates are non-sensible and eternal.[3] Again, the things that enter into and pass out of space are not perfect exemplifications of Ideas but only close approximations to being such; 'with regard to their numbers, their motions, and their powers in general, we must suppose that the god adjusted them in due proportion, when he had brought them in every detail to the most exact perfection *permitted by Necessity* willingly complying with persuasion'.[4] Thus the intermediates form no part of Plato's cosmological scheme, and it seems highly probable that he had come to regard them as fictions necessary for geometry but having no place in reality. It is possible that even when he wrote the *Republic* he had come to think this, and that this is part of his meaning when he speaks of dialectic as annulling the hypotheses of mathematics.[5]

[1] 51 e 6–52 b 5.   [2] 52 a 5.
[3] *Met.* 987^{b}14–18.   [4] *Tim.* 56 c 3–7.   [5] 533 c 8.

XVII

RETROSPECT

THE essence of the theory of Ideas lay in the conscious recognition of the fact that there is a class of entities, for which the best name is probably 'universals', that are entirely different from sensible things. Any use of language involves the recognition, either conscious or unconscious, of the fact that there are such entities; for every word used, except proper names —every abstract noun, every general noun, every adjective, every verb, even every pronoun and every preposition—is a name for something of which there are or may be instances. The first step towards the conscious recognition of this class of entities was, if we may believe Aristotle, taken by Socrates when he concentrated on the search for definitions; to ask for the meaning of a general word was a step from the mere use of such a word towards the recognition of universals as a distinct class of entities. But Socrates seems to have been interested in the defining of one thing at a time, and not to have seen the general significance of what he was doing; Plato did see that what was common to all searches for definitions was the assumption that there are such things as universals. He saw, too, that the objective difference between universals and particulars answers to the subjective difference between science and sense-perception. The senses present to us a world of particular events in which qualities are present almost inextricably conjoined and confused; if we were left to the senses alone we should never be able to disentangle them and reach a clear understanding of the structure of the world. But in reason we have a faculty by which we can grasp universals in their pure form and to some extent see the relations that necessarily exist between them. The best example we have of this power is to be found in mathematics, and Plato was the first thinker who clearly saw this. When we say that 2 and 2 make 4, we are implying not that we have often experienced instances in which this is so, and never found an instance to the contrary, but that we perceive that

Q

from the nature of the system of numbers this must be so; and what is true of '2 and 2 make 4' is true of the most advanced mathematical propositions. In mathematics Plato saw the clearest example of the mind's power of perceiving relations between universals; and that is why in the *Republic* he makes mathematics the necessary introduction to philosophy. But it was, for him, only the introduction. He envisaged the possibility of our similarly perceiving necessary relations between other universals than those treated of by mathematics; and in the *Phaedo* he gives us one, and in the *Sophistes* another, modest instalment of such insight.[1] In the main this is still an unfulfilled aspiration; but we owe it to Plato that we have the aspiration at all. He sometimes expressed the aspiration too sanguinely, as when in the *Republic* he speaks of deducing the whole nature of the system of Ideas from a single unhypothetical first principle. In that he was mistaken; Aristotle was nearer the truth when he maintained—and this is the essence of his theory of syllogism—that it is only by combining two premisses related in a certain way that we can draw fresh conclusions. But, as we have seen,[2] that doctrine of Aristotle's itself owes its origin to a metaphysical principle which Plato had discovered, that there are Ideas so related that one 'drags' another with it—in other words, to his faith that the world of Ideas forms a system of necessary relations. In the face of this community of thought between Plato and Aristotle, the question on which Aristotle lays so much stress, whether universals exist apart from particulars or not, seems almost to be a question of words.

Anyone who writes about the theory of Ideas is bound to state as precisely as he can what Plato's conception of the relation of Ideas to particulars really was. When the Marburg school of Cohen and Natorp was in the ascendant, it was fashionable to give a purely conceptualistic account of Plato's view, and to say that the whole notion of a 'separation' of the Ideas from particulars was foisted on him by Aristotle. This view will not survive examination; it is the expression of what its holders think Plato ought to have said, rather than of what he did say. It would be easy to make a catena of passages drawn from every period of

[1] Cf. pp. 32–3, 111–16.   [2] p. 34.

Plato's literary life, in which objective existence is ascribed to the Ideas. Here are passages from three periods. In the *Phaedo*[1] he says: 'Then we were saying that one thing can come from its opposite, but now we are saying that the opposite itself cannot become opposite to itself—neither that which is in us *nor that which is in nature.*' In the *Parmenides*[2] he says: 'These Forms are, as it were, patterns fixed *in the nature of things*; the other things are made in their image and are likenesses.'

In the *Timaeus*[3] he says:

Is there such a thing as 'Fire just in itself' or any of the other things which we are always describing in such terms, as things that are 'just in themselves'? Or are the things we see or otherwise perceive by the bodily senses the only things that have such reality, and has nothing else, over and above these, any sort of being at all? Are we talking idly when we say that there is such a thing as an intelligible Form of anything? Is this nothing more than a word? . . . If intelligence and true belief are two different kinds, then these things—Forms that we cannot perceive but only think of—certainly exist *in themselves.* . . . We must affirm that they are two different things, for they are distinct in origin and unlike in nature. . . . We must agree that there is, first, the unchanging Form, ungenerate and indestructible, which neither receives anything else into itself from elsewhere *nor itself enters into anything else anywhere*, invisible and otherwise imperceptible; that, in fact, which thinking has for its object. . . . Whereas for an image, since not even the very principle on which it has come into being belongs to the image itself, but it is the everlasting semblance of something else, it is proper that it should come to be *in* something else, clinging in some sort to existence on pain of being nothing at all, on the other hand that which has real being has the support of the exactly true account, which declares that, as long as the two things are different, *neither can ever come to be in the other* in such a way that the two should become at once one and the same thing and two.

Many similar passages could be quoted.

What conclusions can be drawn from passages such as these? First, of course, that Plato consistently thought of Ideas as different from sensible things. Secondly, and with equal certainty, that he thought of them as completely objective, neither as thoughts nor as the 'contents of thoughts' (whatever that phrase may mean), but as entities whose existence is *presupposed* by all our knowledge. Thirdly, that he thought of them as existing separately from sensible things; but to the question whether Plato consistently so thought of them no simple answer can be given. Help may be sought from a study of the words he uses from time to time to express the relation between Forms and particulars. These may be divided into a group of words implying or suggesting the immanence of the Forms, and a group implying or suggesting their transcendence, viz.:

(I) (1) ἐν, εἶναι ἐν, ἐνεῖναι, ἐγγίγνεσθαι, κεῖσθαι ἐν.

(2) κεκτῆσθαι, ἔχειν, ἴσχειν, ἕξις, δέχεσθαι.

(3) μετέχειν, μετάσχεσις, μέθεξις, μεταλαμβάνειν.

(4) παραγίγνεσθαι, παρεῖναι, παρουσία.

(5) προσγίγνεσθαι.

(6) κοινόν, κοινῇ, κοινωνία, κοινωνεῖν.

(7) ἐπεῖναι, ἐπιγίγνεσθαι.

(8) κατέχειν.

(9) ἰέναι εἰς.

(II) (a) παράδειγμα.

(b) αὐτὸ καθ' αὑτό.

(c) βούλεσθαι, ὀρέγεσθαι, προθυμεῖσθαι.

(d) ἐοικέναι, προσεοικέναι, εἰκών, εἰκάζεσθαι, ἀπεικάζεσθαι.

(e) τἀκεῖ.

(f) ὁμοίωμα, ἀφομοιοῦσθαι, ἀφομοίωμα.

(g) μιμεῖσθαι, μίμησις, μίμημα, ἀπομιμεῖσθαι.

The following list of the occurrences of these words in this connexion is doubtless incomplete, but it is near enough to being complete to furnish a true indication of Plato's usage. The 'first part' of the *Parmenides* is omitted, because Plato is there not expressing his view but discussing it. The part of the *Sophistes* in which the 'communion of kinds' is discussed is omitted, because the relation of Ideas to one another is a different matter from their relation to particulars.

Laches. (1) 191 e 10, 192 a 2, b 6.

(2) 192 a 4.

Euthyphro. (2) 5 d 3.   (a) 6 e 4.

Gorgias. (3) 467 e 7.
  (4) 506 d 1.

Hippias Major. (2) 298 b 4, 300 a 9.
  (4) 293 e 11, 294 a 1, c 4, 6.
  (5) 289 d 4, 8, e 5, 292 d 1.
  (6) 300 a 10.
  (7) 300 a 10, 303 a 5.

Lysis. (4) 217 b 6, d 4, 5, 8.

Euthydemus. (4) 280 b 2, 301 a 4.

Meno. (1) 72 e 1, 7.
  (2) 72 c 7.
  (8) 74 d 8.

Cratylus. (1) 390 a 1, b 2, 413 c 3.
  (2) 389 b 10.

Symposium. (2) 204 c 6.   (*b*) 211 b 1.
  (3) 211 b 2.

Phaedo. (2) 103 e 4, 104 b 9, d 2, e 8, 9, (*b*) 78 d 5, 100 b 6.
    105 a 2, 5, 7, b 1, d 11–106 d 4.   (*c*) 74 d 9, 75 b 1, 7.
  (3) 100 c 5, 101 c 3, 4, 5, 102 b 2. (*d*) 74 e 3.
  (4) 100 d 5.
  (5) 100 d 6.
  (6) 100 d 6.
  (8) 104 d 1.

Republic. (1) 402 c 5, 434 d 6–435 c 1. (*a*) 500 e 3.
  (3) 476 d 1, 2.   (*d*) 510 b 4, 8, d 7, e 3, 511 a 6.
  (6) 476 a 7.
  (9) 434 d 3.

Phaedrus.   (*d*) 250 b 4, 5.
  (1) 237 d 6.   (*e*) 250 a 2, 6.
  (6) 265 e 4.   (*f*) 250 a 6, b 3.

Parmenides. (1) 150 a 1, 2, 3.
  (2) 149 e 5, 159 e 5.
  (3) 158 b 6–c 4, 160 a 2.

Theaetetus. (2) 203 e 4.   (*a*) 176 e 3.

Sophistes. (2) 247 a 5.
  (3) 228 c 1.
  (4) 247 a 5, 8.
  (6) 252 b 9, 260 e 2.

Timaeus.   (*a*) 28 a 7, 29 b 4, 39 e 7,
                                    48 e 5, 49 a 1.
                              (*b*) 51 c 1.

Timaeus (*cont.*).

(*d*) 29 b 2, 3, c 1, 2, 52 c 2,
   92 c 7.
(*f*) 50 d 1, 51 a 2.
(*g*) 39 e 2, 48 e 6, 50 c 5.

Philebus. (1) 16 d 2.
   (2) 25 b 6.

Certain things emerge clearly from the consideration of these passages. It is clear that there is a general movement away from immanence towards transcendence. In the early period almost everything speaks of immanence. The one early use of παράδειγμα is no real exception, since Plato is there describing not the relation of particulars to the Idea, but the relation of a human mind to an Idea, 'to which it looks, and uses it as a pattern'. A more significant evidence of the 'transcendental' view is the passage of the *Phaedo*[1] already quoted, where he says: 'Then we were saying that the opposite itself cannot become opposite to itself—neither that which is in us nor *that which is in nature.*'

In the *Parmenides* Plato expressly distinguishes the two views. He there[2] brings the objection of the 'third man' against the view that the Idea is immanent in particulars, and then[3] against the view that it is a pattern which they imitate. But even there the distinction is not quite clear-cut, since he describes 'imitation' not as an alternative to 'participation', but as one way in which 'participation' may be interpreted;[4] and he continues to use both types of phrase in later dialogues.

Though from the *Symposium* onwards Plato begins to use, from time to time, the language of transcendence, and though it is omnipresent in the *Timaeus*, he nowhere answers, or tries to answer, the 'third man' objection which he makes in the *Parmenides* to the transcendentalist view. It is sometimes said that he had already answered it himself by the use he makes in the *Republic*[5] of another infinite regress argument to prove that there cannot be two Ideas of bed. But this is a mistake; to show that the existence of two Ideas of bed would involve the existence of a third Idea behind them has no tendency to show that the exist-

---

[1] 103 b 2–5.   [2] 132 a 1–b 2.   [3] 132 c 12–133 a 7.
[4] 132 d 3–4.   [5] 597 c 1–d 4.

ence of an Idea and of a particular resembling it does not involve
another Idea behind both.

That Plato was not entirely satisfied with the 'transcendent'
view is shown also by the facts that the final argument in the 'first
part' of the *Parmenides*[1] is directed precisely against the 'transcendent', not against the 'immanent' view, that this objection
also is nowhere met by him, and that he continues in later dialogues to use to some extent the language of immanence.

The only conclusion possible seems to be that, while he was not
quite satisfied with either expression, he saw no way of getting
nearer to the truth than by using both, the one stressing the
intimacy of the link between a universal and its particulars, the
other stressing the failure of every particular to be a perfect
exemplification of any universal. He may even have had an ink-
ling of the fact that the relation is completely unique and inde-
finable. Both 'sharing' and 'imitating' are metaphors for it, and
the use of two complementary metaphors is better than the sole
use of either.

Plato's language about the relation of particulars to a universal
would have benefited by a clearer recognition than he seems to
have reached of the distinction between two classes of quality
(and two classes of relation). There are qualities, like heat or
darkness, that admit of degree, and qualities, like straightness or
squareness, that do not. In the case of the former class such
phrases as 'partake of' are appropriate to particulars which have
the quality in some degree. In the case of the latter class, some
things may properly be said to 'possess' them, and some of the
things that do not possess them may fairly be said to approximate
to possessing them or, as Plato said, to 'imitate' them. He nowhere
assigns expressly to either of these classes of quality either of his
two classes of expression for the relation of particulars to a universal, but it may be that the existence of the two classes had a
share in leading him to use the variety of expressions he uses.

That as regards the phase of Plato's thought represented by the
Timaeus Aristotle was justified in ascribing to him[2] a complete

[1] 133 b 4–134 c 8.
[2] *An. Post.* 77[a]5; *Met.* 991[a]12–14, [b]1–3, 1033[b]26–9, 1079[b]12–18, 1086[b]2–13.

separation of the Ideas from sensible things is confirmed by a
consideration of what Plato believed about time and about space.
His conception of the relation of Ideas to time and to space is
clearly stated in the *Timaeus*. Just as change involves time, he
regards time as involving change. Now the nature of the Ideas
for him was (and rightly so) such that they cannot suffer change,[1]
and accordingly, while he describes time as having been brought
into being .by the Demiourgos only simultaneously with the
ordered sensible world, the Ideas, like the Demiourgos, are
eternal.

When the father who had begotten the world saw it set in motion and
alive, a shrine brought into being for the everlasting gods [the stars
and planets], he rejoiced and being well pleased he took thought to
make it yet more like its pattern. So, as that pattern is the Living
Being which is for ever existent, he sought to make this universe also
like it, so far as might be, in that respect. Now the nature of that Living
Being was eternal, and this character it was impossible to confer in
full completeness on the generated thing. But he took thought to make,
as it were, a moving likeness of eternity; and, at the same time that he
ordered the Heaven, he made of eternity that abides in unity an
everlasting likeness moving according to number—that to which we
have given the name Time.[2]

While time is thus made a product of the divine intelligence,
Plato speaks quite differently of space. Space is introduced not
in the part of the *Timaeus* which describes the activity of the
Demiourgos,[3] but in that which deals with 'what happens of
necessity'[4]—i.e. with those features of the world which are not
due to the divine intelligence, but of which it has to take account.
Space is in fact the third fundamental of the system set forth in
the *Timaeus*, coeternal with the Ideas and the Demiourgos. The
Ideas do not enter into it but it is the receptacle for those copies of
the Ideas which form the sensible world.[5]

Thus the Ideas transcend time and are not in space; and since
sensible things are both in time and in space, the independence of
time and space which Plato assigns to the Ideas is the clearest
evidence that he did in fact, as Aristotle says, 'separate' them

[1] *Phaedo* 78 c 1–d 9.   [2] *Tim.* 37 c 6–d 7.   [3] 29 d 7–47 e 2.
[4] 47 e 3–69 a 5.   [5] 48 e 2–52 d 1.

from sensible things. In the early dialogues, written while Plato was completely dominated by the influence of Socrates, it is natural that there should be no trace of transcendentalism; for Socrates was interested, as Aristotle says, only in ascertaining the nature which was common to all just acts, to all beautiful objects, and the like; but as Plato's mind matured he moved gradually towards a transcendental view of the Ideas as entities existing on their own account and only imperfectly mirrored in sensible things and in human actions; and it is naturally of the later Plato, at whose feet he had sat, that Aristotle writes, and against him that he truly formulates the charge that he separated the Ideas from sensible things.[1]

There is much, however, in Aristotle's treatment of Platonic doctrine that is purely captious. It would be tedious to attempt any complete survey of the criticism of Plato which abounds in the *Metaphysics* and elsewhere in Aristotle; but there is one charge the incorrectness of which must be pointed out. Aristotle credits Plato with having recognized two out of the four causes which he himself recognizes—the material and the formal—but accuses him of having ignored the efficient and the final cause.[2]

Incidentally, it is a mistake to say that Plato definitely recognized the material cause. It is no doubt true, as Aristotle says, that Plato, in his latest phase, described the Idea-numbers as 'generated' by the union of a formal element (oneness) with a quasi-material element (the great and small, or indefinite plurality); but Plato nowhere recognizes a literally material element in the being of sensible things. In the *Timaeus*, the only one of his dialogues in which he seriously attempts an account of the sensible world, space is not the matter implicit in the being of sensible things, but only the medium in which they come into being. Aristotle, it is true, identified Plato's 'space' with his own 'matter',[3] but that is an instance of his readiness to read into earlier thinkers adumbrations of his own doctrine. Plato at one point lays himself open to the misunderstanding, when he uses the simile of a plastic

---

[1] For a vigorous defence of the correctness of Aristotle's ascription to Plato of a separation of the Ideas, cf. J. D. Mabbott in *Class. Quart.* xx (1926), 72–9.
[2] 988[a]7–11.   [3] *Phys.* 209[b]11.

material to illustrate his conception of space.[1] But that is no more
to be taken as a precise description of its nature than is his comparison of its function to that of a nurse or a mother.[2]

The passage to which Aristotle points[3] as evidence for the charge
against Plato of having ignored the efficient cause is one in the
Phaedo[4] where Socrates says,

I study no further; I cannot understand those other wise causes which
are alleged, and if a person says to me that the bloom of colour, or
form, or any such thing, is a source of beauty I leave all that, which
is only confusing to me, and singly and simply, and perhaps foolishly,
hold and am assured in my own mind that nothing makes a thing
beautiful but the presence of or participation in beauty in whatever
way or manner obtained; for I do not go so far as to insist on the
manner; but I maintain that by beauty all beautiful things are beautiful. This appears to me to be the safest answer which I can give, either
to myself or to any other, and to this I cling, in the persuasion that this
principle will never be overthrown, but that to myself or to any one
who asks the question, I may safely reply, that by beauty beautiful
things are beautiful.

But Plato does not, of course, forget that in human life beautiful
things are not brought into being except by a craftsman, nor
good deeds except by a doer. Nor is he blind to the problem of
efficient causation on the world scale. Even in the *Phaedo* the
efficient and the final cause are not ignored. The efficient cause
is recognized in the passage in which Socrates criticizes Anaxagoras for not remaining true to his own maxim that reason is the
cause of all things—for falling back on physical causation and
thus failing to distinguish causes from mere conditions.[5] And
with this conception of mind as the efficient cause of the world's
being as it is, there is associated the notion of the good as the final
cause with a view to which mind acts. 'If Anaxagoras said that the
earth was in the centre, I thought he would further explain that
this position was the best, and I should be satisfied with the
explanation given, and not want any other sort of cause.'[6] It is
indeed because Plato has failed to discover the nature of 'the

[1] *Tim.* 50 a 5–b 6.   [2] 49 a 6, 50 d 2–3.
[3] *De Gen. et Corr.* 335[b]7–16; *Met.* 991[b]3–9.   [4] 100 c 9–e 3.
[5] 97 b 8–99 c 6.   [6] 97 e 3–6.

best'—because he does not see his way, for the time being, to a
teleological explanation—that he falls back on explaining by the
presence of Ideas the fact that things are as they are[1]—an
explanation which clearly does not exclude a teleological explanation but may be supplemented by one.

While the Ideas remain his central theme, the twin thoughts of
a divine source of change and a good to which he directs it are
always present in the background of Plato's thought, and find
growing expression in his dialogues. In the *Cratylus*[2] he speaks of
mind or soul as giving life and movement to the body, and as
being the ordering principle of all things. In the *Republic* he speaks
of 'the artificer of the senses',[3] and says that 'the sky with all that
it contains has been framed by its artificer with the highest perfection of which such things are capable';[4] and the thought of an
ultimate *final* cause is clear for all to see, in what he says about the
Idea of good.[5] It has often been thought that the references in the
Republic to a divine being are perfunctory, and that the thought
of such a being is replaced by or merged in that of the Idea of
good. But we have seen that in the *Phaedo* the divine reason is
clearly distinguished from the good to which it looks; and even
apart from that it should be clear, beyond any shadow of doubt,
that Plato could not have confused the notion of a supreme
intelligent being with that of an Idea; an Idea is a nature, not
a being having a nature. That Plato should have thought of an
Idea as thinking or planning or bringing anything into being is
really inconceivable.

There is one passage in the *Republic*[6] where Plato does injustice
to his own view. That is the passage in which he describes God
as making the Idea of bed. To describe any Idea as 'made' is to
deprive it of the complete independence which everywhere else
Plato ascribes to the Ideas. What he is concerned with in that
passage is not metaphysics, but the inferiority of the imitative
to the useful arts, and the exigencies of his argument about this
lead him to use a phrase which he could not seriously have defended. His theme is that the imitative arts—painting, sculpture,

---

[1] 99 c 6–d 3.   [2] 400 a 5–b 7.   [3] 507 c 6–8.
[4] 530 a 3–7.   [5] 504 e 4–509 b 10.   [6] 597 b 5–d 8.

and poetry—produce objects that are removed by two degrees from complete reality. The painted bed is only an imitation of the bed one can sleep in, and that in turn is only an imitation of the ideal bed. And as the painted bed is the work of the painter, and the everyday bed the work of the carpenter, symmetry leads Plato to say that the Idea of bed is the work of God. There is nothing anywhere else in his writings which would justify us in taking this as a serious expression of his real view. As we shall see presently, his scheme requires both a divine intelligence and a system of Ideas, and of these the first is, if anything, thought of as subject to the second; the activity of the divine intelligence is subject to the control exercised by the necessary relations between Ideas.

In the *Republic* the Ideas are the central theme, and the function of God as the efficient cause of change is not emphasized. But the necessity of soul and of reason to account for change is increasingly recognized in later dialogues. In the *Phaedrus* reflection on the origin of change leads Plato to find it in soul, which he describes as self-moving:[1]

Every soul is immortal. For that which is self-moved[2] is immortal; but that which moves another and is moved by another, in ceasing to move ceases also to live. Only the self-moving, never leaving hold of itself, never ceases to be in movement, but is also a fountain and first principle of movement to everything else that is in movement. Now, a first principle is unbegotten; for that which is begotten necessarily has a first principle, but a first principle is begotten of nothing; for if it were begotten of something, then it would cease to be a first principle.[3]

Even when he wrote the *Charmides*[4] Plato had spoken of self-motion as a possibility not to be lightly dismissed; but he does not stress the point; self-motion is mentioned only as one of several relations that a thing might be supposed to have to itself. When he came to write the *Phaedrus*, however, his mind had been at work on the problem of the origin of change. Change in one thing is normally caused by change in another, but that does not provide for an absolute origination of change; that can only be

[1] 245 e 7.
[2] Reading in 245 c 5 αὐτοκίνητον, with the Oxyrhynchus papyrus 1016.
[3] 245 c 5–d 3.   [4] 168 e 9.

if there is something that can originate movement in itself; and
in the *Phaedrus* that which can move itself is identified with soul.
He does not stress the cosmic significance of this; what he is concerned with is to prove the immortality of the human soul. But he
speaks of 'affections and actions of the soul human *and divine*',[1]
and he will later bring out the cosmic significance of the description of soul as self-moving.

In the *Sophistes* he approaches the matter from another side.
He has come to think that his previous treatment of the Ideas as
the only completely real entities, or at least his concentration of
interest on them alone, was mistaken, and he now expresses the
conviction that 'change, life, soul, understanding' are completely
real.[2] In saying that, he does not admit, as he has sometimes been
supposed to admit, change into the world of Ideas; to do that
would be to admit that, for instance, $2+2$ could come to be 5
instead of 4, and that goodness could come to be badness, or
beauty ugliness. In the same passage in which he asserts the
reality of change, he reasserts the unchangingness of the Ideas.[3]

From the *Sophistes* onwards, Plato is growingly occupied with
the problem of the causation of events in the sensible world.
There is a well-known passage in the *Politicus*[4] in which he explains
the presence of both good and evil in the world by the fact that
'there is a time when God himself guides and helps to roll the
world in its course; and there is a time, on the completion of a
certain cycle, when he lets go, and the world, being a living creature, and having originally received intelligence from its artificer,
turns about, and by an inherent necessity revolves in the opposite
direction'. That suggestion is not repeated elsewhere, and if it
stood alone we might suppose it to be only a momentary fancy.
But if we remember the *Timaeus* we shall see in the *Politicus* a first
attempt at explaining the presence of evil in the world, which in
the *Timaeus*[5] Plato explains by the influence of the 'errant cause',
necessity, and which in the *Laws* he ascribes to the action of one
or more evil souls.[6]

All or almost all these thoughts are caught up and systematized

[1] 245 c 2–4.   [2] 248 e 6–249 b 4.   [3] 249 b 8–c 5.
[4] 269 c 4–d 3.   [5] 48 a 6–7.   [6] 896 d 10–e 7.

in the *Timaeus*. The ultimate entities there are three in number—the Ideas, the Demiourgos, and space. The Ideas are mirrored by sensible things in space, and the original mirroring is not ascribed to the action of the Demiourgos; it is, rather, described as happening of necessity. 'Desiring that all things should be good and, so far as might be, nothing imperfect, the god *took over* all that is visible—not at rest, but in discordant and unordered motion—and brought it from disorder into order, since he judged that order was in every way the better.'[1] The Demiourgos is not represented as the creator of the sensible world; for the sensible world just consists of the images of the Ideas in space, and these the Demiourgos 'took over'. Nor is he represented as omnipotent in his dealings with the sensible world; his work is subject to the resistance offered at many points by necessity. He is subject also to the control exercised by the system of Ideas; he cannot make blackness to be whiteness, or vice to be virtue; he cannot override the incompatibilities which, as Plato has pointed out in the *Sophistes*,[2] exist between some Ideas and others. But he is the cause of all order and of all that is good in the world of nature and of man.

The thought of a supreme intelligence which governs the world is found once more in the *Philebus*,[3] where mind is 'the cause of the mixture', of the union of quality with definite intensity which characterizes everything in the sensible world. Socrates says 'Let us begin by asking a question—whether all this which they call the universe is left to the guidance of unreason and chance medley, or, on the contrary, as our fathers have declared, ordered and governed by a marvellous intelligence and wisdom'; and Protarchus answers 'that which you were just now saying appears to me to be blasphemy; but the other assertion, that mind orders all things, is worthy of the aspect of the world, and of the sun, and of the moon, and of the stars, and of the whole circle of the heavens; and never will I say or think otherwise'.

Finally, in the *Laws*,[4] Plato argues that, while one body can move another only by being in motion itself, there must be some-

---

[1] 30 a 2–6.
[2] 252 d 2–253 c 5.
[3] 28 d 3–e 6.
[4] 894 c 10–897 c 10.

thing that can originate movement in itself, and thereby initiate it in other things. This originator of movement he finds, as he had done long before in the *Phaedrus*, in soul. Further, while, to account for the evil in the world, he assumes, not indeed (as he has often been supposed to do) one great evil soul, a sort of Zoroastrian Ahriman, but one or more bad souls,[1] he ascribes the regularity of the movements of the stars and planets, and the general rhythm of the world, to a 'best soul'.[2]

It is clear, then, that in his later period, at least, Plato is far from making the Ideas the be-all and the end-all of his philosophy. He recognizes the necessity of efficient causes as well, and identifies all ultimate originators of change with souls. Nor is he blind to the necessity of final as well as of efficient causes; for among the 'movements' ascribed to soul are wish, consideration, care, deliberation[3]—all of them purposive in character—and the supreme control of the universe is assigned to 'the purpose of a will bent on the achievement of good'.[4]

Thus Aristotle is unfair to Plato when he describes him as recognizing only the material and the formal cause, and ignoring the efficient and the final. The fact is that Aristotle felt so acutely his difference from Plato with regard to the separation of the Ideas from particular things that he was led to do injustice to these other aspects of Plato's system—to his full recognition of mind as the ultimate efficient cause of all change, and of the Good as the final cause to which mind looks.

We often read of 'the hierarchy of the Ideas', and it is important to consider whether the phrase is justified. We may first ask what significance, if any, in this connexion belongs to the method of 'division' preached and practised in the *Sophistes* and the *Politicus*. The importance of this has been exaggerated by some scholars and minimized by others. Stenzel, for instance, has tried[5] to build up an interpretation of the theory of Idea-numbers on the basis of it; Prof. Cherniss[6] minimizes its importance, and treats it as only a heuristic method.

---

[1] 896 d 10–e 7.   [2] 897 c 4–9.   [3] 896 e 8–897 a 3.   [4] 967 a 4.
[5] In *Zahl u. Gestalt* and in *Stud. zur Entw. d. Plat. Dialektik, passim.*
[6] *A.C.P.A.* 46–7.

It is true that the method of division is used in these two dialogues not as a means of attaining insight into the whole structure
of the world of Ideas, but as a device for reaching the definition
of the sophist and the statesman. On the other hand, in the
Phaedrus[1] the method is heralded as *the* method of philosophy, in
a tone which forbids us to under-estimate its importance for
Plato. In the *Sophistes*, indeed, Plato points out that his first
application of the method has led to a variety of discrepant
definitions of the sophist, none of which reveals his true nature.[2]
But that is not because the method is wrong or unimportant, but
because he has not been careful enough in its application, and he
accordingly starts on a fresh application of it, beginning with the
genus to which the sophist essentially belongs, the genus 'contro-
versialist'.[3] In the *Politicus*, again, he points out that excessive
trust in the method may lead us to 'chop off too small a piece' of
the genus, i.e. to omit intermediate stages and treat as a species
what is only a sub-species.[4] But even in saying that not every
'part' of the genus is a species,[5] he implies that there are real
species and that a more careful use of the method would lead us
to these.

We must take account, too, of what he says of the method in the
Philebus:[6]

There neither is nor ever will be a better than my own favourite way,
which has nevertheless often deserted me and left me helpless in the
hour of need . . . one which may be easily pointed out, but is by no
means easy of application; it is the parent of all the discoveries in the
arts . . . a gift of heaven, which, as I conceive, the gods tossed among
men by the hands of a new Prometheus, and therewith a blaze of light;
and the ancients . . . handed down the tradition, that whatever things
are said to be are composed of one and many, and have the finite and
infinite implanted in them: seeing, then, that such is the order of the
world, we too ought in every inquiry to begin by laying down one Idea
of that which is the object of inquiry; this unity we shall find in everything. Having found it, we may next proceed to look for two, if there
be two, or, if not, then for three or some other number, subdividing
each of these units, until at last the unity with which we began is seen

---

[1] 265 c 8–266 c 1.   [2] 231 b 9–232 a 7.   [3] 232 b 1–7.
[4] 262 a 5–c 1.   [5] 263 b 2–11.   [6] 16 b 5–e 2.

not only to be one and many and an infinity of things, but also a definite number; we must not attribute infinity to the many until the entire number of the species intermediate between unity and infinity has been discovered,—then, and not till then, we may rest from division, and without troubling ourselves about each of them may allow them all to drop into infinity.

This, he concludes, as he had done in the *Phaedrus*, is the true dialectic.

Here, years after his first promulgation of the method of division, while acknowledging the difficulties of its application, Plato reasserts his confidence in its possibility and in its importance as laying bare the articulation of the world of Ideas, from the highest genera down to the lowest species, beyond which there is nothing but the infinity of particular instances. It would not be far amiss to say that while in the early dialogues it was his main purpose to affirm the existence of Ideas, in the period which lasted from the *Phaedrus* to the *Philebus* his main object was to assert the importance of discovering the relations between them.

Plato undoubtedly thought, then, that there are minor or departmental hierarchies within the world of Ideas; the question remains whether he thought that there is a grand hierarchy embracing them all. In the *Republic* the Idea of good appears as the supreme Idea, that which gives being and intelligibility to the whole world of Ideas; and in the *Philebus* the Idea of good is at least the highest Idea that comes under discussion. In the *Sophistes*, on the other hand, the 'greatest kinds' or supreme Ideas are existence, sameness, and difference. And in the Idea-number theory the Idea of unity is made the formal principle in all the Ideas. How did Plato think of these various 'highest Ideas' as related? He never tells us, and we are left to conjecture.

These varieties of presentation are to be explained, so far as they *can* be explained, by taking account of the various standpoints from which Plato approaches the subject at different times. In the *Republic*, and again in the *Philebus*, he approaches it from the side of ethics; and in ethics Plato gave the fundamental place to the Idea of good rather than to the only other that might claim that place, the Idea of right; he speaks of 'the essential nature of the Good, from which all things that are good and right (δίκαια) derive their value for us'.[1] It is as the supreme object of human endeavour that the Good first appears,[2] and it is by a rather loose transition that Plato passes from assigning to it the highest place in his ethics to assigning to it the highest place in his ontology. There is a similar loose transition, and combination of the ethical with the ontological standpoint, in the *Philebus*, where he speaks of desiring 'to see the most beautiful mixture, that least torn by faction, and to find in it what it is that is good both in man *and in the universe*'.[3]

Later in the *Philebus*[4] there is what looks like a hint of a hierarchical system, where Plato says, 'If we are not able to hunt the good with one Idea only, with three we may catch our prey, Beauty, Symmetry, Truth.' But these are not three species of the genus good, but, as the sequel shows, three conditions which that which is good must satisfy.

By comparison, the approach to the subject in the *Sophistes* is clear. In calling existence, sameness, and difference 'greatest kinds' Plato means that these are Ideas each of which is predicable of each of the other two, and of all other Ideas as well; and in grouping movement and rest with them he means that one or other of these is predicable of everything that is—'rest' of Ideas, and 'movement' of everything else. But the Ideas in the *Sophistes* do not form a *monarchical* system; existence is given no priority over sameness and difference.

Another Idea came to the front in Plato's latest period; the Idea of One was made the formal principle of all the Ideas. Here again there is not a fundamental change of view, but a difference of standpoint. It was not of the Ideas considered in their total nature, but of the numerical aspect of them—of them considered as implying, each of them, a system of two or more elements—that unity was regarded as the formal principle. It was so regarded because he wished to maintain that each Idea, whatever internal relations it might involve, was itself a unity.

What, we may ask, was the relation of the One to the good, in

[1] 505 a 2–4.
[2] 505 d 11.
[3] 63 e 9–64 a 2.
[4] 65 a 1–2.

this late phase of Plato's doctrine? In his summary account of Plato's teaching, in *Met.* A. 6,[1] Aristotle contents himself with saying that 'he has assigned the cause of good and of evil to his two elements respectively', i.e. the cause of good to the One and the cause of evil to the 'great and small'. Two other passages of the *Metaphysics*[2] deal with Plato's conception of the good but add little to our enlightenment. In 1091ᵃ29–ᵇ3, ᵇ13–15, however, Aristotle returns to the subject. He distinguishes between some thinkers (i.e. the school of Speusippus)[3] who refuse to ascribe goodness and badness respectively to the first principles, and others (i.e. the school of Plato) who do so ascribe them, and of the latter he remarks that 'they say the One itself is the good itself, but treated unity as being its fundamental character'.

Thus in two passages Aristotle makes it clear that for Plato unity, not goodness, was the fundamental character of the first principle which was in fact both one and good. In other words the Idea of One had taken the place formerly occupied by the Idea of good, as the centre of Plato's system. In making this change Plato paid tribute to the fact that while unity is what may be called a primary attribute, goodness is necessarily a secondary or consequential attribute—that nothing can be good except by first possessing some other character. This displacement of the good by the One was at the same time a symptom of the growing mathematization of Plato's system, which leads Aristotle to remark elsewhere[4] that 'for the thinkers of to-day mathematics has come to be philosophy'.

There is one more passage of Aristotle in which the relation between unity and goodness is touched on. In the *Eudemian Ethics*[5] he criticizes the Platonists for deducing from the goodness of things not obviously good that of things obviously good.

They argue that justice and health are goods, since they are arrangements and numbers, on the assumption that goodness is a property of numbers and units because unity is the good itself. But they ought, from what are admittedly goods, such as health, strength, and temperance, to demonstrate that excellence is present even more in

[1] 988ᵃ14–15. [2] 988ᵇ6–16, 1075ᵃ36–ᵇ1.
[3] Cf. 1072ᵇ30–4. [4] 992ᵃ32–3. [5] 1218ᵃ15–24.

the things that are changeless; for all those things in the sensible world are forms of order and rest; if these things, then, are excellent, the things that are changeless are still more excellent, since they have these attributes still more.

Aristotle's comment is a very just one. He objects to its being laid down as axiomatic that oneness or numerical definiteness is good, but is willing to admit that anything that can be found to be a precondition of the goodness of something admittedly good may be inferred to be good itself.

Finally, we must take account of the phrase used by Aristoxenus[1] in describing Plato's lectures On the Good—καὶ τὸ πέρας ὅτι ἀγαθὸν ἔστιν (or ἀγαθόν ἐστιν) ἕν. This has often been translated 'and that limit is the only good', and in view of the stress Plato lays on 'limit' in the *Philebus* that rendering has some attractions; but grammatically it is hardly permissible. Τὸ πέρας must be taken adverbially; the only meaning the phrase can really bear is 'and the lecture culminated in the statement that there is one Good'. That may be what Plato said; it is just against the doctrine that there is only one good, in the sense that 'good' is an unambiguous term, that Aristotle's attack in the *Nicomachean Ethics*[2] is directed. But it is equally possible that Aristoxenus' report is inaccurate, and that what Plato maintained was that the One is good—the doctrine which Aristotle in two passages[3] attributes to him. We do not know, and it would be fruitless to guess.

From all this evidence it follows that it had become a fundamental feature of Plato's system that unity entails goodness. In the absence of further evidence it is impossible to be sure of the precise meaning he attached to this. But we have already seen that in the latest phase of his philosophy, just as the great and small answered to the 'more and less' or the 'unlimited' of the *Philebus*, the One answered to the 'limit' of the *Philebus*, and carried with it overtones that the word 'one' does not suggest to us. The association of limit with goodness was no new thing in Plato's thought. One thinks of his condemnation, in the *Republic*,[4] of unlimited πλεονεξία. The just man, the good musician, the

---

[1] *Harm.* ii. 30 (Meibom).   [2] i. 6.
[3] 988^{b}11–16, 1091^{b}13–15.   [4] 349 b 1–350 c 11.

capable doctor, the wise man, all set limits (he there had said) to their activity; they avoid the too much as well as the too little. One thinks, again, of the passage in the *Politicus*[1] where he insists that moral and artistic excellence alike depend precisely on the avoidance of the too much and the observance of measure; and of the passage in the *Philebus*[2] where he argues that 'in measure, and the mean, and the suitable, and the like, the eternal nature has been found'. It is in the context of such overtones that we must interpret his teaching that unity is the basis of all excellence.

Plato, as we have seen, seems never to have brought his 'highest Ideas' into a single system, but in the Good of the *Republic* and the *Philebus*, the Existence of the *Sophistes*, the Truth of the *Philebus*,[3] and the One of the Idea-number theory, we find the sources of the original list of transcendentals—Bonum, Ens, Verum, Unum—which the schoolmen treated as standing above the categories and being true of all that is.

[1] 283 c 3–285 c 3.   [2] 64 c 1–66 a 8.   [3] 65 a 2.

ENGLISH INDEX

GREEK INDEX

ἀναιρεῖν, 54–7.
ἀνάμνησις, 81.
ἄπειρον, 195.
ἀρετή, 43.
ἀσύμβλητοι ἀριθμοί, 180.
αὐτὸ καθ' αὑτό, 21, 228.
αὐτὸ ὃ ἔστι, 24.
αὐτὸ τό, 17.

βούλεσθαι, 24, 228.

γεγενημένη οὐσία, 137.

δεύτερος πλοῦς, 27.
δημιουργός, 44, 137.
διαίρεσις, 33, 80, 81, 195.
διάνοια, 48, 60, 63, 64, 65, 67, 68, 74,
    75, 76, 77.
δόξα, 48.
δοξαστόν, 69.

εἶδος, 12–16.
εἰκασία, 48, 62, 67, 68, 74, 75, 77–8.
εἰκών, 46, 67, 74, 228.
εἰσιόντα καὶ ἐξιόντα, 124.
ἐκμαγεῖον, 124, 176 n. 3, 222.
ἕν, 92–3.
ἑνάς, 130 n. 6.
ἐπιφέρειν, 34.

ἰδέα, 12–16.

κατὰ ὅλου, 18.
κοινωνία, 29, 33, 37, 111 n. 6, 228;
    γενῶν, 127.

λόγος, 27–8, 51, 163, 198, 199.

μαθηματικά, τά, 59–65.
μέθεξις, 24, 228.
μεταλαμβάνειν, 85, 228.
μετάσχεσις, 29, 228.
μεταξύ, τά, 59.
μίμησις, 24, 228.
μονάς, 130 n. 6.
μονοειδές, 35, 121.

νόησις, 48, 63, 67, 68, 75, 76, 77.
νοητόν, 69.
νοῦς, 48, 60, 64, 65.

ὁμοίωμα, 228.
ὀρέγεσθαι, 24, 228.
οὐσία, 18.

παράδειγμα, 228.
παρουσία, 29, 228.
πέρας, 132, 195, 199, 244.
πίστις, 48, 62, 67, 68, 74, 75, 77.
πλεονεξία, 244.
πολυθρύλητα, 28.
προθυμεῖσθαι, 24, 228.
προσαπτέον, 70, 72.

συναγωγή, 80, 81, 117.

τἀκεῖ, 228.
τετρακτύς, 179.

ὑπερουράνιος τόπος, 81.
ὑποδοχή, 222.
ὑπόθεσις, 27–9, 51, 64 n.

φύσει, 174–5.

χώρα, 125.

PRINTED IN
GREAT BRITAIN
AT THE
UNIVERSITY PRESS
OXFORD
BY
CHARLES BATEY
PRINTER
TO THE
UNIVERSITY

30951